ISBN 978-1-330-99010-0
PIBN 10130532

1 MONTH OF
FREE
READING

at
www.ForgottenBooks.com

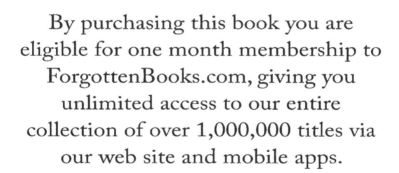

By purchasing this book you are eligible for one month membership to ForgottenBooks.com, giving you unlimited access to our entire collection of over 1,000,000 titles via our web site and mobile apps.

To claim your free month visit: www.forgottenbooks.com/free130532

English
Français
Deutsche
Italiano
Español
Português

www.forgottenbooks.com

Mythology Photography **Fiction**
Fishing Christianity **Art** Cooking
Essays Buddhism Freemasonry
Medicine **Biology** Music **Ancient**
Egypt Evolution Carpentry Physics
Dance Geology **Mathematics** Fitness
Shakespeare **Folklore** Yoga Marketing
Confidence Immortality Biographies
Poetry **Psychology** Witchcraft
Electronics Chemistry History **Law**
Accounting **Philosophy** Anthropology
Alchemy Drama Quantum Mechanics
Atheism Sexual Health **Ancient History**
Entrepreneurship Languages Sport
Paleontology Needlework Islam
Metaphysics Investment Archaeology
Parenting Statistics Criminology
Motivational

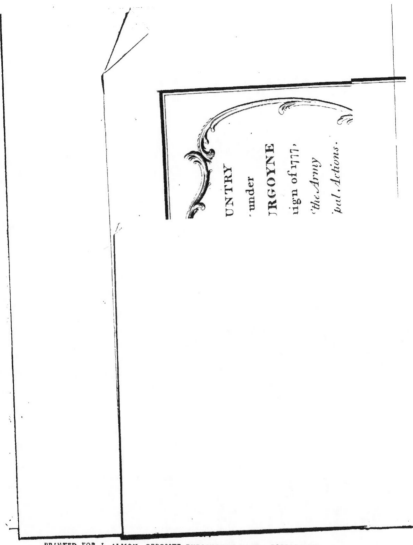

UNTRY
under
JRGOYNE
iign of 1777,
the Army
pal. Actions.

PRINTED FOR J. ALMON, OPPOSITE BURLINGTON-HOUSE, PICCADILLY.
MDCCLXXX.

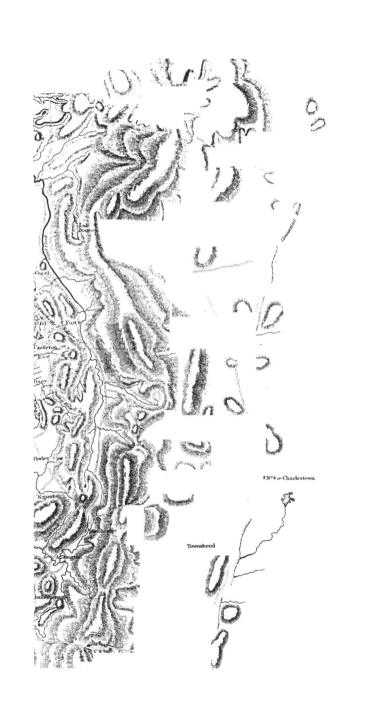

Charlestown.

London. Published as the Act directs Sept. 1780. by W.m Faden Charing Cross.

S T A T E

OF THE

E X P E D I T I O N

FROM

C A N A D A,

AS LAID BEFORE THE

HOUSE OF COMMONS,

BY

LIEUTENANT-GENERAL BURGOYNE,

AND VERIFIED BY EVIDENCE;

WITH A

COLLECTION OF AUTHENTIC DOCUMENTS,

AND

AN ADDITION OF MANY CIRCUMSTANCES WHICH WERE PREVENTED FROM
APPEARING BEFORE THE HOUSE BY THE PROROGATION OF PARLIAMENT.

WRITTEN AND COLLECTED BY HIMSELF,

AND

DEDICATED TO THE OFFICERS OF THE ARMY HE COMMANDED.

———————————

LONDON:

PRINTED FOR J. ALMON, OPPOSITE BURLINGTON-HOUSE, PICCADILLY.

MDCCLXXX.

A

STATE

OF THE

EXPEDITION

FROM

CANADA,

AS LAID BEFORE THE

HOUSE OF COMMONS,

BY

LIEUTENANT-GENERAL BURGOYNE,

AND VERIFIED BY EVIDENCE;

WITH A

COLLECTION OF AUTHENTIC DOCUMENTS,

DEDICATED TO THE OFFICERS OF THE ARMY HE COMMANDED.

TO

MAJOR GENERAL PHILLIPS,

AND THE

OTHER OFFICERS

WHO SERVED IN THE ARMY COMMANDED BY

LIEUTENANT GENERAL BURGOYNE,

UPON AN

EXPEDITION FROM CANADA.

GENTLEMEN,

PROPR͵ETY and affection alike incline me to inscribe to you the follow-ing undertaking. We are mutual and peculiar sufferers by the event of the campaign in 1777. You were witnesses and judges of my actions; but I owed you an account of the principles which directed them.

Another motive for this Address is to avail myself of a proper public op-portunity to repeat to you, what I have omitted no occasion of expressing in Parliament, in correspondence, and in conversation—the fullest approbation of your services. My errors may have been numberless; your conduct has been uniform—faithful, gallant and indefatigable. Debarred of the power of doing you justice before the King, these testimonies are the only means to which my esteem and gratitude can resort.

After vindicating myself as a commanding officer from any inattention to your interest or fame, I next throw myself upon your judgment for my con-duct as a friend.

You will find by this publication, and some others, which though not addressed to you will probably engage your curiosity, that I have been accused of shrinking from the common captivity.

I have

I have been fupported under that afperfion by the confcioufnefs I did not deferve it,' and the confidence that you (to whom chiefly upon that charge I was refponfible) would not adopt it. After the fortunes we have run together, it is not furely unworthy of belief, that I fhould rather have defired, than avoided to partake the clofing fcene : uniting with a due fenfe of perfonal attachments, the prefervation of my military fortune, and a retreat from the diftractions of my country. The defence of your honour and my own, at one time, and refiftance to an affront * which my nature could not bear, at another, alone detained me here.

In regard to my political tranfactions, I have ftated them, and I wifh them to be confidered by my friends, apart from my miltary conduct. I bear very high refpect to fome eminent and ill-treated characters in our profeffion, who in deference to the tranquility of government, have filently refigned the ftations which they could no longer hold with fecurity to their honour, or benefit to the ftate. But the option is not left to thofe, who having a voice in Parliament are obliged to act as citizens as well as foldiers. The number of officers altogether of the army and navy, who with known love to their country and profeffional fpirit equally confpicuous, have voluntarily withdrawn themfelves from employment within thefe two years, exceeds all precedent. I do not place my name in the lift with the fame pretenfions; but it is not arrogant to emulate where we cannot compare; and I am defirous of following the high examples before me in no point more than in that of avoiding to difturb the zeal of thofe who are now employed. The officers who have held it their duty to take part in oppofition, have acted openly and directly in their place in Parliament ; but they may

* The part of my treatment which I call an affront upon this and other occafions, is the refufal of my fervice in this country, even at the head of my own regiment, or as a volunteer, in the time of exigency, and when other officers *precifely in my own fituation*.were employed. My complaint of this partiality has never been officially anfwered ; it has only been evaded by anonymous writers, who have laid it down as a pofition, that I meant to allude to the example of Lord Harrington (with which it certainly has nothing to do) and then have taken a merit in refuting me. The particular example to which I appeal is that of Lieutenant Colonel Kingfton, of the 86th regiment, appointed to that regiment, employed in it for the defence of Plymouth, and actually now embarking with it for foreign fervice, under the fame terms of the convention, and the fame terms of parole to the Congrefs verbatim with myfelf. Other objections, and of a nature that could not be afterwards fupported, were tried againft the Duke of Rutland's recommendation of this excellent officer : but the objection of parole, though fully known to be precifely the fame with that which was fo peremptorily urged againft my pretenfions, was never mentioned.

3

defy

defy malice to fhew an inftance wherein they have not encouraged ardour in their profeffion. They contemplate with one and the fame fentiment the great fupply of honourable men to occupy their places.

You, Gentlemen, ftand high in that defcription; your trials have made you of fterling value; and perhaps it will be better difcerned by men in power, when no longer viewed through the unfavourable medium of my friendfhip. If my exhortations retain their former weight, let me be permitted earneftly to apply them upon this occafion. The examples of generals or admirals who decline employment, refpect only fimilar cafes; your honour is fecure: look not at profeffional difappointments; but point all your views to the true glory of your King and country, and truft for the reward.

O focii (neque enim ignari fumus ante Malorum)
O paffi graviora: dabit Deus his quoque finem.

This paffage will bring to the remembrance of fome among you a hard hour when we before quoted it together, and not without fome *cheer of mind.*——May the end of your enduring be near! And with every other wifh and fentiment that can denote efteem, I have the honour to be,

Gentlemen,

Your moft faithful and moft obedient

humble fervant,

Hertford-Street,
Jan. 1, 1780.

J. BURGOYNE.

INTRODUCTION.

WHEN it becomes neceſſary for men who have acted critical parts in public ſtations to make an appeal to the world in their own juſtification, there are many prudential conſiderations which might lead them to commit the care of it to friends, or, which is in many reſpects the ſame thing, to defend themſelves under an aſſumed character. The charge of vanity uſually made on egotiſm is thus eluded : a fuller ſcope may be given to ſelf-love and particular reſentment : even the lower vexations which attend an author are to a great degree avoided :: the ill-nature of criticiſm is ſeldom awakened by anonymous writings, and the venal pens of party loſe half their gall when the object of it is not perſonally and directly in queſtion.

But there are ſituations, in which, not only general aſſent ſeems to juſtify a man in ſpeaking of himſelf, but in which alſo no little conſideration ought to be admitted to the mind. Such will be the caſe, if I am not deceived, when the intereſts of the public are blended with thoſe of the individual ; and when his very errors may ſerve as inſtruction to others. Misfortunes which awaken ſenſibility will be a further, and a perſuaſive call, upon the *attention* of the public ; and it will amount to a claim upon their *juſtice*, if he can ſhew that he has been injuriouſly treated.

Upon maturely weighing theſe and ſeveral other circumſtances, after I had been denied a profeſſional examination of my conduct, and diſappointed of a parliamentary one, I determined to lay before the public a ſtate of the expedition from Canada, in 1777, in my own name. And my firſt deſign was to do it under the title, and with the latitude of Memoirs ; as a mode by which I could beſt open the principles of my actions, and introduce, with moſt propriety, collateral characters, incidents, and diſcuſſions, as they might occaſionally tend to illuſtrate the main ſubject.

However, in the laſt ſeſſion of Parliament, the enquiry which had not been agreed to the year before, took place. I had preſſed it, and I entered into it under all the diſadvantages which attend a ſtruggle with power, and

the

the prejudice that power can raife againft the perfons it means to deftroy. The utmoft that power could do was done; the Paliament was prorogued pending the proceedings. But though by this contrivance, a final and formal adjudication by that auguft affembly was avoided, their minutes ftand a faered record of truth and juftice, and the moft fatisfactory reliance to which my wifhes could afpire, in offering my actions to the judgment of my country at large.

From that time, therefore, I refolved to publifh, inftead of Memoirs, the Proceedings precifely as they paffed in Parliament, and to continue my defence by fuch Obfervations and Comments upon the Evidence, as I fhould have had a right, and was prepared to make, had the proceedings in the houfe continued.*

Poffibly in this latter part fome colour of my original defign may remain. The fcenes I have been engaged in are uncommon, and it is a natural defire to place them in a full light. The interefts concerned make that defire more urgent; and I dare believe they will be beft guarded by being moft explained.

---

* The order in which the committee in the Houfe of Commons proceeded was, to hear Sir William Howe's Narrative, refpecting his conduct whilft in command in America, and fuch evidence as he thought proper to bring in fupport of it. They next heard my Narrative and Evidence, refpecting the conduct of the expedition from Canada. Lord George Germain then opened a defence on his part, and fummoned witneffes to fupport it. According to the arrangement made by the committee, Sir William Howe and myfelf were afterwards to be heard in reply; but the proceedings were ended by the prorogation of Parliament before the examination of Lord George's fecond witnefs, Mr. Galloway, was clofed, and there were fixteen or eighteen more upon his lift. The order in which the following papers are placed is—1ft. The Prefatory Speech. 2d. The Narrative. 3d. Minutes of the verbal evidence. 4th. Review of the evidence, with Remarks and Explanations, &c. 5th. An Appendix, containing the written evidence.

The SPEECH of Lieutenant General BURGOYNE, prefatory to his NARRATIVE.

MR. MONTAGU,

BEFORE I enter upon the narrative, which the precedent of your late proceedings authorifes me to lay before you, I think it a duty to the committee, to promife that I fhall trouble them with little other matter than fuch as may be neceffary to elucidate the tranfactions of the campaign 1777, in that quarter where I commanded.

I fhall keep in mind, that to explain the caufes of the difafter at Saratoga is the principal point to which all my evidence ought to lead: but at the fame time, I fhall take confidence in the juftice and benevolence of my hearers, that where arguments in exculpation of the commander can aptly be combined with a faithful reprefenta-tion of facts, they will not be deemed foreign to the main object under their confi-deration.

Upon thefe ideas, though fome introductory explanations are requifite, I fhall fupprefs the inclination I at firft conceived, of ftaring my conduct from the time, when, conjointly with my honourable friend who took the lead in this enquiry,* I was called to the unfolicited and unwelcome fervice in America: nor will I enume-rate the complicated circumftances of private misfortune and ill health under which I purfued it. Prudence, as well as other propriety, is, I confefs, confulted in this fuppreffion; for were it feen, that an officer had blended with the refpect due to authority, warm, though difinterefted perfonal attachments; that under a perfuafion of the honour and integrity of the king's fervants, he had united to his zeal for the public caufe an intereft in their private credit and ambition; would it not be con-ceived, that his guilt muft have been atrocious, beyond all excufe or palliation, to induce the very men to whom his endeavours, and his faculties, fuch as they were, had been thus devoted, not only completely to defert him, but to preclude him, as far as in them lay, from every means of defence, and if poffible, to ruin him in the opinion of the king, the army, and the country?

An earneft defire to fave, as much as poffible, the time of the committee, would alfo diffuade me from recurring to any points previous to my inftructions which have been difcuffed upon former occafions; but I find that great ftrefs is ftill laid to my prejudice upon a paper which found its way to the houfe during my abfence: I mean the private letter to the noble lord, fecretary for the American department, dated 1ft January, 1777.*

The noble Lord has frequently ftated that letter to have flipped inadvertently into the parcel deftined for the houfe, and I give credit in that particular to his affertion; becaufe,

See Appendix No. I.

B

* Sir William Howe.

becaufe, whatever other impreffions he might have found it his intereft to make refpecting me, he certainly would not have thought that the imputation on me which
that letter tended to fix, a proper one for *him* to put forward: it is a notorious fact,
or I would not mention it, that it has been held a reflection upon my character (by
the part of the public with whom the noble lord is unpopular) that I addreffed him
as a patron and friend.

This is an imputation to which I muft plead guilty; for at the time I wrote that
letter, I certainly did hold that noble lord as my friend, and I had acted to deferve
he fhould be fo. The next ill tendency of that paper was, as the noble lord
well knows, to imprefs the public with an opinion, that I was endeavouring to
fupplant Sir Guy Carleton in the command of the northern army—an action
abhorrent to the honour of an officer and the liberality of a gentleman; and of
which, thank God, I can prove the falfehood, by irrefragable evidence upon your
table, and in a very fmall compafs. I need only refer to the difpatches to Sir Guy
Carleton by his aid de-camp, dated 22d Auguft, 1776,* four months before I came
home, to fhew that it was at that time determined, that Sir Guy Carleton fhould
remain in Canada; and that determination was made, as I have been informed, not
only upon the political reafoning which appears in that difpatch, but alfo, upon
great law opinions, that he could not, under the commiffion he then held under the
great feal, pafs the frontiers of his province. Sir, this confutation was urged by
me laft year; and were collateral proof neceffary to my juftification upon this fubject, I could bring to your bar a tribe of gentlemen, who had imbibed impreffions
not very favourable to the military proceedings of Sir Guy Carleton in the campaign
of 1776: I could fhew that I feized numberlefs, indeed I feized every poffible occafion to vindicate the judgment, the affiduity, the activity of that highly refpectable
officer, carelefs how ill I paid my court, carneft to meet every attack againft his fame.

I beg leave alfo to call the attention of the committee very particularly to one
other paper, the date of which is previous to my departure from England: it is entitled, "Thoughts for conducting the War from the Side of Canada, by Lieutenant
"General Burgoyne."* Sir, it will be in the recollection of the committee, whether, when the conduct of the war was under confideration laft year in my abfence,
it was not underftood, that the plan of the northern expedition was formed upon that
paper as produced upon your table? If fo, I muft afk the noble lord, why he fuffered that error to prevail? The noble lord knew, (and it was peculiarly his duty to
declare it) that the two propofals, the firft of turning the expedition eventually towards Connecticut; and the fecond, of embarking the army in the river St. Lawrence, in order to effect a junction with Sir William Howe by fea, in cafe the attempt
by land appeared " impracticable, or too hazardous," were erafed while the paper
was in his lordfhip's hands.

*
See Appendix
No. II.

No. III.

From

From that paper, as it appeared without erafures, naturally arofe the conclufion, that the plan I had to execute was completely my own; upon that paper were founded, as naturally, the doubts which have been entertained upon the peremptory tenor of my inftructions. I muft again afk the noble lord, upon what principle of juftice he fuffered thofe impreffions to exift in this houfe? Why, in a debate in which he took a part, did he conceal, that the circumftances in reality were totally different from thofe upon which gentlemen reafoned; that the difcretion referved in the paper before the houfe was taken away, and confequently, that my orders were rendered abfolute in the ftricteft fenfe by his own alterations?

Let any gentleman who has fuppofed I had an implied latitude for my conduct, now compare this circumftance with the wording of the letter to Sir Guy Carleton, dated March 26, 1777, with a copy of which I was furnifhed, and extracts from which were afterwards the only orders I had to act upon. *

I fhall take no particular notice of what is called the faving claufe, in the latter part of the orders, except to give the flatteft contradiction to the fuppofition that I dictated it—a fuppofition that I know is not yet abandoned by the men who firft fuggefted it. I have fpoke to it very fully upon a former occafion;† and I do not wifh, when it can be avoided, to enforce or reiterate the charges of duplicity and treachery, which muft enfue, if that claufe could be fuppofed to have reference to any conduct previous to my arrival at Albany. The circumftance of forbidding me the latitude in the two particulars I had propofed in my plan, and many other circumftances, clearly indicating the decided intentions and expectations of the minifters, rendered the fenfe of the whole order taken together clear and diftinct, and fhewed that the claufe which is pretended to have left me a difcretion as to my main object, had no fort of relation to that object. That claufe evidently related not to my forcing my way, or not forcing it, to Albany, the place of my deftination, but to fuch collateral and eventual operations as might be advifeable in the courfe of my march. It related to the making impreffion upon the rebels, and bringing them to obedience, in fuch manner as exigencies might require, and in my judgment might feem moft proper, previous to receiving orders from Sir William Howe, " of my junction with whom I was never to lofe view."

Notwithftanding there has been fo much difcuffion in debate and print upon the interpretation of abfolute orders, the committee, I am confident, will abfolve me, though, at the expence of a few moments more, I fhould continue a fubject upon which the merit or blame of the future proceedings in great meafure refts.

I do not admit the pofition, that there can be no cafe in which an officer acting at a diftance is bound at every hazard to purfue orders, that appear abfolute *and decifive.*

It

See Appendix No. IV.

† The debate upon Mr. Vyner's motion, May 28, 1778; the fpeech was publifhed.

It is eafy to conceive circumftances, which might juftify a ftate in hazarding an army, for the fake of facilitating great and decifive objects. Gentlemen, converfant in military hiftory, will recollect many examples of this principle : upon a former occafion, I ftated a fuppofed cafe ;* and I now entreat leave to add a real example of peremptory orders, which happened in the courfe of my own fervice. I have ever retained the impreffion, that the circumftance I am going to relate, made upon my mind at the time; and to thofe few who may ftill think, that in any part of my conduct, I rafhly rifked my peace, my intereft or my fame, to forward the wifhes of others, this prepoffeffion may in fome meafure account for, and excufe my imprudence.

In the campaign of 1762, in Portugal, the Count La Lippe, a name, which, if it finds a due hiftorian, will ftand among the firft in military fame, was placed at the head of about 6000 Britifh troops, and a Portuguefe army, the greater part of which was little better than nominal, to defend an extenfive frontier againft the whole force of Spain, and a large body of the veteran troops of France. The falvation of Portugal depended folely on the capacity of that great man, which united the deepeft political reafoning with exquifite military addrefs.

I had the honour to be entrufted with the defence of the moft important pafs upon the Tagus, and my orders were peremptory to maintain it againft any numbers, and to the laft man.

A felect corps of the enemy, greatly fuperior to mine, were encamped within fight on the other fide the river, and our advanced pofts were within half mufquet fhot.

In this fituation, I received intelligence from Count La Lippe, of a defign of the enemy to pafs the Tagus in force, about fix miles above me, and to take poffeffion of the open country in my rear, with a large corps of cavalry, by which means all communication, fupply, or fafe retreat, would be cut off.

Together with this intelligence, the Count's letter expreffed, " That every delay " to the enemy in getting poffeffion of the pafs I guarded, was fo material to his " other plans and operations, that it juftified a deviation from fyftematic rules; that, " therefore, after taking timely precautions to fecure the retreat of my cavalry, I " muft abide the confequence with the infantry; that at the laft extremity, I muft " abandon my cannon, camp, &c. and with fuch provifion as the men could carry

* The cafe alluded to was put in a former debate, as follows: fuppofe the Britifh army that invaded Britany in 1758, had gained a complete victory over the Duke D'Aiguillon; to have marched rapidly towards Paris, abandoning the communication with the fleet, expofing the army poffibly to great want of provifion, and to the impracticability of retreat, would certainly have been a meafure confummately defperate and unjuftifiable, if tried upon military fyftem: yet, will any man fay, that if that meafure muft evidently have produced fuch alarm and confufion in the heart of France, as to have compelled the recall of her whole force from Germany, or fuch part of it, as would have given uncontrouled fcope to the armies under the King of Pruffia and Prince Ferdinand, that the minifter of England would not have been judicious, though at the palpable rifk of the army, as far as capture was concerned, in ordering the general to proceed by the moft vigorous meafures, and to force his way to Paris?

" upon

" upon their backs, throw myfelf into the mountains upon my left, and endea-
" vour, by fmall and difperfed parties, to gain a rendezvous at the northern part
" of the province." I muft obferve, that when thefe peremptory orders were
given, the commander was at a diftance that made all timely communication of circumftances as impoffible, as if the Atlantic had been between us; and I cannot clofe
the example without mentioning the concluding part of Count La Lippe's letter.
" He participated," he laid, " in the feelings with which an officer would be ftruck
" for his reputation, in fuffering himfelf to be cut, and reduced to facrifice his camp,
" his baggage, and twenty pieces of cannon. But *be at eafe*," continued that great
and generous man, " *I will take the meafure entirely upon myfelf, perfevere as I have*
" *directed, and be confident of my defence and protection.*" This was a faving claufe of a
nature very different from thofe it is the practice in the prefent day to pen; and if
any man doubts the quotation, I can bring pofitive evidence to the truth of it verbatim.

Thus much, Sir, I thought it incumbent upon me to ftate in argument againft
the pofition that has been infifted upon, that no orders can be worded fo peremptorily at a diftance, as not to admit of an implied latitude, in cafe of unforefeen and
infurmountable difficulties: but to prevent all future cavil, upon this fubject, I requeft the committee to recollect, what I have again and again repeated; that I by no
means put my defence, in paffing the Hudfon's River, folely upon this reafoning.
On the contrary, fuppofing for the argument's fake, I fhould concede (which I never
have done, nor mean to do) to the noble Lord, and to every other gentleman, all they
can defire to affume upon implied latitude in given cafes, I fhould equally prove that
no fuch cafe did exift, as would have juftified me upon their own principle, in de-
parting from the letter of the orders under which I acted.

Having thus cleared my way to the time of my leaving England, to take upon
me the command of the Northern expedition; I fhall now lay before the committee
a narrative of its progrefs, in as concife and fimple terms, as the nature of the
fubject will allow, endeavouring to imitate the perfpicuity of the honourable gentleman who took the lead in this bufinefs, and not without hope of my endeavours pro-
ducing the fame effect; and that, in the opinion of the houfe, my language, as has
been expreffed of his, will be deemed the language of truth.

N A R

N A R R A T I V E.

IT is my intention, for the more ready comprehenfion of the whole fubject, to divide it into three periods. The firft, from my appointment to the command, to the end of my purfuit of the enemy from Ticonderoga; the fecond, from that time to the paffage of the Hudfon's River; and the third to the figning the convention.

I left London on the 27th of March, and upon my departure from Plymouth, finding the Albion man of war ready to fail for New-York, I wrote to Sir W. Howe by that conveyance, upon the fubject of my expedition, and the nature of my orders. I arrived at Quebec the 6th of May. Sir Guy Carleton immediately put under my command the troops deftined for the expedition, and committed to my management the preparatory arrangements. From thence I wrote a fecond letter to Sir William Howe, wherein I repeated that I was entrufted with the command of the army deftined to march from Canada, and that my orders were to force a junction with his excellency.

I expreffed alfo my wifhes, " that a latitude had been left me for a diverfion to-
" wards Connecticut, but that fuch an idea being out of queftion, by my orders
" being precife to force the junction, it was only mentioned to introduce the idea
" ftill refting upon my mind; viz. to give the change to the enemy if I could, and
" by every feint in my power to eftablifh a fufpicion, that I ftill pointed towards
" Connecticut."

" But," I repeated, " that under the prefent precifion of my orders, I fhould really
" have no view but that of joining him, nor think myfelf juftified by any temp-.
" tation to delay the moft expeditious means I could find to effect that purpofe."

I proceeded to Montreal on the 12th, and as my letters, lately laid before the houfe from that place,* and from Quebec, will fhew the ftate of things, I fhould not reft a moment upon this period, were it not to add one more public teftimony, to thofe I am not confcious of having omitted upon any occafion, of the affiduous and cordial manner in which the different fervices were forwarded by Sir Guy Carleton. I fhould think it as difhonourable to feek, as I know it would be impoffible to find excufe for any fault of mine in any failure on the part of Sir Guy Carleton, or of any per-fons who acted under him, in any matter refpecting the expedition. Had that officer been acting for himfelf, or for his brother, he could not have fhewn more indefatigable zeal than he did, to comply with and expedite my requifitions and defires.

SeeAppendix
No. V.

Certain

Certain parts of the expected force, neverthelefs, fell fhort. The Canadian troops, ftated in the plan at 2000, confifted only of three companies, intended to be of 100 men each, but in reality not amounting to more than 150 upon the whole; nor could they be augmented. The corvées, which are detachments of provincials without arms, to repair roads, convey provifions, or any other temporary employments for the king's fervice, could not be obtained in fufficient number, nor kept to their employments, although Sir Guy Carleton ufed every poffible exertion and encouragement for the purpofe. Drivers for the provifion carts, and other carriages, could not be fully fupplied by the contractor, though no expence was fpared; a circumftance which occafioned much inconvenience afterwards.

To thefe unavoidable difappointments were added the difficulties occafioned by bad weather, which rendered the roads almoft impracticable at the carrying places, and confequently the paffage of the batteaux, artillery, and baggage exceedingly dilatory: we had befides a great deal of contrary wind. Notwithftanding all impediments the army affembled between the 17th and 20th of June, at Cumberland Point, upon Lake Champlain.

On the 21ft I held a conference with the Iroquois, Algonchins, Abenekies, and Outawas, Indians, in all about four hundred.

This conference appears in your papers*. I thought at the time that the cordiality of the Indians over the whole continent might be depended upon, and their firft operations tended to perfuade me into a belief of their utility. The prieft to whom they feemed devoted, and the Britifh officers employed to conduct them, and to whofe controul they engaged to fubmit, gained advantages, and fpread terror without barbariry. The firft party fent out made feveral of the enemy prifoners in the heat of action, and treated them with European humanity.

* See Appendix No. VI.

During the movement of the different corps to this general rendezvous, I wrote a third letter to Sir William Howe. The chief purport of it was to give him " intelli- " gence of my fituation at the time, and of my expectation of being before Ticonderoga " between the 20th and 25th inftant; that I did not apprehend the effective ftrength " of the army would amount to above 6500 men; that I meant to apply to Sir " Guy Carleton to fend a garrifon to Ticonderoga when it fhould be reduced, but " that I was apprehenfive he would not think himfelf authorifed by the King's orders " to comply; that whenever, therefore, I might be able to effect the junction, Sir " William would not expect me to bring near the original number. I repeated my " perfeverance in the idea of giving jealoufy on the fide of Connecticut, and at the " fame time my affurances, that I fhould make no manœuvre that could procraftinate " the great object of a junction."

I ftate thefe different letters to Sir William Howe merely to fhew that my conception of the precifion of my orders was not upon after-thought, and taken up as an

excufe.

excufe when I found the expedition had failed ; but a fixed decided fentiment coeval
with my knowledge of my command.

For a further proof of the fame fact, I beg leave to ftate an extract from my orders
to the army at Crown Point, June 30th.   The words were thefe.

" The army embarks to-morrow to approach the enemy.   The fervices required
" of this particular expedition are critical and confpicuous.   During our progrefs oc-
" cafions may occur, in which, nor difficulty, nor labour, nor life are to be regarded.
" This army muft not retreat." Were it neceffary, I could bring abundant collateral
proof to the fame effect, and fhew that the idea of forcing a way to Albany by vigorous exertions againft any oppofition we might meet, was general and fixt through
the whole army.

My proceedings from the time of affembling the army as before defcribed, to the
date of my public difpatch from Skenefborough, comprehending the manœuvres
which forced the enemy from Ticonderoga, and the actions at Skenefborough, Huberton, and Fort Anne, are related at full in that difpatch.*

See Appendix
No. VII.

It is the lefs neceffary to give the Committee further trouble upon this fubject, becaufe I believe no enemy can be found to arraign my conduct in thofe days of fuccefs ; or if there were one, he could not deprive me of the confolation, that I had his
Majefty's full approbation and applaufe, of which it is known to many, I had a very
honourable and diftinguifhed proof.

All therefore that is neceffary before I quit this firft period of the campaign, is to
give a precife ftate of the effective ftrength of the army, at the time it affembled.

On the 1ft July, the day we encamped before Ticonderoga, the troops confifted of

Britifh rank and file	-	3724
German ditto	-	3016
		6740 regulars, exclufive of artillery-men.
Canadians and Provincials, about	250	
Indians about	-	400
	650	

In regard to the artillery, I think this the proper place to rectify the mifreprefentations that have prevailed refpecting the quantity employed. It has been ftated as far
beyond the neceffary proportion for the number of troops, an incumbrance to their
movements, and one caufe of what has been called the flow progrefs of the expedition.

In order to juftify this charge, a view of the whole mafs has been prefented to the
public without any explanation of its diftinct allotments ; and many have been led
to believe, that the whole was attached to the army throughout the campaign, and
                                                                        fell

fell into the enemy's hands at last—The intention of this reprefentation is obvious: the allegation is falfe.

The facts, as I fhall prove them to the committee, are as follow. The whole original train furnifhed by Sir Guy Carleton confifted of fixteen heavy twenty-four pounders; ten heavy twelve-pounders; eight medium twelve-pounders; two light twenty-four pounders; one light twelve-pounder; twenty-fix light fix pounders; feventeen light three-pounders; fix eight-inch howitzers; fix five and a half inch howitzers; two thirteen-inch mortars; two ten-inch mortars; fix eight-inch mortars; twelve five and a half-inch mortars; and twenty-four four and two fifth-inch mortars. Of thefe two heavy twenty-four pounders were fent on board a fhip for the defence of Lake Champlain, and the other fourteen were fent back to St. John's. Of the heavy twelve-pounders, fix were left at Ticonderoga, four ditto in the Royal George; four medium twelve-pounders at Fort George; one light twelve-pounder at Ticonderoga; two light fix-pounders at Fort George; four light fix-pounders at St. John's; four light three-pounders at Ticonderoga; five light three-pounders at St. John's; two eight-inch howitzers at Fort George; two ditto at St. John's; two five and a half inch howitzers at Fort George; two thirteen-inch mortars in the Royal George; two ten-inch mortars in ditto; four eight-inch mortars in ditto; four five and a half inch mortars at Ticonderoga; four royal mortars in the Royal George; twelve cohorns at Ticonderoga; and eight cohorns in the Royal George.

The field-train therefore that proceeded with the army confifted of four medium twelve-pounders; two light twenty-four pounders; eighteen light fix-pounders; fix light three-pounders; two eight-inch howitzers; four five and a half-inch howitzers; two eight-inch mortars, and four royals.

The carrying the twenty-four pounders (though they were but two) has been fpoken of as an error, and it is neceffary therefore to inform the committee that they were of a conftruction lighter by 800 weight than medium twelves, and to all intents and purpofes field artillery.

This artillery was diftributed as follows.

Frafer's corps, eftimated at three battalions.

Ten pieces, viz.

Four light fix-pounders.
Four light three-pounders, conftructed for being occafionally carried on horfeback.
Two royal howitzers.

German referve, under Colonel Breyman, eftimated at two battalions.
Two light fix-pounders.
Two light three-pounders, and ferved by the Heffe Hanau artillery men.

The line of Britifh, four battalions

C

Germans,

Germans, five battalions.
Total, nine battalions.

Three brigades of artillery, of four fix-pounders each ; viz. one brigade for each wing, and one for the center.

From hence it appears that to fourteen battalions there were allotted twenty-fix pieces of light artillery. The cuftomary allotment is two pieces per battalion, confequently the proportion of artillery was lefs than upon common.fervices.

The forming artillery into brigades, in preference to detaching two guns to each battalion, has been conftantly practifed in moft fervices during laft war under the ableft men, and it is productive of many advantages, as the brigades by that means, either fingly or united, fall under the command of a proportionable number of officers. The fervice is carried on with greater regularity, and the effect of the fire becomes much more formidable than when fcattered along the front of the line.

This mode of fervice was recommended by Major-general Phillips, and adopted, without hefitation by me, my own judgment being confirmed by an officer of his great fkill and experience.

The park artillery confifted of ten pieces, viz:

2 light twenty-four pounders.
4 medium twelve-pounders.
2 eight-inch howitzers.
2 royal howitzers.

I underftood this proportion of field artillery to be the fame as that propofed by Sir Guy Carleton had he commanded; it was the proportion recommended by General Phillips, and I formed my opinion conformably to the fentiments of thofe refpectable officers upon the following reafons, viz. that artillery was extremely formidable to raw troops; that in a country of pofts it was effentially neceffary againft the beft troops; that it was yet more applicable to the enemy we were to combat, becaufe the mode of defence they invariably adopted, and at which they were beyond all other nations expert, was that of entrenchment covered with ftrong abbatis, againft which the cannon, of the nature of the heavieft above defcribed, and howitzers might often be effectual, when to diflodge them by any other means might be attended with continued and important loffes.

In thefe general ideas of the ufe of artillery againft the rebel forces, I have the happinefs to obferve, from the papers before you, the concurrence of Sir William Howe, who ftates fimilar ideas very fully in one of his requifitions to the fecretary of ftate: but further reafons for not diminifhing the proportion of guns of fuperior calibre to fix-pounders in this train, were, firft, their ufe againft block-houfes (a fpecies of fortification peculiar to America); fecondly, a probability that gun-boats might be requifite for the fecurity of the water tranfport, on fome parts of the

3   Hudfon's

Hudſon's River; but principally the intention of fortifying a camp at Albany, in caſe I ſhould reach that place, ſhould meet with a ſufficiency of proviſion there, (as I was led to expect) and ſhould find it expedient to paſs the winter there, without communication with New-York.

With reſpect to the quantity of ammunition attached to this artillery, it is to be obſerved, that the number of rounds accompanying the light pieces, and which were carried in ſmall carts, were not more than ſufficient for a day's action.

Light ſix-pounders	—	124 rounds each.
Light three-pounders	—	300 rounds.
Royal howitzers	—	90 rounds.

The different reſerves of ammunition were chiefly conveyed by water in ſcows and batteaux; it certainly would not have been adviſable, after a communica tion with Canada was at an end, to depend upon precarious ſupplies from the ſouthward, and therefore it became neceſſary (as far as the ſervice would allow) to carry forward ſuch ſtores, as there was every appearance of an abſolute want of, during the courſe of an active campaign.

Had the enemy eſtabliſhed themſelves in force upon the iſlands at the mouth of the Mohawk river, or on other ground equally advantageous, to have diſputed the paſſage of that, or of the Hudſon's River, or had they even waited an aſſault in their works at Still-Water, it is probable, that recourſe muſt have been had to artillery of the heavier nature; in the latter caſe eſpecially they muſt have been uſed in order to derive any advantage from our ſeizing a poſt upon their left flank : I have ſince known, that they had iron twelve and nine-pounders mounted upon thoſe works, which were in other reſpects very formidable.

The Britiſh artillery-men, rank and file, were	— —	245
Recruits, under command of Lieutenant Nutt, of the 33d regiment, attached to the ſervice of the artillery	— — —	150
Heſſian artillery-men, rank and file	— —	78
		473

Add theſe numbers to the former ſtate of the army, and it will be found, that the regular ſtrength when at the greateſt conſiſted of 7213.

I come now to the ſecond period of the campaign, comprehending the tranſactions from the time the purſuit of the enemy from Ticonderoga ceaſed, and the corps of Brigadier-general Fraſer, and the 9th regiment, rejoined the army, after the reſpective actions of Huberton and Fort Anne, to the time when the army paſſed the Hudſon's river to attack the enemy near Still-Water.

It had proved impoſſible immediately to follow the quick retreat of the enemy farther, from the nature of the country, and the neceſſity of waiting a freſh ſupply

of

of provifions. But it appeared evident to me, that could a rapid progrefs towards
Albany be effected, during their difperfion and panic, it would be decifive on the
fuccefs of the expedition.

Queftion has been made by thofe who began at this period to arraign my military,
conduct, whether it would not have been more expedient for the purpofe of rapidity,
to have fallen back to Ticonderoga, in order to take the convenient route by
Lake George, than to have perfevered in the laborious and difficult courfe by land
to Fort Edward? My motives for preferring the latter were thefe : I confidered
not only the general impreffions which a retrograde motion is apt to make upon the
minds both of enemies and friends, but alfo, that the natural conduct of the enemy in
that cafe would be to remain at Fort George, as their retreat could not then be cut
off, in order to oblige me to open trenches, and confequently to delay me, and in
the mean time they would have deftroyed the road from Fort George to Fort Edward. On the other hand, by perfifting to penetrate by the fhort cut from Fort
Anne, of which I was then mafter, to Fort Edward, though it was attended with
great labour, and many alert fituations, the troops were improved in the very effential point of wood fervice; I effectually diflodged the enemy from Fort George
without a blow ; and feeing me mafter of one communication, they did not think
it worth while to deftroy the other.

The great number of boats alfo, which muft neceffarily have been employed for
the tranfport of the troops over Lake George, were by this courfe fpared for the
tranfport of the provifion, artillery, and ammunition.

The fuccefs anfwered this reafoning in every point; for by the vigilance of Gene-
neral Phillips, to whom I had committed the important part of forwarding all the neceffaries from Ticonderoga, a great embarkation arrived at Fort George on July 29th.
I took poffeffion of the country near Fort Edward on the fame day, and independently
of other advantages, I found myfelf much more forward in point of time than I
could poffibly have been by the other route.

Another material motive, which could not be known by ftrangers who have reafoned upon this movement, was, that during the time that my army was employed
in clearing Wood-Creek and cutting roads, and the corps under Major-general
Phillips working to pafs the tranfports over Lake George, I was enabled to detach
a large corps to my left, under Major-general Reidefel, and thereby affift my purpofe of giving jealoufy to Connecticut, and keeping in check the whole country
called the Hampfhire Grants.

It was at this time Major-general Reidefel conceived the purpofe of mounting his
regiment of dragoons. In the country he traverfed during his detached command,
he found the people frightened and fubmiffive, He was induftrious and expert in
procuring

procuring intelligence in parts of the country more remote than Bennington, and entertained no doubt of fuccefs, were an expedition formed under the command of Lieutenant-colonel Baum.

On the arrival of the army at Fort Edward, the great objeſt of attention was the tranſports from Fort George. The diſtance was about ſixteen miles, the roads wanting great repair, the weather unfavourable, the cattle and carriages ſcarce; part of the latter inconvenience was occaſioned by the number of both that were neceſſarily detained at Ticonderoga, for the purpoſe of dragging the boats and the proviſions over the carrying places, between Lake Champlain and Lake George; another part of the inconvenience was cauſed by the unavoidable delays, in bringing the different diviſions of horſes as they were collected in Canada through the defart, for ſuch moſt of the country is between St. John's and Ticonderoga.

It was ſoon found, that in the ſituation of the tranſport ſervice at that time, the army could barely be victualled from day to day, and that there was no proſpeſt of eſtabliſhing a magazine in due time for purſuing preſent advantages. The idea of the expedition to Bennington originated upon this difficulty, combined with the intelligence reported by General Reideſel, and with all I had otherwiſe received.

I knew that Bennington was the great depoſit of corn, flour, and ſtore cattle; that it was guarded only by militia; and every day's account tended to confirm the perſuaſion of the loyalty of one deſcription of the inhabitants and the panic of the other. Thoſe who knew the country heſt were the moſt ſanguine in this perſuaſion.

Had my intelligence been worſe founded, I ſhould not have heſitated to try this expedition with ſuch troops, and under ſuch inſtructions as I gave to the commanding officer, for ſo great a purpoſe as that of a ſupply ſufficient to enable the army to follow at the heels of a broken and diſconcerted enemy. The German troops employed were of the beſt I had of that nation. The number of Britiſh was ſmall; but it was the ſelect light corps of the army, compoſed of choſen men from all the regiments, and commanded by Captain Fraſer, one of the moſt diſtinguiſhed officers in his line of ſervice that ever I met with. The inſtructions recommended the utmoſt caution reſpeſt-ing poſts and ſecurity of retreat, attention againſt expoſing the ſolid part of the detach-ment to affront, or committing it in any inſtance, without a moral certainty of ſucceſs. I touch with tenderneſs and with great reluſtance points that relate to the dead. My defence compels me to ſay, my cautions were not obſerved, nor the reinforcement advanced with the alacrity I had a right to expeſt. The men who commanded in both inſtances were brave and experienced officers. I have ever imputed their failure partly to deluſion in reſpeſt to the enemy, and partly to ſurpriſe and conſequent confuſion in the troops.

For further explanation of my motives, and the circumſtances attending the con-

I   duſt

* See Appendix No. VIII.

duct of the expedition, I beg leave to refer the committee to the letter laid before the houfe laft year, and more particularly to the private letter laid before the houfe lately.*

The fame letter will fhew the only refource that remained for proceeding towards Albany, after the difappointment of this expedition, viz. to prefs forward a neceffary fupply of provifion, and other indifpenfible articles, from Fort George. I fhall bring proof to your bar to this point, and I truft I fhall fhew beyond a doubt, that no poffible exertion was omitted. It is not uncommon for gentlemen, unacquainted with the peculiarities of the country to which I am alluding, to calculate the tranfport of magazines, by meafuring the diftance upon a map, and then applying the refources of carriage, as practifed in other countries. I requeft permiffion to fhew their miftake. The firft ftage from Fort George to Fort Edward is by land. The diftance and the roads were defcribed before. At Fort Edward the Hudfon's River becomes navigable for a certain extent, and it is the conftant practice in all tranfports to refume the water carriage. Were it not, new impediments would arife from hills, worfe roads, and fuch an increafed diftance, as would prevent the cattle returning to Fort George the fame day. About fix miles below Fort Edward lie the falls of Fort Miller, where there is another carrying-place, which, though of no confiderable length, makes it neceffary to unload the boats, to place the contents in carts, and to replace them in frefh boats, at the place the river again admits of navigation. The boats unloaded, return to Fort Edward againft a rapid ftream.

Upon this fhort ftate of facts, gentlemen will judge of our embarraffments. In the firft place, it was neceffary to bring forward to Fort Edward fourfcore or a hundred boats, as mere carriage-veffels for the provifions, each boat made a hard day's work for fix or more horfes, including the return of the horfes. At the next carrying-place, as above defcribed, it was neceffary to place a confiderable relay of horfes to draw over, firft, a portion of carriage boats, and afterwards the provifion, as it arrived. I have not mentioned the great number of other boats neceffary to be brought forward, to form bridges, to carry baggage and ammunition, and the number of carriages framed to tranfport the boats themfelves at the enfuing carrying-places, as we fhould proceed to Albany. This will be fhewn in detail at the bar, if the committee chufe to hear it; and I pledge myfelf, it will appear, that the diligence in this fervice was extreme; that it was performed in the moft expeditious manner poffible, regard being had to our refources, and that no delay was occafioned by the artillery, becaufe the horfes appropriated to it were fupernumerary to thofe for which we had carts, and the artillery, not already with the army, at laft was all brought up by its own horfes in two days.

On the 13th of September, the ftore of provifion, amounting to about thirty day's confumption, was completed. I have ftated, in my letter to the fecretary of ftate, my reafons againft proceeding with lefs quantity. And it is now time to enter upon the

the confideration of that object, which is held by fome to be conclufive upon the executive part of the campaign, the paffage of the Hudfon's River.

Two errors, refpecting this paffage, though of oppofite and incompatible natures, are fuppofed to have contributed to the ill fuccefs that enfued; the one, the error of delay, the other, that of precipitation. In defence againft the firft, I refer to my effort at Bennington to procure fupplies, and to the impediments, I have juft now ftated, after that effort failed. Againft the latter, I refer to the reafons laid down in my private letter to the fecretary of ftate, dated 20th of Auguft. * The ftate of things at this important crifis, and my reafoning upon it, are expreffed ftill more at large in my difpatch from Albany; I will now only touch them fhortly. On the one hand, my communications were at an end;. my retreat was infecure, the enemy was collected in force; they were ftrongly pofted; Colonel St. Leger was retiring from Fort Stanwix. Thefe were difficulties, but none of them infurmountable. On the other hand, I had diflodged the enemy repeatedly, when before in force, and more. ftrongly pofted; my army, was confcious of having the fuperiority, and eager to advance; I expected co-operation; no letters from Sir William Howe removed that expectation; that to Sir Guy Carleton had never weighed upon my mind, becaufe it was dated early in April, and confequently long before the fecretary of ftate's inftructions, which I muft have fuppofed to relate to co-operation, could be received. The letter of 17th July,* mentioned that General's return to my affiftance, fhould Wafhington turn his force towards me; indicated, as I thought, an expectation of my arrival at Albany; and informed me, that Sir Henry Clinton was left at New-York, and would act as occurrences might direct. I did *not* know Sir Henry Clinton's force. I *did* know, that confiderable reinforcement might be then expected at New-York from England: After all, fhould co-operation from below fail, the whole force of Colonel St. Leger, and Sir William Johnfon, was to be expected from above, in time to facilitate a retreat, though not in time to affift my advance. Under thefe different fuggeftions, and thofe that are more copioufly ftated in the difpatch, to which I have referred, I read again my orders.(I believe for an hundredth time) and I was decided.

And I am ftill convinced, that no proof that could have been brought from appearances, intelligence or reafoning, could have juftified me to my country, have faved me from the condemnation of my profeffion, or produced pardon within my own breaft, had I not advanced, and tried a battle with the enemy.

I will conclude this fubject, with again afferting upon my honour, what I hope to fupport by evidence, though it is impoffible to bring pofitive proof to a negative, that neither General Frafer, nor General Phillips, ever offered, as has been reported, nor can be fuppofed to have conceived any objection againft the paffage of the Hudfon's River.

This

* See Appendix No. IX.

* No. X.

This refolution being taken, I truft, the manner of approaching the enemy, when explained by witneffes, will not be difgraceful to me as a foldier.   The action, which enfued on the 19th of September, verified my opinion of the valour of my army; and I muft, in truth, acknowledge, a very refpectable fhare of that quality in the army of the enemy. To the general defcription given in my difpatch, it will be fit to add, by evidence, the peculiar merits of the troops in that action. The honour of three Britifh regiments, in continual and clofe fire for four hours, all of them fuffering confiderable lofs, and one remaining with lefs than fixty men, and four or five officers, ought not to lofe its due applaufe, becaufe it is faid, their opponents were irregulars and militia.

A victory was at laft obtained, but the clofe of day unavoidably prevented any immediate advantages. On the day following, it was known from prifoners and deferters, that the enemy were in a poft ftrongly fortified; but from the thicknefs of the wood, it was impoffible to catch a view of any part of their pofition. All that could be done, therefore, was to take up ground as near them, as the nature of the country would admit with regard to military arrangement. It appears from the difpatch already alluded to, that the army remained in this pofition till the 9th of October, when the fecond action enfued, employed in fortifying their camp, and watching the enemy, whofe numbers it was now known, had been greatly fuperior to ours in the action.

It may here be afked, why, as foon as it became palpable that no ufe could be made of the victory, I did not retreat?

It will be fhewn, that on the fecond day after the action, I received intelligence from Sir Henry Clinton, of his intention to attack the highlands about that time, and I was hourly in expectation, I thought a juftly founded one, of that meafure operating to diflodge Mr. Gates entirely, or to oblige him to detach a large portion of his force. Either of thefe cafes would probably have opened my way to Albany. In thefe circumftances, could the preference upon thefe alternatives admit of a moment's reflection? To wait fo fair a profpect of effecting at laft the great purpofe of the campaign, or to put a victorious army, under all the difadvantages of a beaten one, by a difficult and difgraceful retreat; relinquifhing the long expected co-operation, in the very hour of its promife, and leaving Sir Henry Clinton's army, and probably Sir William Howe's, expofed, with fo much of the feafon of the campaign to run, to the whole force of Mr. Gates, after he fhould have feen me on the other fide of Hudfon's River.

Some of the fame confiderations, and other concomitant circumftances, will, in part, ferve to account for my not attacking the enemy during this interval; for in this fituation, as in former ones, my conduct has been arraigned upon oppofite principles.
                                                                          The

The committee will obferve, that after receiving intelligence of Sir Henry Clinton's defign, different meffengers were difpatched by different routes, to inform that officer of my fituation, and of the time I thought I could continue in it. To have hazarded a repulfe, under fo reafonable an expectation of a powerful diverfion, would, in my opinion, have been very unjuftifiable; but when I add, that from the backwardnefs, or defection, of the few Indians that remained, the numbers of rifle-men, and other irregulars employed on the enemy's out-pofts, and the ftrength and darknefs of the furrounding woods, it had not yet been practicable to gain any competent knowledge of their pofition, I truft every man will go with me in the fentiment, that all thefe circumftances confidered, an attack would have been confummate rafhnefs.

Another very powerful reafon, that operated on the fide of delay, was the ftate of. my fick and wounded. Numbers of the latter were recovering faft; many excellent officers in particular; and the more I delayed the ftronger I grew. The time alfo entitled me to expect Lieutenant Colonel St. Leger's corps would be arrived at Ticonderoga, and fecret means had been long concerted to enable him to make an effort to join me, with probability of fuccefs.

Upon mature confideration of thefe and other circumftances attending this period, come to my knowledge fince, I am clearly of opinion, that had the reinforcements from England arrived in time, to have enabled Sir Henry Clinton to have effected the ftroke he afterwards fo gallantly made in the highlands, any time between the two actions, I, fhould have made my way.

The difpatch alluded to, proceeds to ftate the reafon that induced me to make the movement on the 7th October. I fhall only add, to obviate a fuppofed error, in not advancing my whole line, that the part remaining in my camp, operated as effectually to keep the enemy's right wing in check, from fupporting their left, as if it had moved, with this additional advantage, that it prevented the danger of their advancing by the plain, near the river, and falling upon my rear.

I have reafon to believe my difappointment on that day proceeded from an uncommon circumftance in the conduct of the enemy. Mr. Gates, as I have been informed, had determined to receive the attack in his lines; Mr. Arnold, who commanded on the left, forfeeing the danger of being turned, advanced without confultation with his general, and gave, inftead of receiving battle. The ftroke might have been fatal on his part had he failed. But confident I am, upon minute examination of the ground fince, that had the other idea been purfued, I fhould in a few hours have gained a pofition, that in fpite of the enemy's numbers, would have put them in my power.

Difagreeable as is the neceffity, I muft here again, in juftice to my own army, recur to the vigour and obftinacy with which they were fought by the enemy. A more determined perfeverance than they fhewed in the attack upon the lines, though they were

D

finally

finally repulfed by the corps under Lord Balcarras, I believe, is not in any officer's experience. It will be the bufinefs of evidence to prove, that in the part, where Colonel Breyman was killed, and the enemy penetrated, the mifchief could not be repaired, nor under it the camp be longer tenable.

The tranfactions of the enfuing night, the day of the eighth, and the whole progrefs of the retreat to Saratoga, will be laid before the committee minutely in the courfe of my evidence, as well as every circumftance, from the time the army arrived there to the figning the convention. I have only to premife, that, I truft, I fhall be able to prove, to the fatisfaction of the committee, that even in this fituation, I had the chance of a favourable event. The enemy had intended to attack by the plain of Saratoga. On the morning of the 11th, a confiderable column had actually paffed the Fifh Kill for that purpofe during the fog, which at that feafon was regular till fometime after fun rife. The intention was prevented taking place, by intelligence one of their generals received from a deferter, that I had a line formed behind the brufh-wood, to fupport the poft of artillery, which was their immediate object of attack. The general inftantly retreated his column, and prevented a general action, which my pofition, compared with the propofed one of the enemy, gave me reafon to hope would have been to my advantage.

I have likewife a fatisfactory confidence, that I fhall demonftrate that the intelligence I ftated to the councils of war, refpecting the ftrength of the enemy, did not fall fhort in any part, and in fome parts much exceeded my own belief, particularly on the only poffible routes of my retreat; and that thofe pofts were not taken up during my ftay at Saratoga, as has been reported, but fome of them previous to the action of the 7th, and the reft immediately after it.

I fhall clofe the whole of this by delivering at your table, from the hands of my fecretary, an authenticated return of the force of General Gates, figned by himfelf, and the truth of it will be fupported from ocular teftimony, by every officer of the Britifh army. Many of them are now in England, and after what has been infinuated, not to fay charged in this Houfe, it becomes the duty of the accufers, not only to examine clofely the officers I have called, but to produce any other witneffes, that in their thoughts may be qualified to fpeak to the good or bad order of the rebel troops, when they marched by in their prefence, and to their behaviour, when oppofed to our troops in action.

I cannot clofe this long trefpafs upon the patience of the committee, without expreffing one humble hope, that in forming a judgment upon the whole, or any diftinct part of thefe tranfactions, they will be confidered as they muft have appeared at the time; for, I believe, where war is concerned, few men in command would ftand acquitted,

quitted, if any after-knowledge of facts and circumstances were brought in argument against decisions of the moment, and apparent exigencies of the occasion.

I submit all I have said, some of it, I fear, not sufficiently prepared or arranged, with true respect to the committee. I shall not mention *all* the disadvantages, under which I have pressed this business upon their attention. I have cause to regret the absence of a most confidential friend in Major General Phillips; zealous advocates, I trust, in Major General Reidesel and Brigadier Hamilton. Much of my vindication is in the grave with General Fraser; much with Colonel Ackland your late member. I trust my zeal, in promoting this enquiry, as I have done, will be one mark of the sense I bear of the general character of this house; that however men may be biassed by political attachments upon common occasions, when the honour of an individual is committed to their hands, they will alone be guided by truth and justice. And the next inference I should wish to be drawn, from my earnestness for a public appeal, is this; that however others may impute errors to my conduct, I am myself conscious of the rectitude of my intentions.

EVIDENCE.

Jovis 20° *die Maij,* 1779.

Committee to confider of the feveral Papers which were prefented to the Houfe by Mr. De Grey, upon the 19th Day of March laft, purfuant to their Addrefs to his Majefty.

Mr. F. Montagu in the Chair.

SIR GUY CARLETON was called in and examined by General Burgoyne as follows:

1. Q. **D**O you recollect having received a letter from the fecretary of ftate, mentioning the reafons that made it expedient for you to remain in the province of Quebec?
    A. Yes, very well.
2. Q. What was the date of it?
    A. I think the 12th of Auguft, 1776—I am fure it was in Auguft.
3. Q. Was not the date of that letter long before the return of General Burgoyne from Canada to Great Britain?
    A. Yes.
4. Q. During the winter, preceding the campaign of 1777, was not the artillery prepared at Montreal for field fervice, upon the fuppofition that you was to command the army beyond the frontiers of the province?
    A. It was.
5. Q. Was the proportion allotted to General Burgoyne for field fervice more than was intended, had you fo commanded?
    A. I don't precifely recollect that—It does not ftrike me there was any great difference.
6. Q. Was the quantity of artillery decided on in concert with Major-General Phillips, and on his recommendation?
    A. The artillery I had prepared for the campaign, on a fuppofition I was to go myfelf, was in concert with General Phillips. That department, as well as others, was put under the command of General Burgoyne on his arrival; and, I fuppofe, he followed the fame method fo far as regarded the artillery.
7. Q. Did General Burgoyne apply to you for troops from Canada to garrifon Ticonderoga when he advanced?
    A. He did.
8. Q. What was the purport of your anfwer?
    A. That I did not think myfelf juftified to grant it by my orders—My anfwer will appear more precifely by a copy of my anfwer to General Burgoyne.

Q. Do

Q. Do you recollect that General Burgoyne informed you of the motives on which 9.
he proceeded from Skenesborough to Fort Edward by land in preference to the route by
Ticonderoga and Lake George?

A. I do.

Q. Did you concur in his fentiments?   10.

A. I remember my anfwer was an anfwer of approbation.

Q. Do you know of any circumftance of General Burgoyne's military conduct, 11.
while under your command, that you difapproved?

A. I had no reafon to difapprove of any part of his conduct while under my command.   [*Withdrew.*

Again called in, and examined by other Members of the Committee.

Q. Whether, when you propofed to take that train of artillery with you that you 12.
have mentioned, it was with a view to the reduction of the forts at Ticonderoga; or
whether you propofed to have taken with you the fame train of artillery in cafe you had
marched forward in the country toward Albany?

A. It was with an intention to reduce the forts and lines at Ticonderoga; the train
of artillery was calculated for that fervice.

Q. Whether you know what proportion of artillery was carried forward by the ar- 13. By Gen.
my under General Burgoyne's command after the reduction of Ticonderoga?   Burgoyne.

A. I don't recollect.

Q. Would you not, in cafe you had reduced Ticonderoga and marched forwards 14.
towards Albany, have carried with you a train of field artillery?

A. I probably fhould have taken artillery with me.

Q. Had you forefeen a neceffity of fortifying a camp at Albany, would you not 15.
have carried fome guns of the calibre of twelve pounders and light twenty-fours?

A. It is really a very difficult matter off hand to run into all the minute operations
of a campaign; every meafure of that fort muft have been a matter of confideration
and deliberation, and there are a thoufand circumftances that might have determined
me upon the fpot—I don't wifh to conceal from this Houfe any thing that I would
have done—but I hope they will confider, that every gentleman may have different
ideas of the ftate and fituation of the army, as expreffed by the queftion afked, and the
leaft inaccuracy of expreffion on my part may convey ideas very different from what
I could wifh—In general, fo confiderable a corps as that was, very feldom moves
without artillery, but the precife number muft depend on a variety of circumftances,
which the difcretion and judgment of the officer who commands muft determine.

Q. Were not the orders you received from government pofitive, for General Bur- 16.
goyne to march to Albany?

A. The orders have been publifhed I underftand—Every gentleman in this Houfe
muft be a judge of thofe orders whether they were pofitive or not.

Q. Did you not receive a letter, dated the 5th of April, from Sir William Howe, 17.
informing you that he could not fend any force to affift the operations of General
Burgoyne's army?

A. I received a letter from Sir William Howe relative to his operations, a copy of
which was fent to General Burgoyne—I think it was not juft in thofe terms, but a
copy of the letter is on the table.

Q. Whether

18.   Q. Whether on that information, you confidered that you had any difcretionary power to detain General Burgoyne after that information ?

A. Certainly not.

19.   Q. Whether in cafe of any difficulty that General Burgoyne might meet with on his march, there was any latitude given to him (General Burgoyne) to retreat ?

A. I faid before, that the orders were before the Houfe, who are competent to judge on that point.

20.   Q. Did you yourfelf underftand thofe orders to General Burgoyne to be pofitive ?

A. That is giving an opinion upon what perhaps may be a queftion in the Houfe; whereas I have already faid, the Houfe are as competent to judge as I am.

21.   Q. Is the Committee to underftand from that anfwer, that you have any objection of giving your opinion on that queftion ?

A. I have an objection to give an opinion on almoft all points.

22.   Q. Did you give it in orders to General Burgoyne, in cafe he met with any difficulties during his march in Canada, under your command, not to proceed ?

A. I fhould have taken care that General Burgoyne met with no difficulties in his march in Canada ; nor do I well fee how he could.

23.   Q. Where do the boundaries of the province of Canada end ?

A. Between the Illinois and Point au Fer.

24.   Q. Is the fortrefs of Ticonderoga in Canada ?

A. No.

25.   Q. Did your commiffion, as commander in chief of the troops in the northern divifion, extend beyond the boundaries of Canada fo Ticonderoga ?

A. That commiffion as commander in chief, I underftood, did extend fo far ; but by the orders already alluded to, or by thofe which General Burgoyne brought out in the fpring 1777, I underftood that my command was reftrained to the limits of the province, and that General Burgoyne was entirely from under my command, as foon as he paffed the limits of the province.

26.   Q. Did you apply to the fecretary of ftate for a reinforcement of 4000 men, as neceffary for the campaign of 1777 ?

A. I recollect when General Burgoyne was coming home in the fall of 1776, as I was perfectly fatisfied with his conduct in the preceding campaign, I talked over with him, in confidence, what I thought neceffary for the following campaign ; among other things I defired him to make a memorandum to demand 4000 men, as a reinforcement for the enfuing campaign, or at leaft for four battalions. I think I have feen thofe memorandums were accurately ftated and laid before the Houfe.

27.   Q. What part of that 4000 men which you thought neceffary for the campaign of 1777, was actually fent out to Canada in that year ?

A. I do not accurately remember how many—I think a very fmall part—You may have a very precife account from the returns.

28.   Q. Of that fmall part fent in 1777, did not a certain proportion arrive very late in the year ?

A. Yes, a part arrived late.

Q. After

Q. After you had received your orders from the fecretary of ftate, did you appre- 29.
hend that General Burgoyne, as long as he was within the province of Canada, was
pofitively under your command?

A. Yes, I did: as long as he was in the province of Canada, I looked on him to be
pofitively under my command; but the load of the expedition being on his fhoulders, I thought it proper that he, in all things fhould direct; and therefore I gave out
immediate orders, that not only the troops he was to command out of the province, but all the departments neceffary for the affifting his expedition, fhould comply
immediately, and without delay, with every requifition and order he fhould give.
The reafon of my doing fo was, that no time might be loft. I only required that
they fhould report to me what orders they had received from General Burgoyne. I
believe thofe orders are alfo on the table.

Q. Will you explain to the Committee what you mean by the words, *load of the* 30.
expedition lying on General Burgoyne's fhoulders?

A. I had no particular meaning; they are words I fhould have ufed on any expedition of importance.

Q. If General Burgoyne had met with very confiderable difficulties to impede his 31.
progrefs within the province of Canada, would you have thought yourfelf juftifiable in giving any orders to General Burgoyne, different from thofe tranfmitted to
General Burgoyne, through you, from the fecretary of ftate?

A. Had there been any difficulties in Canada, I would not have given him up
the command.

Q. Having given up the command to General Burgoyne, and having ordered all 32.
the troops to obey him, only reporting their proceedings to you, would you after
that, have thought yourfelf juftifiable to change the order to General Burgoyne,
upon his meeting with great difficulties on the frontiers of the neighbouring provinces?

A. I really did not mean to evade the queftion in the leaft. It did not appear to me
poffible that there could be any difficulties. I don't mean to fay there could not, from
the nature of the country, be difficulties in the march that might occafion delay, but
by the nature of the queftion I underftood difficulties from the enemy. In that cafe
I fhould not have thought myfelf juftifiable in giving up the command.

Q. If you had heard, that on the frontiers, and within the province of Canada, 33.
there was the greateft reafon to think, that the refiftance of General Burgoyne's army
was fo great as to make it, in your opinion, exceedingly difficult for that General to
force his way to Albany, would you think yourfelf juftifiable in giving different orders to General Burgoyne, from thofe given by the fecretary of ftate; or would you
have thought the fecretary of ftate's orders for General Burgoyne's army fo peremptory that it would not be proper for you to interfere?

A. If I underftood the queftion as it now ftands, it is what I would have done, had
the province been invaded, or clofe on the point of being invaded, and the enemy
entering the province.

Q. The queftion does not mean an invading army, but a refiftance from the enemy 34.
to the progrefs of General Burgoyne's army, in the cafe ftated in the laft queftion?

A. In

A. In that cafe, that an enemy fhould be found (within the limits of my command) I fhould have ordered all the troops deftined for the defence of the province,
to have immediately joined thofe deftined for General Burgoyne, and have reaffum-
ed the command of all, until thofe obftructions had been removed, within the
limits of my authority.

35. Q. Suppofe no enemy within the province of Canada, but pofted in fuch a manner
upon the line of communication with Albany, as to make it exceeding difficult for
General Burgoyne to obey the orders given to him, would you think yourfelf juftifiable in giving different orders to General Burgoyne, from thofe given by the fecretary of ftate ; or would you have thought the fecretary of ftate's orders for
General Burgoyne's army fo peremptory that it would not be proper for you to
interfere ?

A. I could not change General Burgoyne's orders one tittle, that was my opinion ; he
received his orders from the fame power that gave me my authority ; when once he
paffed the limits of my command, I neither could give him orders, nor would he
be juftified in obeying them.

36. Q. Do you mean the latter part of that anfwer as an anfwer to a queftion which
fuppofes General Burgoyne within the limits of the province of Canada ?

A. No : while he was within the limits of the province of Canada, I would
have given General Burgoyne orders in all cafes of difficulty and danger. There
being no fuch cafe when General Burgoyne arrived in Canada, in 1777, nor a poffibility of an event of that fort, I put the troops and all things under his command, which concerned his expedition, that he might arrange and combine their
motions according to his own plan of operation for the campaign, that no time might
be loft by any unneceffary applications to me, which the ftrict forms of my command
might otherwife require.   [Withdrew.

Again called in.

37. Q. Should you, if you had been in General Burgoyne's fituation, and acting under the orders which you know he received, have thought yourfelf bound to
purfue them implicitly, or at liberty to deviate from them ?

A. I fhould certainly have thought myfelf bound to have obeyed them to the utmoft of my power ; but, to fay as a military man, that in all cafes poffible, I
muft have gone on, is a very nice thing to fay indeed ; it muft have thrown me, and
I fuppofe every officer, into a moft unpleafant and anxious fituation, to have debated within himfelf, whether he was or was not to go on. Every man muft decide
for himfelf. What I would have done, I really don't know ; the particular fituation,
and a man's own particular feelings, muft determine the point. If I might be indulged, I would beg leave to fay, that I did not mean to evade any queftion ; I meant to
anfwer directly ; yet queftions may be put to me, of fo delicate a nature, and perhaps
no man in the world is in a more delicate fituation, with refpect to the prefent cafe in
queftion, and the bufinefs of this Committee, than I am ; when fuch queftions are
put to me, I fhall pray the indulgence of the Committee, to be excufed anfwering

3   them

them, but I will not evade them. As I now underftand the meaning of the right honourable member in the former queftions to be, Whether I fhould have taken upon me to fuperfede the King's orders, fuppofing I knew of any unfurmountable difficulties in the way, as that I had information of 20,000 men at Ticonderoga, before General Burgoyne left the province of Canada, I fhould have told General Burgoyne my information? But it was General Burgoyne who was to carry the orders into execution, and not me, and therefore it was upon his own judgment he was to determine ; I fhould have given him my opinion, but I think I had no right to give him orders under thofe circumftances.

Q. Who was it that made the arrangement and diftribution of the troops that 38. were to be left for the defence of Canada, independent of thofe under the command of General Burgoyne?

A. The orders that are before the Houfe are very full, and I thought very clear. The Committee will fee in thofe orders the troops that were deftined for General Burgoyne's expedition, and the troops that were to remain for the defence of the province.

Q. Who made that diftribution? 39.

A. It came to me from the fecretary of ftate.

Q. Did not the orders from the fecretary of ftate go to the detail of the fmalleft 40. pofts within the province?

A. The letter is before the Committee.

Queftion repeated.

A. I fhould beg for the letter to be read; I don't wifh to avoid any queftion, but 41. I wifh to be accurate.

Q. Was the diftribution of the troops prefcribed to you by the fecretary of ftate, or 42. left to your difcretion?

A. In mentioning the number of troops which were to remain in that province, it was there faid that thofe troops would be fufficient for garrifoning fuch and fuch places, particularizing them.

Q. Did you ever know an inftance, in your military life, of a minifter making a 43. diftribution of troops for the defence of a province, without taking the opinion or leaving a great deal to the difcretion of the governor of that province, that governor being an acting military officer of very high rank?

A. I never had the honour to correfpond with a fecretary of ftate till I was appointed to the command of that province.

Q. Whether you was confulted upon the practicability of penetrating from the 44. frontiers of Canada to Albany by force, with the ftrength allotted to General Burgoyne for that purpofe?

A. No ; I was not.

Q. Are you acquainted with the paffage from New York to Canada by the Hud- 45. fon's River.

A. I have gone that way.

Q. Have you obferved it with a view to military operations? 46.

A. No; I never made the tour having any military operations in view.

E   Q. Are

47.   Q. Are you acquainted with the forces which Sir William Howe had under his immediate command at and about New York, on the 17th of July, 1777?

A. I am not.

48.   Q. Suppofing Sir William Howe had 12,000 effective men, befides a fufficient force lodged in New York, Staten Ifland, and Long Ifland, to defend them againft General Wafhington's army, fuppofing General Wafhington's army in the Jeffies, near Quibble Town, and that Sir William Howe had received accounts of General Burgoyne's fuccefs at Ticonderoga, and was acquainted with the orders under which General Burgoyne acted; is it your opinion that the beft movement Sir William Howe could have made for the purpofes of forwarding the execution of the orders, under which General Burgoyne acted, would have been to have failed with his army from New York to Chefapeak Bay?

A. Had I had the honour to have commanded on that fide, I do not know what I fhould have done myfelf.

49.   Q. After you received the letter from Sir William Howe, informing you of his intended expedition to the fouthward, whether you did expect that Sir William Howe's army could co-operate on the Hudfon's River with the northern army that feafon?

A. I don't know.

50.   Q. Whether you thought, after the receipt of that letter, that it was probable there would be a co-operation from the fouthern army?

A. I took it for granted, that Sir William Howe knew what he was about, and would do what he thought beft for the public fervice: I really was fo little informed of all the particular circumftances of his fituation and of the provinces under his command, that I could form no judgment of the propriety or impropriety of his conduct, or of the effects of his meafures.

51.   Q. Did your information lead you to believe, that the inhabitants between Saratoga and Albany, were fo well affected to bis Majefty and Great Britain, as that there would be much advantage derived from their affiftance to the King's army in the profecution of General Burgoyne's expedition?

A. I had frequent accounts from that part of the country, that there were numbers ready to take arms and join the King's troops if they fhould penetrate fo far.

52.   Q. Do you mean, by *penetrating fo far*, to Albany, or to the length the army got?

A. The whole extent of the inhabited country, according to the information brought to me.

53.   Q. Had you no information that a formidable militia might be raifed in that country to oppofe his Majefty's arms?

A. Yes; I had fuch information.

54.   Q. Did you think that the force which General Burgoyne carried with him from Ticonderoga towards Albany was fufficient to oppofe fuch force?

A. I really muft beg leave to be excufed anfwering that queftion.

55.   Q. If you had been confulted refpecting General Burgoyne's expedition, knowing the nature of that country, and the force General Burgoyne had, would you or not have advifed fuch an enterprize?

A. If

A. If I had had the honour to command in that campaign as I had in the former, I don't precisely know what I should have done myself.

Q. Did you give any advice for employing the savages? 56.

A. I don't recollect that I said any thing about them. [*Withdrew.*

Jovis 27° *die Maii,* 1779.

Earl of Balcarras called in and examined by General Burgoyne.

Q. IN what station did your Lordship serve in the campaigns in America, in 1776, 1. and 1777?

A. I commanded the British light infantry.

Q. Was the British light infantry continually attached to the corps under the 2. command of Brigadier General Fraser?

A. Yes.

Q. Had you occasion to observe that General Burgoyne and General Fraser lived 3. together in friendship and confidence?

A. Yes, I had.

Q. Had you reason to believe that General Fraser was consulted by General Bur- 4. goyne in all material operations?

A. I had reason to believe that General Fraser was consulted in many material operations.

Q. Does your Lordship know or believe that the proportion of artillery, at- 5. tached to General Fraser's corps through the whole campaign, was according to his requisitions and desires?

A. I understood from General Fraser, that the proportion of artillery allotted to him was agreeable to his own requisitions.

Q. Do you recollect the number of killed and wounded in General Fraser's corps, 6. at the affair of Huberton?

A. I don't recollect exactly; I think it was about 150.

Q. What was your opinion of the behaviour of the enemy on that day? 7.

A. Circumstanced as the enemy was, as an army very hard pressed in their retreat, they certainly behaved with great gallantry.

Q. Was it practicable, the nature of the country, the fatigue of the King's troops, 8. the care of the wounded, and other circumstances considered, to have pursued the enemy farther after that action?

A. It was not

E V I D E N C E.   [Earl of Balcarras.

9.   Q. Do you recollect on what day General Fraſer's corps rejoined the army at Skeneſborough?
A. On the 9th of July; I think that it was on that day.

10.   Q. On what day was the action at Huberton?
A. On the 7th of July.

11.   Q. Do you recollect the difficulties of removing the wounded from Huberton to the hoſpital at Ticonderoga?
A. From the diſtance and badneſs of the roads, the difficulties attending the removing of the hoſpital muſt have been very great.

12.   Q. Was it practicable, unleſs the wounded had been left expoſed to the enemy, to have rejoined the army ſooner?
A. It was not.

13.   Q. Does your Lordſhip recollect how the army was employed between that time and the march to Fort Edward?
A. The Britiſh were employed in opening the country and making roads to Fort Anne; the Germans under General Reideſel were detached about fourteen miles to the left.

14.   Q. Do you recollect the poſt the enemy abandoned upon the aſcent from the Low Country to the Pitch Pine Plains, in the march from Fort Anne to Fort Edward?
A. I do recollect ſuch a place.

15.   Q. Had the enemy maintained their ground on that poſt, do you apprehend that a conſiderable portion of artillery would have been neceſſary to diſlodge them?
A. Artillery would certainly have been of great uſe to diſlodge the enemy.

16.   Q. Did you ever ſee an inſtance, during your ſervice in America, that the rebels continued twenty-four hours on the ſame place without entrenching; and was it not alſo their general practice to add abbaties to their entrenchments?
A. The rebels were always indefatigable in ſecuring themſelves by entrenchments, and in general they added an abbatis to thoſe entrenchments.

17.   Q. Do you remember the poſition the enemy abandoned at Schuyler's Iſland?
A. I do remember to have paſſed ſuch an poſt once.

18.   Q. Does you Lordſhip think that poſition could have been forced without a numerous artillery or heavy loſs?
A. I do not think it could.

19.   Q. From the nature of that country, do you think that poſt could have been turned?
A. Not without greatly riſquing the boats and portable magazines.

20.   Q. Is it poſſible at any time in that country, and with a ſmall army, to quit the navigable rivers, without leaving the boats and portable magazines expoſed?
A. I imagine it is not.

21.   Q. Did you live in habits of intimacy and communication with General Fraſer?
A. I did.

22.   Q. Was General Fraſer of a warmth and openneſs of temper that generally made him communicative of his ſentiments, when they differed from the ſentiments of thoſe with whom he acted?
A. General

A. General Frafer's temper was warm, open, and communicative, but referved in matters of confidence.

Q. Did you ever hear General Frafer exprefs difapprobation of the meafure of paf- 23. fing Hudfon's River ?

A. I never did.

Q. Was not a bridge conftructed of rafts, and fome boats thrown over that 24. river, a little before the time of the attack on Bennington ?

A. There was.

Q. Did not General Frafer's corps pafs the river by that bridge, and take poft on 25. the heights of Saratoga ?

A. It did.

Q. Do you remember that bridge being carried away by the torrents and bad 26. weather, whereby the communication was cut off between that corps and the main body of the army ?

A. I do.

Q. Was General Frafer's corps recalled after that action, and obliged to repafs 27. the river in boats and fcowls ?

A. It was.

Q. Do you remember General Frafer expreffing his forrow for being obliged to re- 28. turn back over the Hudfon's River ?

A. I remember General Frafer mentioning it with regret.

Q. Had the rear guard of General Frafer's corps been attacked during that paf- 29. fage over the river, would not a powerful fire of artillery from the oppofite fhore have been of great ufe, if not the only means of protecting them ?

A. If the enemy had attacked General Frafer, they would have found him in a very bad pofture ; it was impoffible to take a better, and, as they could not be fupported by the line, the only means of fafety muft have been to get under cover of the fire of our artillery.

Q. Was there not an expectation and impatience of the troops in general to pafs 30. Hudfon's River, and advance on the enemy ?

A. There was.

Q. Was there not a general confidence and alacrity on the occafion ? 31.

A. There was.

Q. From thefe circumftances, and your other knowledge of the army, do you not 32. believe that to have made no further attempt on the enemy would have caufed difappointment and dejection in the troops, and reflections on the general ?

A. The troops were in the higheft fpirits, and wifhed to be led on.

Q. Does your Lordfhip recollect the march up to the enemy on the morning of 33. the 19th of September ?

A. I do.

Q. Was the combination of the march fuch, as, that notwithftanding the paf- 34. fage of the ravines and the thicknefs of the woods, the column of General Frafer's march, and that of the Britifh line, led by General Burgoyne, were in a fituation to fupport each other, and fpeedily to form in line of battle, at the time the enemy began the attack ?

A. After

A. After the columns had paffed the ravines, they arrived at their refpective pofts with great precifion in point of time, and every fortunate circumftance attended the forming of the line.

35. Q. How long did that action laft?
A. The Britifh were attacked partially about one o'clock. The action was general at three, and ended at feven o'clock.

36. Q. From the nature of the country, was it poffible to difcern the enemy's pofition or movements, to form any judgment what attacks were in force, and what were feints?
A. I think not.

37. Q. Did we remain mafters of the field of battle?
A. We did.

38. Q. Had the field of battle been well difputed by the enemy?
A. The enemy behaved with great obftinacy and courage.

39. Q. Was it too dark to purfue with effect at the time the action ended?
A. It was.

40. Q. Did the King's troops take up ground nearer to the enemy, the morning after the action?
A. It was rather nearer to the enemy.

41. Q. How near were the out-pofts of General Frafer's corps to the out-pofts of the enemy from that time to the action of the 7th of October?
A. I fhould imagine within half a mile.

42. Q. From the nature of the country, and the fituation of the enemy's out-pofts, was it poffible to reconnoitre their pofition?
A. From the nature of the country, the difficulties attending reconnoitering muft have been very great.

43. Q. Were not the riflemen, and other irregulars, employed by the enemy at out-pofts and on fcouts, an overmatch for the Indian or provincial troops that were with the army at that time?
A. They were.

44. Q. Was not General Frafer's corps continually at work during the interval abovementioned, in feeuring their own pofts, and opening the front to oppofe the enemy?
A. They were.

45. Q. After General Frafer received his wound, on the 7th of October, on whom did the command of his corps devolve?
A. On me.

46. Q. Was you in a fituation on that day, to obferve the general difpofition of the army, made by General Burgoyne, previous to the action?
A. I remember two redoubts having been erected on the left, to cover the boats and provifions to enable General Burgoyne to make a detachment from his army.

47. Q. Was you in a fituation to obferve the difpofition made immediately before the attack by the enemy?
A. I only recollect the fituation of the two battalions of the advanced corps.

Q. After

Q. After the retreat to the lines, were the lines attacked, and with what de- 48.
gree of vigour?

A. The lines were attacked, and with as much fury as the fire of small arms can
admit.

Q. Does your Lordship remember that part of the lines where you commanded, 49.
being visited by General Burgoyne during the attack?

A. I don't recollect to have seen General Burgoyne.

Q. Was the cannon of great use in the repulse of the enemy in your post? 50.

A. Of very great use.

Q. Do you think that post would have been tenable next morning, the enemy 51.
having possession of Colonel Briemen's post?

A. I do not think it would.

Q. Would the possession of the post by the enemy, together with the possef- 52.
fion of Colonel Briemen's posts, have laid open the flank and rear of the camp of
the line?

A. It would.

Q. Was the retreat in the night, and the new disposition of the whole army made 53.
in good order and without loss?

A. It was.

Q. Did the army remain under arms, and in momentary expectation of battle, 54.
the whole of the day of the 8th?

A. It did.

Q. Do you remember the confusion and difficulties attending the line of baggage 55.
in the retreat, in the night of the 8th?

A. I do.

Q. Was not the retreat neverthelefs made in good order by the troops, and 56.
without loss?

A. It was.

Q. Does your Lordship remember the weather, the state of the roads, the state 57.
of the cattle, and the difficulty of passing the Fish Kiln, in the retreat to Saratoga,
in the day and night of the 9th?

A. It rained incessantly, consequently the roads were bad; the cattle were nearly
starved for want of forage, and the bridge over the Fish Kill had been destroyed by
the enemy; the troops were obliged to ford the river.

Q. Had there been no enemy to oppose us, or no bridges or roads to repair, would 58.
it have been possible, from the state of the fatigue of the troops, to have continued
the march farther immediately after the arrival at Saratoga?

A. The troops were greatly fatigued, and the artillery had been left on the other side
of the Fish Kill.

Q. Why were they left on the other side of the Fish Kill? 59.

A. The bridge had been destroyed by the enemy; it was exceeding dark, and I do
not know whether the ford was passable for the artillery without being first examined.

Q. Do you remember the enemy opening a battery on the opposite side of Hudson's 60.
River, and the circumstances attending the opening that battery?

A. The

A. The corps I commanded was at that time posted, and they fired on us at that time, but I do not know from what direction.

61.   Q. Does your Lordship remember the shot from that battery going over the table when you and several officers were at dinner?

A. I did not dine with General Burgoyne that day—I recollect hearing a cannon shot had discomposed the company at the general's table.

62.   Q. Consequently must not that battery have commanded the ford over the Hudson's River?

A. I believe I said, I did not recollect from what direction the shot came, but they had a battery which commanded that ford.

63.   Q. Do you recollect on what day you was called, with other commanders of corps, to the first council of war?

A. On the 13th of October.

64.   Q. Was there a spot in the whole position to be found for holding that council, which was not exposed to cannon or rifle-shot?

A. We were not so fortunate as to find one.

65.   Q. Do you recollect that General Burgoyne, after stating to the council the difficulties of the situation, declare, that nothing should induce him to propose terms to the enemy without the general concurrence of the generals and field officers of the army, and that he was ready to take the lead in any measure that they should think for the honour of the British arms, or words to that effect?

A. I remember words to that effect.

66.   Q. Was the concurrence unanimous for treating on honourable terms?

A. I hope I shall stand justified with the members of that council, when I have the honour to declare to this House, that our situation appeared to them so decided as not to admit of one dissenting voice.

67.   Q. When Colonel Kingston brought back the first proposition, wherein it was specified by Major General Gates, that the army should lay down their arms in their entrenchments and surrender prisoners of war, does your Lordship remember, that General Burgoyne, when he read them to the council, declared, he would not set his hand to those conditions, or words to that effect?

A. I think the words of the proposal from General Gates were, That the British army should be ordered, by word of command from their adjutant general, to lay down their arms in the entrenchments. It was rejected with disdain by General Burgone, and the council concurred in his indignation.

68.   Q. Were the counter proposals, penned by General Burgoyne, unanimously approved?

A. They were.

69.   Q. When those proposals had been agreed to by General Gates, but copies not signed by either party, do you remember General Burgoyne informing the council of intelligence he had received from a spy in the night, and submitting to their consideration, whether it was consistent with public faith, and if so, expedient to suspend the execution of the treaty and trust to events?

A. I do remember it.

70.   Q. Does your Lordship recollect what was the result of that consideration?

A. The

A. The determination of the council, on the queftion being put, was, that the public faith was *bona fide* plighted.

Q. Though that was the opinion of the majority, was there not a difference of opinion in the council ?   71.

A. There was.

Q. Were the opinions of the feveral commanding officers afked refpecting the condition of their refpective corps, and what might be expected from them feverally in defperate cafes ?   72.

A. It was.

Q. Was there not on that queftion alfo difference of opinion ?   73.

A. There was.

Q. After the Convention took place, did your Lordfhip fee the army of General Gates pafs in review before General Burgoyne and General Phillips ?   74.

A. I did.

Q. From the manner and filence of their march, the order obferved in keeping their divifions, and an apparent attention to their officers, did that army appear difciplined ?   75.

A. They marched in good order and were filent, and feemed to pay attention to their officers. Thefe are effential points of difcipline, but I faw nothing farther of it.

Q. From the general behaviour of the rebel troops in the different actions in which you was prefent in the courfe of the campaign, did you think them difciplined and refpectable troops ?   76.

A. When I anfwered the laft queftion, I fpoke to the manœuvre I faw upon the fpot. At all times when I was oppofed to the rebels, they fought with great courage and obftinacy.

Q. Judging by your eye, and the time the rebel army was marching in review, did you form any judgment of their number ?   77.

A. It requires great experience to make a computation of numbers by feeing them pafs : as far as I could judge on the occafion, they feemed to me to amount to thirteen or fourteen thoufand rank and file under arms.

Q. Has your Lordfhip reafon to know or believe, that the troops that paffed in review were exclufive of thofe corps that had been pofted on the other fide of the Hudfon's River ?   78.

A. They were exclufive of thofe corps.

Examined by other Members of the Committee and by General Burgoyne occafionally.

Q. What was the general opinion of the army of General Burgoyne's behaviour in action and in difficulty ?   79.

A. It appeared to me, that General Burgoyne always poffeffed himfelf in every fituation of danger and difficulty, and, I may venture to fay, it appeared fo to the army.

. Q. Had General Burgoyne the confidence of the army ?   80.

A. He had.

Q. After the arrival of the troops at Cambridge, were the officers and foldiers of   81.

F   the

the army fatisfied with the general's efforts to contribute to their comfort, and redrefs their grievances ?

A. They were.

82.   Q. Was the army fatisfied with the general's behaviour at the court martial held on Colonel Henley ?

A. He carried on that profecution in perfon, and as fuch they were fatisfied with him.

83.   Q. Did your Lordfhip ever hear any officer or foldier of that army exprefs any diffatisfaction at the general's returning to England ?

A. I did not.

84.   Q. Does your Lordfhip think that the officers of that army wifh to have their refpective merits ftated to their Sovereign, by the general in perfon who had the honour of commanding them ?

A. It was the wifh of that army that General Burgoyne fhould go to Europe, to juftify not only his own conduct, but the conduct of the army he commanded.

85.   Q. Does your Lordfhip apprehend, that the return of General Burgoyne to that army, under perfonal difgrace, and without any diftribution of preferment among the diftinguifhed officers of that army, would be any fort of confolation to the troops under captivity ?

A. General Burgoyne, at all times, fhared the dangers and afflictions of that army in common with every foldier; as fuch they looked on him as their friend, and certainly would have received him in perfon, or any accounts of him, with every mafk of affection.

86.   Q. Your Lordfhip having faid that if the rebels had maintained their poft, at the afcent from the Low Countries to the Pitch Pine Plains, in the march from Fort Anne to Fort Edward, artillery would have been of great ufe to diflodge them; will your Lordfhip fay what kind of artillery, of what calibre, would have been neceffary for that purpofe ?

A. Any of the artillery officers now under the order of the Houfe can give a much more fatisfactory anfwer to that queftion than I poffibly can.

87.   Q. Did you fee that poft ?

A. I think I faid I did fee it.

88.   Q. With what kind of work was that poft fortified ?

A. I fpoke of it merely from its fituation.

89.   Q. Were there then any works or none ?

A. I don't recollect there were any works.

90.   Q. If the army, after taking Ticonderoga, had been embarked, and proceeded directly to South Bay, would there have been any occafion to have attacked the poft at Pitch Pine Plains at all ?

A. The army did proceed by South Bay, excepting a detachment of General Frafer's corps, and fome Germans to fupport him; and the army affembled at Skenefborough on the 9th or 10th of July.

91.   Q. Was it neceffary to go to the poft at Pitch Pine Plains, in order to go to South Bay ?

A. They had no fort of connection with each other.

92.   Q. Might not the army have proceeded to Fort Edward, and omitted the attack of that pafs, fuppofing it had been meant to be defended ?

A. There

A. There were two routes to Fort Edward. General Burgoyne might ftill go the fame route without any neceffity of attacking that poft, as there might have been many different ways of diflodging the enemy from that poft without attacking it.

Q. In how many inftances do you remember the rebels defending their entrench- 93.
ments after they had made them?

A. We never got a view of any of their entrenchments but fuch as they had voluntarily abandoned.

Q. Is it then to be underftood that they never defended any entrenchments ?   94.

A. They never did.

Q. Did you ever hear General Frafer exprefs his approbation of the paffing of the 95.
Hudfon's River ?

A. I never did.

Q. Did you ever hear General Frafer exprefs his approbation of the Bennington 96.
expedition ?

A. That detachment was made, and the bufinefs concluded, before I ever heard of the project or execution.

Q. Have you occafion to know, when the firft detachment was fent out under Co- 97.
lonel Baume, where they were ordered to rejoin General Burgoyne, after they had performed the fervice they were fent on ?

A. I don't know.

Q. Whether, in your Lordfhip's opinion, after the lofs the rebels had fuftained over 98.
night, in the action of the 19th of September, if they had been attacked brifkly at break of day, the next day, there was a probability that they could have ftood their ground ?

A. I have not hefitated to give an opinion upon fuppofed matters, which muft have been attended with evident and demonftrable confequences ; but I beg the indulgence of the Houfe in declining to give any opinion upon any queftion relative to fpeculation or judgment. Had any general officer of that army under General Burgoyne been prefent in this country, I fhould have confined myfelf merely to the manœuvres of the corps I commanded. As there is no general officer here, I wifh to give this Houfe every information confiftent with my rank in the army.

Q. Had you any information that might indicate to you that the rebels were pre- 99.
pared to decamp after the action of the 19th of September ?

A. I was ignorant of any fuch intelligence being received.

Q. Had you any information of their baggage being packed up ?   100.

A. I have already anfwered, that I had no information at all about it.

Q. In the action of the 7th of October, on which fide did the rebels force our lines 101.
and make a lodgement ?

A. The lines to the right were ftormed and carried.

Q. Were the lines attacked to the left ?   102.

A. To the left of that poft they were, but not to the left of the army.

Q. Did not the poffeffion of Fort Edward, and the country thereabouts, cut off 103.
the retreat of any garrifon that might have been in Fort George ?

A. It undoubtedly did.

Q. Had the army proceeded to Fort George by Ticonderoga and Lake George, 104.
might not the enemy have remained at Fort George till the trenches were opened, and have ftill had their retreat fecure ?

A. That is a matter of opinion upon speculation.

105. Q. Do you not think that the British army, being well provided with artillery, was a probable reason for their not defending entrenchments?

A. The reason they did not defend their entrenchments was, that they always marched out of them and attacked us.

106. Q. Does your Lordship think it would have been adviseable, in point of prudence, or just to brave troops, who had suffered severe loss, to attack an enemy the morning after that loss, posted within entrenchments, which it was impossible to reconnoitre?

A. That attempt was tried on the 7th of October, and did not succeed.

107. Q. Were not the enemy reinforced between the 19th of September and the 7th of October?

A. I think it is likely they were.

108. Q. Were they likely to be in better spirits to repel an attack the day after they had been repulsed with great loss, or when they had been reinforced, and seen an army lie three weeks inactive in their camp?

A. I do not judge of the spirit of the enemy but when I was opposed to them myself.

109. Q. On the first day of the action, when the enemy was repulsed on the 19th of September, had not our army suffered very considerably?

A. They suffered very considerable loss.

110. Q. Was not the army recruited, and in better order, on the 7th of October, than they were on the 20th of September?

A. Numbers of the men who had been wounded and disabled in the action of the 19th, joined their corps on the 7th of October.

111. Q. Was the behaviour of the enemy, opposed to your Lordship, in the actions you have seen, such as to make them contemptible in the eye of a soldier?

A. I have already mentioned, that they fought at all times with courage and obstinacy.

112. Q. Whether the behaviour of the enemy was such as to make advantages obtained by them over his Majesty's troops more humiliating and disgraceful to the British arms than the same advantages obtained by an equal number of any other troops?

A. I myself felt more humiliation until I considered that those advantages proceeded from the nature of the country, and not from the want of zeal or bravery in the British troops.

113. Q. Whether the enemy's troops were such bad troops as to make it more disgraceful to have an advantage obtained by them over the King's troops than by the like number of any other enemy over a like number of his Majesty's troops in the same circumstances of country?

A. The advantages gained by the rebels over the British troops proceeded from their local situation, and not from the want of courage in the British troops. We were taught by experience that neither their attacks nor resistance was to be despised.

114. Q. Did you ever serve against any other troops?

A. I commenced my service in America.

Q. Whether

Q. Whether the army under General Burgoyne, in general, expected co-operation 115.
in their efforts to go to Albany, from the army under the command of Sir William
Howe?

A. General Burgoyne gave it out in general orders, that he had every reason to
believe that powerful armies were acting in co-operation with the army he had the
honour to command.

Q. Do you know at what time that order was given out? 116.

A. The adjutant general's books will shew it: I think it was about the 3d of
October.

Q. Does your Lordship believe that if the army under General Howe had co- 117.
operated up the North River with the army under General Burgoyne, that the
army under General Burgoyne would have been obliged to have made the convention
it did?

A. That is a matter of judgment. The army looked forward to that co-operation,
which they were led to understand, by the orders General Burgoyne had given out,
with pleasure.

Q. What was the general opinion of the officers of the army in which you served, 118.
on that subject of co-operation?

A. I do not think my rank in the army entitles me to give my opinion on that subject; I shall still less presume to give that of others.

[Withdrew.

Then he was called in again, and several parts of the examination, particularly that
which immediately follows the place where it is said that his Lordship was examined
by other members of the Committee, were read, and then the last question which was
put to his Lordship immediately before he withdrew, was repeated, with this addition,
" To the best of your recollection and information." 119.

A. I have already declined answering that question.

Q. When did you first know that there was to be no co-operation from General 120.
Howe's army, and that Sir William Howe had carried his army to Chesapeak
Bay?

A. I did not know that we were to expect no co-operation, until after the convention was signed.

Q. When did you first hear that Sir William Howe was gone to the south- 121.
ward?

A. It was reported so in the army about the beginning of the campaign, before
we crossed the river.

Q. When was that report first confirmed so as to make it a matter of belief? 122.

A. I never knew it was confirmed at all.

Q. Whether you yourself was not surprised or disappointed, or both, when you 123.
first understood that there was not to be any co-operation from Sir William Howe,
but that Sir William Howe's army was gone to Chesapeak Bay?

[Withdrew.

Again

Again called in.

124.   Q. Whether you yourself was furprifed or difappointed, or both, when you
first heard that Sir William Howe's army was gone to Chefapeak Bay?
A. I neither knew the object of the campaign nor its expectations, and therefore cannot fpeak to any manœuvre of which I could not know the tendency.

125.   Q. Did the army in general exprefs themfelves pleafed at the news of Sir William Howe's being gone to Chefapeak Bay?
A. The anfwer to the laft queftion, as it relates to me in particular, relates to
them in general.

126.   Q. Whether your Lordfhip, as a matter of fact, in the confideration you had in
the army, on the news of Sir William Howe's being gone to Chefapeak Bay,
heard thofe you converfed with exprefs themfelves pleafed, or talk of that expedition to Chefapeak, as a powerful co-operation with General Burgoyne?
A. I think that queftion is fully anfwered in the two preceding ones.

127.   Q. Whether you did not think General Howe's fighting General Wafhington's
grand army, at the battle of Brandywine, was a very capital co-operation with the
army under General Burgoyne?
A. I was not at Brandywine.

128.   Q. Whether you was not furprifed when you returned home to this country, to
learn that the fecretary of ftate for the American department, had information
from General Howe, of his intentions of going to the fouthward, before General
Burgoyne departed from this country, and never communicated that information
to General Burgoyne before his departure for Canada?
A. I have the honour to ftand before this Houfe as a military man, and
not as a politician, and cannot anfwer any queftion but thofe relative to my own
profeffion.

129.   Q. What was your Lordfhip's opinion of the fpirit of your own corps?
A. The opinion I gave in the council of war, relative to the fpirit of the corps I
commanded was, that they were willing and zealous to undertake any enterprife
that General Burgoyne would pleafe to employ them upon.

130.   Q. When advice was received that Sir Henry Clinton was coming up the North
River, did you apprehend the treaty of convention had gone fo far that it could
not be broken?
A. My opinion was, with refpect to that queftion, that all military negotiations
were fair and juftifiable, to make delays and to gain time; I therefore thought and
declared my fentiments, that General Burgoyne was at full liberty to break off
that treaty in the ftage it then was; and I could not conceive that the public
faith was engaged, until the treaty was actually figned and exchanged.

131.   Q. Whether the opinion of General Burgoyne, of General Phillips, of Brigadier
By General   Hamilton, and feveral other officers, did not coincide with your opinion in all the
Burgoyne.   matters comprifed in the laft queftion?
A. As General Burgoyne feems defirous that I fhould anfwer that queftion, I de-
clare his fentiments were the fame with thofe I have now delivered. I hope that

the

the other members of that council, will foon be in a fituation to ftand forward and to declare the opinion they gave on that and every other queftion.

Q. When the queftion relative to the point of public faith was decided, by the majority of the council, was not the concurrence for figning the convention unanimous ?   1 32. By General Burgoyne.

A. It was.

Q. What day was it firft known that Sir Henry Clinton had taken the highlands, and was coming up the North River ?   1 33.

A. In the night of the 16th of October.   [*Withdrew.*

CAPTAIN MONEY called in and examined by General Burgoyne.

Q. WAS not you deputy quarter mafter general of the army under General Burgoyne, in 1777 ?   1.

A. I was.

Q. After Lieutenant Colonel Carleton returned to Canada, was you the fuperior officer in that department ?   2.

A. I· was.

Q. As fuch, did you make it your bufinefs from the beginning of the campaign to get a knowledge of the country ?   3.

A. Whenever there was any occafion to obtain the knowledge of any particular part of the country, a party was always fent with me for that purpofe, but the woods were fo thick that it was impoffible to go without a party.

Q. Was you well acquainted with the country between Skenefborough and Fort Edward ?   4.

A. I was.

Q. How long was the army employed in making the roads practicable between Skenefborough and Fort Edward ?   5.

A. About fix or feven days in making the road between Skenefborough and Fort Anne, and between Fort Anne and Fort Edward. I do not believe the army was delayed an hour on that account ; there was a very good road made by the rebels the year before, between Fort Anne and Fort Edward, in which road the rebels had cut down fome few trees which took the provincials in our army fome few hours to clear.

Q. Does not the poffeffion of the country in the neighbourhood of Fort Edward, neceffarily prevent the retreat of a garrifon that might be in Fort George ?   6.

A. It

A. It prevents the getting off any artillery or ſtores ; but a garriſon might get through the woods, in caſe we were in the poſſeſſion of the ground in the neighbourhood of Fort Edward.

7. Q. Did not the garriſon of Fort George evacuate the fort upon the approach of the King's troops toward Fort Edward ?

A. I heard they did ; I was not near enough to ſee.

8. Q. Had the army taken their route by South Bay, Ticonderoga, and Lake George, how many bateaux do you imagine it would have taken to carry the troops ſolely over Lake George, excluſive of proviſions and ſtores ?

A. I think between three and four hundred, which bateaux muſt have been carried up out of Lake Champlain to Lake George.

9. Q. What time would it have taken, as you imagine, to have drawn thoſe bateaux over the land, between Lake Champlain and Lake George, with the horſes then at Ticonderoga ?

A. I ſuppoſe a fortnight—Four hundred bateaux.

10. Q. Though there were no troops paſſed over Lake George, how long did it take before the firſt tranſport of proviſions arrived at Fort George ?

A. I can't recollect preciſely.

11. Q. Conſidering the length of time it took to tranſport the proviſions, without the troops, over Lake George, was not the army forwarder in their way to Albany, in point of time, by the route they took, than they could have been by the route of Ticonderoga and Lake George ?

A. I have already ſaid, that it would take a fortnight to tranſport the 400 bateaux from Lake Champlain to Lake George ; it therefore would have delayed the army a fortnight longer than they were delayed to have returned from Skeneſborough by Ticonderoga, and gone acroſs Lake George.

12. Q. Was you commiſſary of horſe, as well as deputy quarter maſter general ?

A. It was.

13. Q. What is the nature of that department ?

A. It was to take charge of all the horſes furniſhed by contract for General Burgoyne's army, by any letter of inſtructions from General Burgoyne. I am directed to give proper orders and directions to the drivers, furniſhed by that contract, for the purpoſe of tranſporting proviſions and ſtores brought to Fort George, for the uſe of the army.

14. Q. Did you report from time to time to Major General Phillips, and take orders from him, as well as from General Burgoyne ?

A. Yes.

15. Q. Were not the orders from both the generals invariable, preciſe, and preſſing, for uſing all poſſible diligence in forwarding the tranſport of proviſions ?

A. They were. There was one order which I will read, as it will fully anſwer that queſtion : it is dated Auguſt the 18th, Duer-Camp, and is in theſe words ;
" It having been a practice for officers to order to be taken from the proviſion train,
" in the ſervice of the King for this army, the carts and horſes, for the carrying
" baggage and other purpoſes, to avoid for the future the danger and inconve-
" niencies to the ſervice, it is in the moſt poſitive manner ordered, that no cart or
" horſe are to be uſed but for the public tranſport of the army ; nor is any officer,

2   " accidentally

" accidentally coming to any particular post, to interfere with the provision train,
" in any other manner than to give it every aid and assistance, which he is on all
" occasions to do."

Q. Was not the transport of merchandize, and even sutler's stores, as well 16.
as of officers' baggage, positively forbid till the transport of provision should be
over ?

A. There was such an order, and a seizure made of two barrels of Madeira,
and two barrels of rum, which were ordered to the hospital.

Q. Do you recollect General Burgoyne's expressing, at several times, particular 17.
anxiety on the subject of expediting the transport of provisions ?

A. I do remember once to have heard General Burgoyne express his concern at
our not being able to bring forward a greater quantity of provision to enable him
to proceed with the army.—I do recollect to have heard him say with very great
earnestness to General Phillips and Colonel Carleton, that one- month's provision
at that particular time (it was about the latter end of August) would be worth
100,000l. to Great Britain.

Q. Do you think that the commissary of the waggons, and other carriages, 18.
was authorised to buy or hire ox-teams wherever they could be had, and that all
draught cattle taken, were appropriated to the transport ?

A. He received such directions.

Q. How many carts and ox-teams could be mustered at any one time ?
A. I think only 180 carts could at any one time be mustered ; the number of 19.
ox-carts I really forget, but I believe between 20 and 30.

Q. About how many days provision for the troops, and all other persons fed 20.
from the King's stores, could that number of carriages convey ?

A. There never was any trial made, but if I may presume to judge from the
proportion brought forward, over and above the daily confumption of the army,
should suppose all those carriages would not carry more than four days provisions at
most. I am speaking at random, as no trial was made.

Q. Did it not sometimes happen, from accidents of weather, and roads, and the 21.
tired state of the cattle, that not more than one day's provision could be brought
forward in a day ?

A. It did.

Q. How many hours did it take, one hour with another, to draw a bateau 22.
from Fort George to Fort Edward ?

A. In general about six.

Q. Was not the unloading the carts at Fort Edward, and embarking the contents 23.
in bateaux, unloading the bateaux at the upper falls of Fort Miller, and a second
time unloading them at the lower falls, dilatory as it was, a more expeditious method
than it would have been to have carried the provisions the whole way in carts ?

A. I do apprehend it was not possible, in the feeble state I found the horses furnished by contract, to have brought forward the daily confumption of provisions for
that army down to Fort Miller. In the month of August, in the latter end of that
month, at which time I was appointed a commissary general of horse, I made, on
　　　　　　　　　　　　　　G　　　　　　　　　　　　　the

the firſt of September, a general muſter, and found 30 horſes unſerviceable, from fatigue and hard labour.

24.   Q. Was the tranſport of proviſions at any time impeded by the bringing forward the artillery from Fort George?

A. The artillery had a ſeparate contract for horſes, with which they brought forward their own ſtores. I don't recollect that any part of the proviſion train were ever employed in bringing forward artillery or artillery ſtores.

25.   Q. Was it poſſible, with the means we had, to collect a month's ſtore of proviſions ſooner than it was collected?

A. I believe not, without the utter ruin of the horſes furniſhed by contract for the purpoſe of tranſporting ſtores.

26.   Q. Was you preſent in the action of the 19th of September?

A. I was.

27.   Q. Did the enemy diſpute the field that day with obſtinacy?

A. They did, and the fire was much heavier than ever I ſaw it any where, unleſs at the affair of Fort Anne.

28.   Q. Do you know how long the regiments of the Britiſh line were under that fire?

A. The three Britiſh regiments (the 20th, 21ſt, and 62d) were engaged from three o'clock in the afternoon till ſeven in the evening; and whilſt I was a priſoner I heard the rebel quarter-maſter general ſay, they had nine different regiments in the field, oppoſed to the three Britiſh I have named.

29.   Q. Do you know the loſs the three Britiſh regiments ſuſtained?

A. I can't ſay.

30.   Q. Do you remember the ſtrength of the 62d regiment when they came out of the action?

A. I can't ſpeak to the particular ſtrength of the regiment when they came out of action; but I heard that they were not 100 rank and file.

31.   Q. How many officers were left in that regiment at the end of the action?

A. I can't anſwer that queſtion.

32.   Q. From the general ſtate of the three Britiſh regiments, do you think that they would have been in a proper condition to have attacked the enemy the next morning?

A. Certainly not; nor to go on any ſervice whatever.

33.   Q. About what time of the day did the enemy finally give way?

A. They gave way very often; finally about ſeven in the evening.

34.   Q. Was it practicable, at that time of the evening, and in that kind of country, to have purſued?

A. I ſhould think not.

35.   Q. Was you not often employed, between the day of that action and the action of the 7th of October, to reconnoitre?

A. I was.

36.   Q. Was you able to obtain a view of the enemy's poſition?

A. I obtained a view of the poſition of the right of the rebel entrenchments.

37.   Q. What was the nature of their poſition to the right, with regard to entrenchments?

A. They

A. They were pofted on a hill that came very near the river. On the top of the hill was a ftrong breaft-work, at the foot an abbatis.

Q. Did it appear to you that that wing of the enemy was attackable ?   38.

A. It is a queftion that is fcarcely in my line of fervice to anfwer; but as there are no general officers, nor older officers than myfelf, who ferved under General Burgoyne, I hope no military man will think me prefuming to give my opinion on that fubject. I do think that we could not have attacked the right wing of the rebel entrenchments without rifking the lofs of the whole army, and with little probability of fuccefs.

Q. Could you obtain a view of the left wing of the enemy ?   39.

A. I never faw the left wing of the enemy's entrenchments till I was taken prifoner and conducted through their works.

Q. On the 7th of October was you in a fituation to fee the enemy advancing to the   40. attack of your left ?

A. Yes.

Q. Did they advance under a well ferved fire of grape-fhot from our artillery ?   41.

A. I was in a fituation that gave me an opportunity of feeing the directions of the rebels' columns; and I was very much aftonifhed to hear the fhot from the enemy fly fo thick, after our cannonade had lafted a quarter of an hour.

Q. When the Britifh grenadiers were forced laft from their poft, what enfued ?   42.

A. I did not fee the Britifh grenadiers forced back. I faw them on their march, as I apprehended, taking a different pofition; at that time feveral of them broke their ranks, but on fome aid du camps calling to them for fhame, to continue their rank, they marched away to their ftation in good order. A battalion of Brunfwickers that were on the left of the artillery quitted their ground as foon as the firing began, and, to the beft of my recollection, I did not fee they left a man behind them on the ground. I would add, that after fome difficulty that battalion was brought to make a ftand in the rear of the artillery, but in no order.

Q. Was not that battalion brought to that ftand by the activity and exhortation of   43. Major General Reidefel ?

A. I did not fee General Reidefel endeavour to ftop the battalion; but I faw an aid du camp of his and a brigade major, with their drawn fwords, keeping them up. I did fee General Reidefel immediately afterwards, on the right of the artillery, with the battalion perfectly formed, and in good order.

Q. Do you imagine that the giving way of the battalion you firft defcribed was   44. the caufe that the artillery on that fpot was taken, and yourfelf and Major Williams being made prifoners ?

A. I believe it contributed, in fome meafure, towards the lofs of the action on that day; but before Sir Francis Clarke died of his wounds, he told me that he received his wound in bringing orders for the artillery and the whole of the detachment to return to camp; and to the circumftance of Sir Francis Clarke's being wounded, I do attribute the lofs of the artillery, if not the lofs of the whole army ?

Q. Had you an opportunity, after you was prifoner, to fee the left of the enemy's   45. entrenchments ?

A. I had.

Q. Was

46.   Q. Was the ground within cannon ſhot of the left open and commanding it?
      A. All the ground I ſaw was cleared and entrenched.

47.   Q. Was there not ground within cannon ſhot that would have commanded that
entrenchment on the left?
      A. There was.

48.   Q. Had we gained poſſeſſion of that ground, and been able to erect batteries of
our heavieſt guns, would not the whole line of the enemy have been enfiladed?
      A. The ground alluded to was entrenched, and commanded the whole of the
rebel camp and lines. If the army had got poſſeſſion of that ground, I do not believe
the rebels would have ſtaid one hour in their camp.

49.   Q. Did you ever hear, in converſation with the rebel officers, that General Arnold, foreſeeing that inconvenience, had marched out of his lines, and attacked,
without orders from General Gates?
      A. I did hear that General Arnold had marched out on the 7th of October, without
orders from General Gates. I did alſo hear that he adviſed the going out to meet General Burgoyne on his march, and engaging him before he approached their lines; and the
reaſon he gave was this: If General Burgoyne ſhould ever come near enough their
lines to be able to make uſe of his artillery, that he would certainly poſſeſs himſelf of
their camp; that their troops in that caſe would never ſtand any where; but if, on
the other hand, the rebels ſhould be defeated in the woods, the troops would, after
that, have confidence in their works, for which reaſon Arnold adviſed riſking an
action in the woods before General Burgoyne came near enough to ſee their works.

Examined by other Members of the Committee, and by General Burgoyne occaſionally.

50.   Q. Did not your ſituation, as deputy quarter maſter general, lead you to mix very
much with the different officers of the army?
      A. It did.

51.   Q. What do you apprehend to have been the general opinion of the officers of
General Burgoyne's conduct, as well in action as in the many trying occaſions which
have been ſtated by you at the bar?
      A. They entertained a very high opinion of General Burgoyne's conduct.

52.   Q. Had General Burgoyne the full confidence of the army under his command to
the laſt moment?
      A. He certainly had.

53.   Q. What was the army's opinion of the rebels after their retreat from Ticonde-
toga?
      A. The army in general did not think, after they had evacuated Ticonderoga, that
they would make a ſtand any where.

54.   Q. What was the reaſon given in your army for the expedition to Bennington?
      A. I believe I cannot anſwer that queſtion better than by reading an abſtract of the
General's orders the day after that action.

                                                        " *Auguſt*

"*August* 17, *Duer Camp*.

" It was endeavoured, among other objects, by the expedition which marched to
" the left, to provide such a supply of cattle as would have enabled the army to proceed
" without waiting the arrival of the magazines.   That attempt having failed of success,
" through the chances of war, the troops must neceffarily halt some days for bringing
" forward the tranfports."

Q. Why did the army remain from the 16th of Auguft to the 13th of September, 55.
before they croffed the Hudfon's River to engage the rebels as Stillwater?

Q. To bring forward a fufficient quantity of provifions and artillery, to enable
the general to give up his communication.

Q. What was the opinion of the army on their croffing the Hudfon's River?   56.

A. They did think it was their indifpenfible duty to proceed forward and fight the
rebels, which we heard were then at Stillwater.

Q. Did you ever forage to the right of General Frafer's camp before the 7th of 57.
Auguft?

A. We never foraged to the right of the camp at Freeman's Farm, at any
one time; on the 7th of October, while the troops were in the field, General
Frafer ordered all the batmen and drivers, belonging to his brigade, to come and
forage in the rear of the troops.

Q. Do you know what was General Frafer's opinion on your foraging to the 58.
right?

A. I do know that General Frafer mentioned to me, on the 5th of October,
that there was forage on the right of his camp; but at that time the ground on
which that forage was to be met with was in poffeffion of the rebels' advanced
poft.

Q. Do you think your army would have been loft, if even the expedition from 59.
New York had taken place a few days fooner?

A. If the troops had arrived at New York foon enough to have enabled Sir
Henry Clinton to have made his expedition up the North River a week fooner, I
do conceive that our army would not have been loft.

Q. What was the opinion of the rebels on Sir William Howe's going to the 60.
fouthward.

A. I was not acquainted enough with the rebel leaders, to hear their opinion
on that queftion.   I do not think that the peafants of the country were judges of
the propriety of Sir William Howe's conduct.

Q. What was the opinion of the officers of General Burgoyne's army, after it 61.
was loft, relative to the croffing Hudfon's River.

A. They did think that the alternative of retreating with their army to Canada, or proceeding to Stillwater, under the neceffity of giving up his communication, to be an unfortunate fituation; but I never heard any officers fay that
they thought General Burgoyne had done wrong; many faid, that if they had retreated without rifking an action, at the time Sir Henry Clinton was coming up the
North River, the army would never have forgiven him, nor would he ever have
forgiven himfelf.

Q. Was you at New York after the lofs of General Burgoyne's army?   62.

A. Yes.

3

A. Yes.

63.   Q. What was the opinion or the language of the military at that place, relative to
Sir William Howe's expedition to Penſylvania?
    A. Whatever opinion was formed of Sir William Howe's expedition to Penſyl-
vania, or is formed previous to this enquiry, ſuch an opinion muſt have been ill:
founded, as Sir William Howe's reaſons were not known, nor his inſtructions communicated to the public.

64.   Q. From your laſt anſwer, is the committee to underſtand that the opinions that
were formed reſpecting Sir William Howe's expedition to Philadelphia, before this
enquiry, were not in favour of that expedition?
    Queſtion objected to.   [Withdrew.

Again called in.

65.   Q. You have ſaid that the army thought it their indiſpenſible duty to paſs over
Hudſon's River—Why did they think that that meaſure was particularly their indiſpenſible duty?
    A. If the Hudſon's River had not been there, the army would have thought
it their indiſpenſible duty to have gone and riſked an action before they returned to
Canada. If I recollect right, I ſaid, that if the army had returned to Canada,
without fighting, that the army would - never have forgiven the general, nor the
general have forgiven himſelf.

66.   Q. Do you know the nature of the country, between the place where we paſſed
the Hudſon's River and Albany, on the eaſt ſide of the river?
    A. Yes, I do.

67.   Q. Could the army have taken that route, in order to paſs the river oppoſite or
near to Albany?
    A. The army could not have taken that route, as part of the way was a ſwamp,
and on the right of the rebel entrenchments was a mountain very rugged, and not
paſſable nearer than two miles from the river.

68.   Q. Was it not a neceſſary conſequence then, that the boats muſt have been abandoned, if the army had taken that route?
    A. I think I have ſaid the army could not take that route; if the army had
marched on the eaſt of the Hudſon's River, they could not have marched near
enough to have covered their proviſion bateaux from the rebel force, on the weſt
ſide of the river.

69.   Q. Did the army under General Burgoyne, on their approach to Albany, expect a co-operation of the army under Sir William Howe, upon the North
River?
    A. They did; and this is the order of General Burgoyne, given October the
3d at Freeman's Farm:
    " There is reaſon to be aſſured, that other powerful armies are actually in co-
" operation with theſe troops; and although the preſent ſupply of proviſion is ample,
" it is highly deſirable, to prepare for any continuance in the field that the King's
" ſervice may require, without the delay of bringing forward further ſtores for
                                                                          " thoſe

" thofe purpofes; the ration of bread or flour is, for the prefent, fixed at one
" pound."

Q. Are you acquainted with the North River, from New York to Al- 70.
bany?

A. I am not.

Q. How many days march from Fort Edward to Albany, if no interruption from 71.
an enemy?

A. I cannot anfwer that queftion, unlefs I am to fuppofe that a bridge was
ready formed for the troops to pafs over, on fome part of Hudfon's River,
between Batten Kill and Fort Edward, or that there were veffels ready to tranfport
the troops over Hudfon's River.

Q. Is the diftance fo great between Fort Edward and Albany, that the army 72.
could not carry provifions with them to fupport them during the march?

A. Certainly Albany is not at fo great a diftance from Fort. Edward, but
that a corps of troops might certainly carry provifions fufficient for the march
to Albany.

Q. Was it not underftood, that if you had arrived at Albany, that the army 73.
would find plenty of provifions there?

A. It was generally believed, and I believe it myfelf firmly, that if the army
had got to Albany, we fhould have found a number of loyal fubjects, that would
have joined and done every thing in their power to have eftablifhed the army
at that place.

Q. Muft not the army, to march from Fort Edward to Albany, have neceffa- 74.
rily carried a number of boats to form a bridge to pafs the river?

A. There was no paffing the river well without a bridge of boats, and there
were not fcouls enough on that river, to make a bridge.

Q. Would not the neceffary delay, arifing from carrying forward thofe boats, 75.
and throwing a bridge, fit to pafs an army, have confumed more time than it
was poffible for that army to fubfift with fuch provifion as they could carry with
them?

A. I fhould think it would.

Q. You will give the committee what information you can, refpecting a road 76.
from Fort Edward to Albany, on the left fide of the river.

A. I have anfwered that fully.

Q. Whether by taking a pretty large circuit, the army would have reached Al- 77.
bany, and avoided the fwamps you mentioned?

A. Certainly not on the eaft-fide of the river, becaufe the enemy being on the oppofite fhore, would certainly have oppofed General Burgoyne's army croffing the
Hudfon's River at Albany, the river being three times the width it is at Saratoga.

[*Withdrew.*

Martis

Martis 1° *die Junii,* 1779.

Mr. F. Montagu in the Chair.

EARL OF HARRINGTON called in and examined by General Burgoyne.

1. Q. IN what capacity did your Lordſhip ſerve in America in the campaign
1777 ?
    A. I was captain in the 29th regiment of foot, and went on the expedition with
General Burgoyne, with the command of the grenadier company ; I was afterwards appointed ſupernumerary aid du camp to the general.

2. Q. While acting as captain of the grenadier company, was you at the action
of Huberton ?
    A. I was.

3. Q. What was the behaviour of the enemy on that day ?
    A. They behaved in the beginning of the action, with a great deal of ſpirit ; but
on the Britiſh troops ruſhing on them with their bayonets, they gave way in great
confuſion.

4. Q. From the nature of the country, was it practicable to purſue the enemy further than they were purſued on that occaſion ?
    A. Certainly not.—I think we ran ſome riſque even in purſuing them ſo
far.

5. Q. At what time of the campaign was it that General Burgoyne requeſted your
Lordſhip to act as his aid du camp ?
    A. I think about the 12th of July.

6. Q. Was you preſent a few days after that time, at a council held with the Indians of the remote nations, then juſt arrived, under the conduct of Major Campbell and Mr. St. Luc ?

7. A. Yes.
    Q. Was you preſent at a former council of the Indians held at Lake
Champlain ?

8. A. Yes.
    Q. What was the tenor of General Burgoyne's ſpeeches and injunctions at both
thoſe councils reſpecting the reſtraint of barbarities ?
    A. He abſolutely forbid their ſcalping, except their dead priſoners, which they
inſiſted on doing, and he held out rewards to them for bringing in priſoners, and
enjoined them to treat them well.

Q. Do

Q. Do you remember being with General Burgoyne, foon after the laft council, 9.
upon a vifit to an out poft near Fort Anne?

A. I perfectly recollect it.

Q. Had General Burgoyne a confiderable efcort of Indians with him? 10.

A. He had.

Q. Did part of that efcort, on a fcout from that poft, fall in with and take 11.
a part of the enemy, who were laid in ambufh for the purpofe of killing or taking
the general, and thofe who were with him?

A. They did.

Q. What were the fentiments of the captain taken on that occafion refpecting 12.
his treatment from the Indians?

A. He faid he was treated with much humanity, and I perfectly remember that
prifoners brought in on many other occafions by the Indians, declared that they had
been ufed with the fame degree of humanity.

Q. Does your Lordfhip remember General Burgoyne's receiving at Fort Anne, the 13.
news of the murder of Mifs M'Rea?

A. I do.

Q. Did General Burgoyne repair immediately to the Indian camp, and call them to 14.
council, affifted by Brigadier General Frafer?

A. He did.

Q. What paffed at that council? 15.

A. General Burgoyne threatened the culprit with death, infifted that he fhould
be delivered up; and there were many gentlemen of the army, and I own I was
one of the number, who feared that he would put that threat in execution. Motives of policy, I believe alone, prevented him from it; and if he had not pardoned
the man, which he did, I believe the total defection of the Indians would have enfued, and the confequences, on their return through Canada, might have been
dreadful; not to fpeak of the weight they would have thrown into the oppofite fcale, had they gone over to the enemy, which I rather imagine would
have been the cafe.

Q. Do you remember General Burgoyne's reftraining the Indian parties from 16.
going out without a Britifh officer or proper conductor, who were to be refponfible for their behaviour?

A. I do.

Q. Do you remember Mr. St. Luc's reporting difcontents amongft the Indians, 17.
foon after our arrival at Fort Edward?

A. I do.

Q. How long was that after enforcing the reftraints above mentioned? 18.

A. I can't exactly fay; I fhould imagine about three weeks or a month.

Q. Does your Lordfhip recollect General Burgoyne's telling Mr. St. Luc, that 19.
he had rather lofe every Indian, than connive at their enormities, or ufing language to that effect?

A. I do.

Q. Does your Lordfhip remember what paffed in council with the Indians at 20.
Fort Edward?

H　　　　　　　　　　　　　　　　　A. To

A. To the beſt of my recollection, much the ſame exhortation to act with humanity, and much the ſame rewards were offered for ſaving their priſoners.

21.　Q. Do you recollect the circumſtance of the Indians deſiring to return home at that time ?

A. I do, perfectly well.

22.　Q. Do you remember that many quitted the army without leave ?

A. I do, immediately after the council, and the next morning.

23.　Q. Was it not the general opinion that the defection of the Indians, then and afterwards, was cauſed by the reſtraint upon their cruelties and habits of plunder ?

A. It was.

24.　Q. Had you reaſon to believe that the expedition to Bennington was much deſired by General Reideſel, and that it was his wiſh to have it conducted by Lieutenant Colonel Baume ?

A. It was always imagined in the army, that it was his wiſh, and that Colonel Baume was appointed to the command of it in compliment to him.

25.　Q. Did you know the corps of Britiſh, commanded by Captain Fraſer, which made part of that expedition ?

A. They were volunteers from the Britiſh regiments, and alſo ſtood very high in the opinion of the army, from their gallant behaviour on all occaſions.

26.　Q. Do you remember General Burgoyne's viſiting the detachment after it was aſſembled, and conferring with Colonel Baume ?

A. I do.

27.　Q. Did Colonel Baume appear ſatisfied with the ſtrength of his corps ?

A. I converſed with Colonel Baume, and with ſeveral officers under his command, and they appeared perfectly ſatisfied, at leaſt I heard no complaint from them ; the only anxiety they expreſſed was, leſt the deſtination of that corps ſhould become known to the enemy.

28.　Q. Does your Lordſhip remember General Burgoyne's receiving, in the night, a letter from Lieutenant Colonel Baume, expreſſing he found the enemy in greater force than he expected ?

A. I do.

29.　Q. Do you remember Sir Francis Clarke, General Burgoyne's aid du camp, being ſent with orders to Colonel Breyman to march immediately to ſupport him ?

A. I do.

30.　Q. Did you communicate the ſame order to General Reideſel at the ſame time ?

A. I did.

31.　Q. Was Colonel Breyman the neareſt corps for the purpoſe of that ſupport ?

A. It was.

32.　Q. Did Brigadier General Fraſer at all times treat your Lordſhip with great confidence ?　　　　4

A. I was

A. I was often with General Frafer, and he frequently talked without referve upon matters which he was not particularly bound to conceal. There were certain matters of intelligence which it would have been improper for him to mention to any body. In this cafe I cannot boaft fo much of his confidence, as to fuppofe that he would have opened his mind to me on matters which he would have concealed from the reft of his friends.

Q. Have you not frequently been prefent when General Burgoyne and General 33.
Frafet difcuffed the objeft of the campaign, and converfed freely on the circumftances of the time?

A. I have.

Q. Did your Lordfhip ever, in prefence or abfence of General Burgoyne, hear Ge- 34.
neral Frafer exprefs a difapprobation of paffing the Hudfon's River?

A. I never did?

Q. Do you know or believe that the idea of forcing our way to Albany was pre- 35.
valent throughout the army?

A. In every converfation I had with different officers of the army, I never remem-ber once to have heard it doubted, but that we were to force our way.

Q. Did the army pafs the Hudfon's River with alacrity?   .   36.

A. It is impoffible for any army to have been in higher fpirits than they were at that time, or more defirous of coming to an engagement with the enemy.

Q. Do you not conceive, that to have remained pofted behind the Hudfon's 37.
River, at the time the army paffed it and advanced, would have caft a damp on the fpirits of that army and a reflection on their General?

A. From the eagernefs of the army to advance and the great uneafinefs that was difcernible through it on every delay, I apprehended that it could not have been otherwife; and I think that General Burgoyne's character would not have flood very high either with the army, this country, or the enemy, had he halted at Fort Edward.

Q. Do you recollect the march up to the enemy on the 19th of Septem- 38.
ber?

A. I do.

Q. Will you pleafe to defcribe it? 39.

A. The army marched in three divifions; the German line flanking, the artillery and baggage purfued the courfe of the river through the meadows, and formed the left hand divifion; the Britifh line marched parallel to it at fome diftance through the woods, and formed the centre divifion; General Frafer's corps, with the grena-diers and light infantry of the Germans, were obliged to make a large detour through the woods, and formed the right hand divifion or column. Beyond this, on the right, there were, as I underftand, flanking parties of light infantry and Provin-cials?

Q. Was the country, over which the army paffed, interfected with a deep 40.
ravine?

A. It was one of the deepeft I ever faw.

Q. Which column was firft attacked?   ' 41.

A. The advanced party, confifting of the picquets of the centre column, being fent
H 2   forwards,

forwards, under the command of Major Forbes, to explore the way by which that column was to pass, fell in with a considerable body of the rebels, posted in a house and behind fences, which they attacked, and after a great deal of fire, the detachment nearly drove in the body of rebels; but on finding that the woods quite round them were filled with the enemy, they were obliged to retire to the main body.

42.   Q. Was the march so performed that when General Burgoyne formed the line of the British infantry, General Fraser's corps were ready upon their right to support them ?

A. General Fraser, on hearing the fire of Major Forbes's party, detached two companies to support them, which came up just after that engagement was over; and on their appearance the enemy finding that our troops were in strength, quitted the post they had before occupied, and, immediately after this, the whole line was formed with the utmost regularity.   I would explain, that when I speak of the line, I do not include the left hand column which was composed of Germans, and which did not come into the line or into action till late in the day.

43.   Q. How long did the action last ?
A. From three o'clock, I think, till very near eight.

44.   Q. How long were the 20th, 21st, and 62d regiments engaged ?
A. During the greatest part of that time.

45.   Q. Was the action well disputed by the enemy ?
A. It was, very obstinately.

46.   Q. Was your Lordship near the person of General Burgoyne during that action, except when you were employed to carry orders ?
A. Yes.

47.   Q. Were not different attempts made by the General's orders to charge the enemy with bayonets, and did not those attempts fail by the heaviness of the enemy's fire and thickness of the woods ?
A. There were many attempts made for that purpose, and they all failed except the last, when the British troops finally drove them out of the field.

48.   Q. When part of the German troops did get into action that day under General Reidesel, how did they behave ?
. A. I heard their behaviour spoke of in the highest terms ; they marched up to the enemy with great coolness and steadiness, and gave them, as I was told, three vollies by word of command from their officers.

49. . Q. Can your Lordship speak to the loss sustained by the three British regiments, the 62d in particular?
A. The loss was very considerable ; but I don't recollect the numbers.

50.   Q. Were those three British regiments in a condition to have attacked the enemy the next morning ?
A. Their numbers were so reduced, that I apprehend they were not.

51.   Q. From the loss of killed and wounded, particularly of officers, would it have been desirable to have brought those three regiments into action for the next ten days ?
A. In less than ten days the state of those regiments certainly would not have
been

been much mended; I therefore apprehend, that if they were not in a condition to be brought into action the next morning, their inability would have still continued for those ten days.

Q. Had the army made a movement to gain the left of the enemy's entrench- 52. ments before the redoubts were constructed that commanded the plain near the river, would not all the bateaux, stores, and hospitals have been exposed to attack?

A. It certainly would have been so.

Q. Do you recollect the scarcity of forage on the west-side of the river? 53.

A. I do perfectly.

Q. Would not the bridge of boats, constructed for the purpose of foraging to 54. the east side, have also been exposed before the redoubts, above mentioned, were raised?

A. They certainly would, had it not been for those redoubts and a work called the *Tête du pont*, which was raised for the protection of the bridge.

Q. Do you recollect how long it took to raise those redoubts, to throw the bridge, 55. and raise the *Tête du pont?*

A. If I recollect right, the bridge itself was finished in one night; the making and compleating the other works took some days.

Q. Does your Lordship remember General Burgoyne mentioning to you in 56. confidence, the receipt of a letter from Sir Henry Clinton, and his hourly ex- pectation of his attacking the Highlands, and his opinion that his success there must dislodge the enemy without attacking their entrenchments?

A. I perfectly recollect the General's mentioning all this to me.

Q. Was you near General Burgoyne in the action of the 7th of October? 57.

A. I was.

Q. Do you recollect what orders you carried? 58.

A. I do.

Q. What were they? 59.

A. The first orders I recollect to have carried, were to post fifty men under the command of a captain of the 20th regiment, to the left of the detachment of the army, in order, in some measure, to join them to the advanced works of General Fraser's camp, and, in case of any accident, to protect the detachment, should they find it necessary, to retire thither.

The next orders I carried were to Major General Phillips, at the end of the action, acquainting him, that as that detachment seemed much disordered from the enemy having turned both their flanks, that it was necessary to draw it as soon as possible back to the camp, which seemed menaced with an attack; the care of this General Burgoyne committed to General Phillips, while he himself returned to the camp, in order to take proper measures for its defence. On our return thither the works of the camp were actually attacked as General Burgoyne had foreseen, and I was then em- ployed to collect what troops I should meet, and to order them to those parts where they were most wanted. Soon after this, the enemy having got round the right of our camp, we expected an attack upon our rear, and I then was dispatched with orders from General Burgoyne to Brigadier General Hamilton, for all the works in

3   the

the rear of the camp, which had been previoufly conftructed, to be manned with fuch foldiers as he could fpare from the defence of the front.

60. Q. Does your Lordfhip know what orders Sir Francis Ciarke was charged with, at the time he received his wound?

A. I met Sir Francis Clarke as I was fearching for General Phillips, and acquainted him with my orders, telling him at the fame time, that as the thicknefs of the wood might prevent my finding General Phillips directly, I wifhed he would affift me, in order that no time might be loft in delivering thofe orders; that was the laft time I faw Sir Francis Clarke, and I believe that foon afterwards he received the wound of which he died?

61. Q. Was it dark before General Burgoyne had a certainty that Col. Breyman was killed, and his poft carried by the enemy?

A. It was fo dark that the officer, who I believe firft brought the intelligence of it, feeing a number of men round the fires of that camp, took them for Germans, and was not convinced of his error till he was fired upon by them, as they proved to be a party of the enemy who had forced the works.

62. Q. Did General Burgoyne ufe any efforts to rally the Germans who were returning from the action, and to perfuade them to recover Colonel Breyman's poft?

A. He certainly did his utmoft endeavours for that purpofe, which however were ineffectual from the darknefs of the night, and the entire confufion in which they were.

63. Q. Were any other troops at hand that could have been fpared for that purpofe?

A. There certainly were not; every regiment was occupied in defence of its own lines which were not certainly overmanned.

64. Q. In the heat of the action do you recollect feeing General Reidefel about the time that the Germans, on the left of the Britifh artillery, were giving way?

A. I do.

65. Q. Was not General Reidefel exerting himfelf to reftore order in his troops?

A. General Reidefel appeared to me to have behaved, on that occafion, in every way as became a brave and intelligent officer.

66. Q. Was the retreat of the army in the night of the 7th made in good order, and a new pofition taken by the time it was day-light?

A. It certainly was.

67. Q. Was the army under arms the whole day of the 8th, and in continual expectation of action?

A. They were, and indeed were cannonaded during the greateft part of that day, and the advanced corps in particular, who were pofted on a hill, were under almoft a continual fire from the riflemen of the enemy.

68. Q. Do you recollect the circumftance of General Frafer's funeral on the afternoon of that day?

A. I do, perfectly well; the redoubt in which he was buried was very heavily cannonaded during the ceremony, and even previous to this they fired at thofe who attended

attended the corpfe on its way thither, which I fuppofe was accidental, and proceeded from the enemy's feeing a number of people together.

Q. Who were the chief pe.fons who attended that funeral ?   69.

A. All the generals of the army, their aid du camps, and I believe all thofe who
were not attached to any particular poft, which at that time were very few.

Q. Was the retreat of the army on the night of the 8th, and on the day and part   70.
of the night of the 9th, made in good order ?

A. It was made in perfect good order.

Q. What was the weather on the day of the 9th ?   71.

A. Exceeding wet.

Q. What was the ftate of the troops, in point of fatigue, when they arrived at   72.
Saratoga ?

A. They certainly muft have been much fatigued, from the length of time they
had been under arms, and more particularly fo from the badnefs of the roads, occafioned by the rains.

Q. When it was day-light the next morning, did you fee any part of the enemy   73.
upon the plain at Saratoga, on the ground where our artillery was afterwards
pofted ?

A. I don't recollect.

Q. Does your Lordfhip recollect feeing a corps of the enemy on the other fide the   74.
Hudfon's River oppofite to Saratoga ?

A. Perfectly well; and they feemed in force.

Q. Do you remember the circumftance of a battery opening from that corps ?   75.

A. I do perfectly well. The general, General Phillips, and feveral other gentlemen were at dinner. We were all obliged to remove, from finding ourfelves in
the range of that battery.

Q. We being in the range of that battery, muft it not neceffarily have com-   76.
manded the ford on the Hudfon's River ?

A. It certainly did command that ford.

Q. Do you recollect Lieut. Col. Sutherland being fent with a detachment of   77.
regulars and provincials from Saratoga, to cover a party of workmen employed-to
repair bridges, and render the road practicable?

A. I perfectly recollect it.

Q. Do you recollect for what reafon Colonel Sutherland and the regulars were re-   78.
called ?

A. I underftood it was on the apprehenfion of an action.

Q. Does your Lordfhip recollect different fcouts bringing reports of the enemy's   79.
being in poffeffion of the country between Saratoga and Fort Edward, on both fides
of the river ?

A. I do.

Q. Do you remember General Burgoyne's mentioning, in confidence to you, dif-   80.
ferent ideas of forcing the ford over Hudfon's River; of cutting away by the enemy's right, and attempting a rapid march to Albany ; or by a night march to gain
the fords above Fort Edward ?

A. I do perfectly remember that he mentioned to me all thofe ideas.

Q. Did

81. Q. Did you ever hear of an offer made by General Phillips to make his way to Ticonderoga with a body of troops?

A. No.

82. Q. In the intimacy in which you lived with Major General Phillips, myself, and the officers in General Phillips's family, do you not think you should have heard of such an offer had it been made?

A. I apprehend that I should have heard of it.

83. Q. Did your Lordship hear of General Phillips offering to attempt an escape through the woods, with one or two guides, for the purpose of putting himself at the head of the troops at Ticonderoga, for the future defence of that place?

A. I heard it mentioned since I came to England, in some common conversation; but I never heard it hinted at while I was in America.

84. Q. The day before the council of the generals and field officers was called, can your Lordship speak of the state of things in general at Saratoga?

A. The state of our army was certainly as bad as possible. Their numbers were few, their provisions short, and their position not a good one, owing to the nature of the country, which rose to the distance of some miles, one hill overtopping that which was next to it.

85. Q. Do you know any officer of that army who, in that situation, thought we had a right to more than honourable terms?

A. Our situation, in the apprehension of every one there with whom I conversed, did not entitle us to more.

86. Q. Did the army in general look on the terms obtained, namely, the power of serving their country in other places, to be advantageous as well as honourable, and more than they had a right to expect?

A. I believe they certainly did; and that few persons in the army expected so good terms as those which were granted.

Examined by other Members of the Committee, and by General Burgoyne occasionally.

87. Q. Did the Indians leave the army till after the battle of Bennington?

A. Great numbers did, and at many different times.

88. Q. Were not some Indians on the expedition to Bennington?

A. There were.

89. Q. Was the expedition originally sent out to Bennington?

A. My situation in the army not entitling me to be in the council of war, and not being employed on that expedition, I was of course not entrusted with the orders that were given to Col. Baume.

90. Q. Have you reason to suppose that General Reidesel or Colonel Baume had a particular knowledge of that part of the country, so as to make it particularly proper to give Colonel Baume the command of that expedition?

A. I believe there was no officer in that army of sufficient rank to have commanded such an expedition, who ever had been in that particular part of the country.

Q. The

Q. The intention of the expedition being, as appears by the papers on the table, 91.
to found the difpofition of the people of that country, was that part of the country peopled with Germans, as many other parts of the country are?

A. I can't exactly fpeak to the defcription of the people of that country, as I
was never there myfelf; but there were employed on that expedition numbers of
provincials, many of whom were of that very country; and I apprehend that the
common foldiers of a regular army are not the immediate people who are expected
to found the minds of any country to which they are fent.

Q. As your Lordfhip mentioned the alacrity with which the army paffed the 92.
Hudfon's River, did the army in general think themfelves at that time inadequate to
the purpofe of forcing their way to Albany?

A. The opinions of an army, who cannot be acquainted with the intelligence that
has been received, are often erroneous. The army was in high fpirits, and did not,
I believe, doubt of reaching Albany.

Q. Did the General then doubt of reaching Albany?　　　　93.
A. I really don't know.

Q. Were the rebels' entrenchments completed on the 19th of September?　　94.
A. I never faw the entrenchments at all.

Q. How was our army employed between the 19th of September and the 7th of 95.
October?

A. The army itfelf was employed in ftrengthening its pofition.

Q. Did it take the army eighteen days to ftrengthen its pofition before it made any 96.
movement?

A. I can't exactly fay. They were working all the time.

Q. What works were executed in that time? 97.
A. There were numbers of redoubts erected; the tête-du-pont; lines before the
camp; outworks to the lines, in which guards and picquets were placed; and batteries.

Q. How many redoubts were erected? 98.
A. I think in all there muft have been five or fix.

Q. Was the erecting thofe works full employment for eighteen days? 99.
A. I am not an engineer, or I certainly fhould endeavour to anfwer that queftion.

Q. Were all thofe works neceffary, in your opinion, for an army that meant to 100.
march forward and attack the enemy?

A. They were neceffary in our particular fituation, being within half a mile of the
enemy, to whom we were oppofed, and being inferior in numbers.

Q. Does your Lordfhip know whether the enemy thought it neceffary to fortify 101.
themfelves with redoubts?

A. I don't know what the fpecies of their fortification was; but I have been
always told that great labour had been employed on their works; and what fmall part
I faw of them convinced me of it.

Q. Had you not information from deferters or friends what the enemy was 102.
doing?

A. My fituation in that army did not entitle me to receive that intelligence. When
any perfon came to me to inform me that he had been employed in gaining fuch intelligence, my duty was to bring him to the General.

I

Q. Was

103. Q. Was it not a matter of notoriety in the army, that the enemy received reinforcement between the 19th of September and the 7th of October?

A. The manner of receiving intelligence in an army seldom transpires; the army might guess, but I believe they knew nothing.

104. Q. Was it understood that the rebels had suffered a much greater loss than the king's troops on the 19th of September?

A. It was.

105. Q. Was not the whole, or nearly the whole, of the rebel army engaged?

A. I don't know; I apprehend the whole was not engaged.

106. Q. Was our army in general, in your apprehension, in as good a condition on the 20th of September as the rebel army, who had suffered much more?

A. The rebel army was so numerous that their loss was not equally felt with ours.

107. Q. What number had you reason to suppose the rebel army consisted of on the 19th of September?

A. I always understood they were very numerous. I never heard their numbers exactly.

108. Q. Was not the scarcity of forage foreseen by every body?

A. Those with whom I conversed did not foresee it to the extent in which we experienced it.

109. Q. Was it prudent, in your Lordship's opinion, to bring, or attempt to bring, upwards of fourteen hundred horses to attend the army, in a country so destitute of forage?

A. I never heard that the horses in our army were thought too numerous. On all occasions a scarcity of them was complained of.

110. Q. Do you know how many horses were allowed for the baggage of each regiment?

A. I don't know.

111. Q. Does your Lordship know how many horses were employed about the train of artillery?

A. I don't recollect; but the returns are on the table.

112. Q. Was the heavy artillery brought back from Stillwater, on the retreat of the army to Saratoga?

A. We had lost some small part of it, and the rest was brought to Saratoga.

113. Q. Did the bringing back of that artillery delay that retreat or not?

A. An army with cannon certainly cannot march so rapidly as one without cannon; but cannon always creates a delay which armies have been content to put up with.

114. Q. Was it necessary, in your opinion, in the situation in which the army retreated, to make their retreat as expeditious as possible?

A. The army appeared to me that it did make its retreat as expeditious as possible.

115. Q. Would the leaving of heavy artillery behind, in your opinion, have made a difference of four miles in the march?

A. I can't conceive that it would. The enemy were in force behind us; not having numbers to contend with them, it would have been a very desperate circumstance to have abandoned our cannon, in case of an attack.

Q. Was

Q. Were the heavy artillery, in effect, of any use in that retreat? 116.

A. I don't recollect as it happened, that they were of any other use than that of their not being turned against us.

Q. Might not those cannon have been spiked, and their trunnions have been 117. knocked off, to have rendered them useless?

A. I understand that the spikes in cannon are easily removed, and that it is not an easy matter, I believe almost an impossibility, with any tools that are carried in an army, to knock off the trunnions of brass cannon.

Q. Might not the retreat have been accelerated by leaving behind a great part of 118. the baggage?

A. I don't think it would. I do not remember that we were stopt on account of any particular impediment.

Q. Does your Lordship know at what time intelligence was received in General 119. Burgoyne's army of the failure of Colonel St. Leger's expedition?

A. I think it must have been in the month of August.

Q. Was not that before the passing of Hudson's River? 120.

A. I don't recollect the exact date of receiving that intelligence.

Q. Was it in the month of August? 121.

A. I cannot tell. I heard of it some time after by accident.

Q. Was there any heavy artillery with the army, properly so called? 122.

A There was none of the heavy sort; we had medium twelve-pounders, and two twenty-four pounders, which we took from the enemy at Quebec, which were very much lighter than those twelve-pounders.

Q. From the state of the fatigue of the troops, when they arrived at Saratoga, 123. do you apprehend they could have continued their march though there had been By Gen. Bur- no artillery? goyne.

A. The army was certainly very much fatigued. I believe they could have got but very little further. They certainly were not in a state for a long march.

Q. If the battle expected at Saratoga had been on the plain, would not the 124. heaviest artillery we had have been one of our best dependencies? By General

A. It certainly would; it would have given us a manifest superiority in that Burgoyne. particular.

Q. If the army had not been provided with the number of horses they had, by 125. what means would their provisions or bateaux have been transported in places where By General the river was not navigable? Burgoyne.

A. The transportation of the bateaux and provisions could not certainly have been carried on.

Q. Were there not such places on the Hudson's River between Fort Edward 126. and Albany? By General

A. There were. Burgoyne.

Q. Is it not at any rate a principal object with every army, and of a retreating one 127. in particular, to preserve their artillery if it be possible, even at the expence of By other some labour and delay; and for the use they might be of to them afterwards, as members. well as on the retreat?

A. I apprehend the cannon are feldom abandoned, but through abfolute neceffity.

128. Q. Whether in general you can inform the committee, whether the army had a confidence in the general?

A. They certainly had a confidence in the general, and I do not believe that they have altered their opinion.

129. Q. Did the army then in general, and the officers in particular, entertain a favourable opinion of the general's conduct, capacity, and attachment to them in the various fcenes in which he was engaged, and more particularly on very trying occafions?

A. I don't recollect that any officer, with whom I have had converfation, has ever expreffed himfelf in different terms, and I believe there never was an army more defervedly pleafed with the conduct of their general.

130. Q. Whether the army expreffed any diffatisfaction at the general's return home; that is, whether they thought he came with any purpofes not friendly to them, or looked on themfelves as deferted by him?

A. I was not with the army when General Burgoyne came away; but I have converfed with many officers who have come from it, and they exprefs no diffatisfaction on that head, much lefs looked on or confidered General Burgoyne's intentions as inimical to them.

131. Q. What was the ftate of the American artillery, and how was it ferved?

A. Except on a few occafions, I do not remember their having made much ufe of their cannon; I thought on thofe occafions that they ferved them flowly, but not ill.

132. Q. Whether all circumftances confidered at the time of the affair of Saratoga, the retreat of the army was practicable, either with or without artillery?

A. I thought it was impracticable.

133. Q. Whether after the convention at Saratoga you went to Albany?

A. Yes.

134. Q. Whether you had any opportunity of obferving the nature of the country, if it was ftrong or woody, clear or open?

A. Very ftrong and woody, and a great number of hills.

135. Q. What was the diftance?

A. I don't exactly recollect; about thirty-two miles.

136. Q. Was the fituation of Albany a ftrong fituation, or was it commanded by hills round it?

A. The fituation of Albany was in a bottom very much commanded.

137. Q. If the army had penetrated to Albany, from whence might they have drawn their fubfiftence, if the country had been againft them?

A. I don't know enough of the country to anfwer that queftion.

138. Q. Muft they not have drawn their fubfiftence from New York?

A. I apprehend fo, if they were not mafters of the Mohawk country.

139. Q. Had you any opportunity of obferving the extent of clear or cultivated country round Albany?

A. I can't very juftly defcribe it, not having gone out of the town of Albany, from the time I came into it, till I embarked for New York.

Q. Do

Q. Do you think that, circumstanced as the army was after the engagement of 140.
the 19th of September, it would have been more advantageous to have returned than
to have stayed and fortified the camp?

A. As matters have turned out, it certainly might; but I believe no one thought
so at that time.　　　　　　　　　　　　　　　　　　　　　　　[*Withdrew.*

MAJOR FORBES called in and examined by General Burgoyne.

Q. WAS you major of the 9th regiment, and present with that regiment in 1.
the action near Fort Anne?

A. I was.

Q. What was the behaviour of the enemy on that occasion? 2.

A. At half past ten in the morning, they attacked us in front with a heavy and
well-directed fire; a large body of them passed the creek on the left, fired from a
thick wood across the creek on the left flank of the regiment; they then began to
re-cross the creek, and attack us in the rear: we then found it necessary to change
our ground, to prevent the regiments being surrounded; we took post on the top
of a high hill to our right. As soon as we had taken post, the enemy made a
very vigorous attack, which continued for upwards of two hours; and they certainly would have forced us, had it not been for some Indians that arrived and
gave the Indian whoop, which we answered with three cheers; the rebels soon after that gave way.

Q. What command had you on the 19th of September? 3.

A. I commanded the picquets of the British.

Q. Was you attacked on the march, and with what degree of vigour? 4.

A. I was attacked with great vigour from behind railed fences, and a house, by
a body of riflemen and light infantry.

Q. Was you wounded in that affair? 5.

A. Very early in the day.

Q. Do you remember General Burgoyne bringing up the British line to sup- 6.
port you, and forming at the first opening of the wood?

A. I do.

Q. Did General Fraser's corps arrive precisely in time to occupy the heights on 7.
the right of the British line when the action began?

A. It did, and two companies of light infantry came to my support.

Q. Where did General Burgoyne post the 9th regiment? 8.

3　　　　　　　　　　　　　　　　　　　　　　　　　　　　A. As

A. As foon as they came out of the wood, they filed off to the right, and were drawn off at a fmall diftance from the left of General Frafer's corps, with orders to occupy two houfes, one company in each, and defend them to the laft extremity.

9.   Q. Had you an opportunity in that fituation to obferve the ftrefs of the action?

A. I had while we remained in that pofition.

10.   Q. What was the progrefs of it?

A. The twenty-firft and fixty-fecond regiments were drawn up on our left, and were attacked about three o'clock on the fame ground where the picquets had been attacked. About that time I heard a great deal of firing to my right with the advanced corps; an officer came up to General Burgoyne, and acquainted him that the enemy were endeavouring to turn the left of the fixty-fecond regiment, on which he difpatched an aid-de-camp with orders to the twentieth regiment to form on the left of the fixty-fecond; immediately after, fome companies of the light infantry came to occupy the ground the ninth were drawn up on; the ninth were then ordered behind a deep ravine, to form a corps-de-referve I faw nothing of the action after that.

11.   Q. What was the ftrength of the ninth regiment on that day before they fuftained any lofs?

A. On the 15th of the month the weekly return was given in, and, to the beft of my recollection, they were two hundred and fifty and odd rank and file fit for duty.

12.   Q. What was the ftrength of the other regiments in the Britifh line?

A. I cannot fpeak with any certainty, as I did not fee the returns; but on talking with different commanding officers: the four Britifh regiments were about one thoufand one hundred, and the advanced corps about one thoufand two hundred.

13.   Q. Where was the twenty-fourth regiment?

A. With the advanced corps.

14.   Q. Where was the forty-feventh regiment?

A. Six companies of the forty-feventh regiment that were with that army, were employed as a guard to the bateaux and provifions, and two with the advanced corps.

15.   Q. Where were the other two companies of that regiment left?

A. One at Fort George, and another on an ifland in Lake George.

16.   Q. Of the eleven hundred which compofed the line on that day, do you know how many were loft and difabled in the action?

A. I have heard the furgeon of the hofpital fay, that there were more than fiv   of the whole in the hofpital, but I can't fpeak to how many of the hundred

17.   Q. Can you fay how many were killed?

A. I can't.

18.   Q. Can you fay how many officers were killed and wounded?

A. I can't immediately.

Q. Were

Q. Were the Britifh troops in a condition to have attacked an enemy in in- 19.
trenchments after the action?

A. After the action of the 19th, I went to the hofpital to get my wounds
drefled, and did not join the regiment till the 8th of October; I can't therefore give an opinion of my own: but I have heard feveral officers fay, they
did not think it would have been prudent or right from the lofs they had fuftained
the day before.

Q. Did the regiments begin to be encreafed in their ftrength from the recovered 20.
men to any confiderable degree in lefs than eight or ten days?

A. Not that I know of. I was at the hofpital at the time.

Q. Being in the hofpital, had you occafion to know that the regiments were 21.
ftronger from the receipt of their recovered men on the 7th of October, than
they were at any time between the 19th of September and that day?

A. I know that feveral men were difcharged from the hofpitals fo far recovered as to enable them to do their duty.

Q. At what time did the troops arrive at Saratoga?   22.

A. About eight o'clock at night on the 9th.

Q. Do you know how long the troops had then been under arms, and without 23.
repofe or regular refrefhment?

A. From the 7th in the morning.

Q. Had they been in action, or in continual expectation of action, during that 24.
whole time?

A. I was in the front of the army, and I heard a great deal of firing in the rear,
and we conftantly expected and looked for an attack.

Q. Did the battery of the enemy on the other fide of the river at Saratoga com- 25.
mand the fort on that river?

A. It did.

Q. Was the ground fuch on our fide as would have enabled our artillery to have 26.
fileuced that battery?

A. It did not appear to me that it could.

Q. Had the paffage of the ford been effected, and the army have proceeded to- 27.
wards Fort Edward, on the eaft fide of the river, muft they not neceffarily have
paffed Batten Hill?

A. Undoubtedly.

Q. Do you remember the ford at Batten-Hill?   28.

A. Yes.

Q. Would it have been poffible for the army to have paffed that ford without 29.
artillery to cover them, and the enemy pofted on the other fide?

A. Certainly not. I had an opportunity of feeing the twentieth regiment pafs
that ford without an enemy to oppofe them, and they took a confiderable time,
owing to the depth of the water, the rapidity of the current, and the ftones being
remarkable flippery, fo that feveral of them fell into the river.

Q. Was you prefent at all the councils of war to which the field officers of the 30.
army were called at Saratoga?

A. I was.

Q. Do

51.   Q. Do you remember whether General-Burgoyne ftated the difficulties of the time, and that he mentioned his readinefs to undertake any meafure they fhould think for the honour of the Britifh arms ?
A. I do remember it.

32.   Q. Was the council unanimous to treat with the enemy on honourable terms?
A. They were.

33.   Q. When the firft terms propofed by General Gates were read to them, were they unanimous to reject them ?
A. They were.

34.   Q. After it was decided by a majority of the council that the treaty could not be fufpended without breach of faith, were not the council then unanimous to fign it on that day ?
A. As the majority of the council had given it as their opinion that the public faith was pledged, the council thought that there was no time to be loft, and that it ought to be figned immediately.

Examined by other Members of the Committee and by General Burgoyne occafionally.

35.   Q. Do you know or apprehend that the rebel camp was completely entrenched on the 19th of September ?
A. I don't know.

36.   Q. Had you any reafon to believe from information that they completed their en-trenchments afterwards ?
A. I underftood they had—I don't fpeak from authority.

37.   Q. Had you reafon to think that the rebels received confiderable reinforcements between the 19th of September and the 7th of October ?
A. I did not hear that they had.

38.   Q. Suppofing the rebels to have received reinforcements, could any acceffion of ftrength to our army from the recovery of any number you can fuppofe of the 500 that were in the hofpital, be equal to a reinforcement of even 500 men received by the enemy ?
A. I cannot take upon me to fay.

39.   Q. From being in the hofpital yourfelf, how many of the 500 do you judge joined the army ?
A. I can't pretend to fay.

40.   Q. Do you judge in your own opinion, putting all the circumftances you can toge-ther, whether the enemy were more likely to be forced on the 20th of September or a day or two after, than on the 7th of October ?
A. It is impoffible for me to judge—I did not know their ftrength on the 19th of September, or what reinforcements they received before the 7th of October.

41.   Q. Did you apprehend the army might have made their retreat good to Canada immediately after the action of the 19th of September ?
A. That

A. That depended entirely on circumſtances.

Q. Judging from the circumſtances you then knew, what is your opinion ? 42.

A. I was not more acquainted with the circumſtances of the 19th of September than with thoſe of the 7th of Oĉtober.

Q. If the army had had three weeks more proviſions when they began their retreat, 43. would not that have been a material circumſtance to them towards making good their retreat ?

A. The army could have defended themſelves longer in their entrenchments at Saratoga if they had had more proviſions.

Q. Had you known, immediately after the aĉtion of the 19th of September, that 44. a letter had been received from Sir Henry Clinton, mentioning his intention to attack *By General* the highlands about that time, would you have thought either a retreat or an immediate *Burgoyne.* attack on the enemy adviſeable ?

A. Certainly not.

Q. Do you know whether a council of war was called on the 20th of September, 45. or immediately after the engagement of the 19th of September ? *By other Members.*

A. I don't know that there was.

Q. Did the army in which you ſerved, in its approach to Albany, expeĉt a co-ope- 46. ration from Sir William Howe on the North River ?

A. We did.

Q. Do you believe if the army under Sir William Howe, inſtead of going 47. by ſea up the Cheſapeak to Philadelphia, had operated upon the North River to effeĉt a junĉtion with General Burgoyne's army, conſidering alſo the panic that prevailed after the taking of Ticonderoga, that the army under General Burgoyne would have been made priſoners ?

A. I ſhould think not.

Q. Did you expeĉt any great oppoſition from the rebel army after the taking 48. Ticonderoga ?

A. I did not.

Q. Upon what grounds did you ſo poſitively expeĉt a co-operation with Sir Wil- 49. liam Howe's army ?

A. From General Burgoyne's orders.

Q. Did you ever ſee General Burgoyne's orders ? 50.

A. Every day during the campaign.

Q. By what orders of General Burgoyne did you expeĉt a co-operation ? 51.

A. Early in Oĉtober General Burgoyne gave it out in orders that there were powerful armies of the King's then co-operating with ours.

Q. Did not thoſe orders give ſpirits to General Burgoyne's army ? 52.

A. Situated as our army was, every proſpeĉt of reinforcement muſt certainly give us ſpirits.

Q. Did you ever hear of any co-operation before thoſe orders of General Burgoyne's 53. in Oĉtober ?

A. It was generally talked of in the army, but not by authority.

Q. Whether, if the operations of Sir Henry Clinton on the North River had taken 54. place in time, it would not have been looked on as a very advantageous co-operation with General Burgoyne's army ?

K A. It

A. It might have been attended with very good confequences.

55.   Q. What fituation in general, and particularly with regard to provifions, was General Burgoyne's army in, at the time you mentioned thofe encouraging hopes of co-operation in his orders?

A. The army was put on fhort allowance at that time.

56.   Q. Whether in military affairs a powerful diverfion, if well executed, is not known often to anfwer very effectually the purpofes of co-operation?

A. Certainly very good effects have accrued from powerful diverfions.

57.   Q. If there had been a council of war on the 20th of September, or immediately after the engagement of the 19th, fhould you have known of it?

A. I think I muft have heard of it.

58.   Q. Whether, confidering the circumftances of Sir William Howe's having carried his army to Chefapeak Bay, you fuppofed, or ever heard it fuppofed, that Sir Henry Clinton would have attempted his operations up the North River fooner than he did, or previous to the arrival of his reinforcement from Europe?

A. Not knowing Sir Henry Clinton's ftrength, or his orders, nor the force the enemy had to oppofe him, it is impoffible for me to anfwer that queftion.

59.   Q. What effect had it on the fpirits of General Burgoyne's army when they found there was to be no co-operation between that army and the army of Sir William Howe?

A. We never knew but that there was to be a co-operation.

[Withdrew.

CAPTAIN BLOOMFIELD, of the Artillery, called in, and examined by General Burgoyne.

1.   Q. IN what capacity did you ferve in the campaign in America in 1776 and 1777?

A. I was major of brigade of the royal artillery.

2.   Q. Was you employed by General Phillips, on your return to England, after the campaign of 1776, to folicit a further fupply of artillery for the fervice of the enfuing campaign?

A. On my leaving General Phillips at St. John's, in the month of November, 1776, I was charged with a letter to Sir Guy Carleton, wherein he recommended
4   it

it to make a demand of a further fupply of artillery and ftores for the complete equipment of an additional number of gun-boats for the fervice of Lake Champlain in the enfuing campaign, and likewife for the boats themfelves to be fent out in frame-work. Sir Guy Carleton, on perufing the letter, difapproved of the boats being fent out, but approved of the demand of the ftores and artillery agreeable to General Phillips's requeft, and they were accordingly fent out in the beginning of the year 1777.

Q. At what time did you join the army in the campaign of 1777 ? 3.
A. I joined the army at Ticonderoga on the 23d of July.

Q. Did you live in the family of General Phillips, and had you occafion to 4. know his fentiments refpecting the artillery department?
A. I did chiefly live with the general, and had frequent occafion to know his fentiments on the fubject of the artillery in the courfe of my duty as brigade-major.

Q. Did you know, or had you reafon to believe, that the proportion of ar- 5. tillery employed that campaign was according to the opinion and recommendation of General Phillips ?
A. I can have no doubt but that an officer of General Phillips's rank and extenfive experience muft have determined that point.

Q. What was the diftribution of the artillery after the enemy evacuated Ti- 6. conderoga ?
A. The light brigade of artillery proceeded with the army by the way of Skenefborough ; the park brigade and ftores were conveyed acrofs Lake George in bateaux.

Q. Was not a confiderable portion of artillery of the heavieft kind either left 7. at St. John's, fent back from Ticonderoga, or difpofed of in veffels ?
A. It was : there were left at Ticonderoga fix heavy twelve-pounders, one light twelve-pounder, four light three-pounders, four royal mortars and twelve cohorns. Left on board the Royal George, two heavy twenty-four-pounders, two thirteen-inch mortars, two ten-inch mortars, four eight-inch mortars, four royal mortars and eight cohorns. Sent back to St. John's in the Radau, fourteen heavy twenty-four-pounders, two eight-inch howitzers. Left at Fort George, four medium twelve-pounders, two light fix-pounders, two eight-inch howitzers, two royal howitzers. With Colonel St. Leger's expedition to Fort Stanwix were fent two light fix-pounders, two light three-pounders, four cohorns. Left at St. John's, four light fix-pounders, five light three-pounders, four cohorn mortars : that was the diftribution of artillery that remained after the army had quitted Fort George. The quantity of artillery brought forward with the army were four medium twelve-pounders, two light twenty-four-pounders, eighteen light fix-pounders, fix light three-pounders, two eighteen-inch howitzers, four royal howitzers, two eight-inch mortars, four royal mortars.

Q. Was not that park artillery, tho' confifting of fome twenty four-pounders 8. and fome twelve pounders, properly field artillery ?
A. They certainly were, and have ever been confidered as fuch on all field fervices. Heavy artillery is of a diftinct nature, and confiderably heavier than guns of the fame calibre which we had in the army.

K 2

Q. Have

9.   Q. Have you ever known a lefs proportion than the brigaded artillery, which was attached to the line and to the advanced corps, allotted to the fame number of trooPs ?

   A. The proportion of field artillery certainly fhould vary both in quantity and nature according to the variety of circumftances under which the army is to act ; the ufual allotment of light field pieces are two to each battalion ; and from a calculation of the number and ftrength of General Burgoyne's army, I do not conceive that our light field artillery exceeded that proportion.

10.   Q. What do you apprehend was the propofed ufe of artillery in the country in which we were to act ?

   A. To diflodge the enemy from fuch pofts as every where prefent themfelves in that part of the country, and from which it may be impoffible to diflodge them without artillery of a more confiderable calibre than light fix-pounders.

11.   Q. Do you remember the pofition which the enemy evacuated at Schuyler's Ifland ?

   A. I do perfectly.

12.   Q. Had that pofition been maintained, would not artillery of the heaviet nature we had have been particularly ferviceable ?

   A. Provided the poft could not have been turned, and the enemy had made ufe of every advantage which the ground gave them, I have no doubt but the park artillery would have been abfolutely neceffary.

13.   Q. Had the paffage of the Hudfon's River, or of Batten Kill been difputed, would artillery of that nature have been ferviceable ?

   A. Doubtlefs it would.

14.   Q. Had the enemy taken a pofition at the Forks of the Mohawk River, would artillery of that nature have been ferviceable ?

   A. From the imperfect manner in which I faw that ground, it appeared capable of being made extremely defenfible, and, of courfe, that fort of artillery would have been ferviceable.

15.   Q. Had the army reached Albany, and it had been found expedient to fortify a camp there for the winter, would artillery of that nature have been neceffary ?

   A. There can be no doubt of it.

16.   Q. What do you apprehend to be the chief ufe of howitzers and fmall mortars in the field.

   A. I apprehend they are of infinite fervice againft all kinds of log work, abbaties, and againft entrenchments. The fmall mortars are particularly ufeful againft redoubts and other works where the enemy are confined within a fmall fpace.

17.   Q. Are not log works a fpecies of fortification peculiar to that country ?

   A. I never faw any elfewhere.

18.   Q. Was the carrying forward the artillery from Lake George to the place where the army croffed the Hudfon's River any impediment to the tranfport of provifions ?

   A. The tranfport of our artillery and ftores were conftantly made by horfes

attached

attached to our department, and therefore I do not conceive it did in any manner interfere with the transport of provisions—I mean to confine myself in this answer to the transport from Fort George to the Hudson's River; for after crossing the river we had some oxen and horses attached to the service of the artillery, which I believe were before employed in bringing forward provisions and bateaux.

Q. What time did it take to bring forward the park artillery from Fort George 19. to the bridge of boats over the Hudson's River?

A. The light brigade and the artillery of the park, with their proper proportion of stores and ammunition, had their horses, carriages, and drivers constantly attached to them ; it therefore required no more time to carry those stores than was necessary for the carriages themselves to pass from Fort George to the Hudson's River ; but with respect to the reserve which was afterwards transported by water in bateaux, I believe two days with all our carriages would easily have conveyed them to the Hudson's River.

Q. Do you remember the position of the King's troops from the time of the 20. attack on the 19th of September to the attack on the 7th of October?

A. Yes.

Q. Had the army made a movement to gain the left of the enemy's en- 21. trenchments without previously constructing redoubts on the heights that commanded the plain, would not the bateaux, provisions and hospital have been left open to an attack from the enemy's right?

A. They would have been left exposed undoubtedly.

Q. Were not the largest guns we had the properest pieces of artillery for those 22. redoubts?

A. I think it was a service that was exactaly adapted to them.

Q. Do you remember the disposition made by General Burgoyne on the 7th 23. of October?

A. I do.

Q. At what time was you wounded in that attack? 24.

A. I believe in about twenty minutes after it commenced.

Q. What circumstance of the action did you observe before you was wound- 25. ed, particularly respecting the artillery and the enemy's advancing under the fire of the artillery, and what happened to the troops posted immediately on the left of the artillery?

A. The ground on which the artillery was posted was a clear spot, in a great measure surrounded by woods, the skirts of which on our left was distant about two hundred yards where the attack first began. The two medium twelve-pounders were posted on a small eminence, nearly in the center of this cleared spot between the German picquets and a detachment of the Hesse Hanau regiment. On the enemy's column approaching, the fire of the twelve-pounders and the four sixes was immediately directed towards the enemy's column, notwithstanding which, they drew up along the skirts of the wood behind trees, and after driving in the Germans, kept a pretty warm fire of musketry on the guns and the troops posted about them ; soon after this I heard a firing on the right

towards

3

towards a eleaied fpot, feparated from us by a wood on which the light infantry were pofted on very commanding ground. On their retreating, as alfo the twenty-
fourth regiment who was drawn up in the wood on our right, the enemy made
their appearance on an eminence on our right, and cut off the retreat of the artillery—At this moment I received my wound, and therefore can give no farther
account of the circumftances of that day's action.

Examined by other Members of the Committee.

26. Q. What was the number of horfes in general employed for the artillery after the march from Ticonderoga ?
A. The whole number of horfes detached with the Britifh artillery, previous
to the paffing the Hudfon's River, was about four hundred.

27. Q. How many would have been neceffary for the field pieces attached to the
battalions only ?
A. Eighteen fix-pounders at four horfes each ; fix three-pounders at three
horfes each, and two royal howitzers at three horfes each : the remainder were for
park artillery, ammunition, and ftores of all kinds to accommodate the army on
its march.

28. Q. Was the forage for thefe horfes procured in the country on their march,
or brought from a diftance ?
A. A quantity of oats was brought forward from Canada, but with refpect to
other forage they were under the neceffity of collecting it in the neighbourhood
of the encampment.

29. Q. How many waggons might the bringing on that quantity of oats employ ?
A. I believe the quantity of oats after paffing Fort Edward was fo trifling
that I don't believe it loaded one waggon.

30. Q. After the army arrived at Fort Edward, did any delay or not arife to its
forward progrefs from bringing on the park artillery, waiting for horfes and drivers for that purpofe, or to provide forage ?
A. The park artillery remained at Fort Edward no longer than was neceffary
during the time the army remained in that neighbourhood : I do not know of
any delay whatever from the want of horfes and drivers. Had the park artillery
moved forwards fooner, no end could have been anfwered by it, before the bridge
was thrown over the Hudfon's River.

31. Q. Were there any gun-boats fent out to Quebec for the campaign 1776 ?
A. There were.

32. Q. Were there a fufficient number fent out, in your opinion ?
A. It appeared that the naval force was fuperior to that of the rebels, from the
event of that engagement ; and therefore I conclude, that for the ufes of that campaign there were a fufficient number.

33. Q. Did you apprehend, before the event of the action on the lakes, that the number was fufficient, and went out in time ?

A. We

A. We had received very exaggerated accounts of the rebel force on the lakes, and therefore uncommon exertions were uſed to render our force as formidable as poſſible ; and probably ſome time was loſt, and the campaign in ſome degree retarded, from that circumſtance.

Q. Would the campaign have been retarded ſo long if a greater number of gun-boats had been ſent out ?　34.

A. Certainly not.

Q. What number of artificers were ſent to Canada for the campaign in 1776.?　35.

A. I don't immediately recollect the exact number ; but I think Colonel Chriſtie engaged about two hundred. I know of no others being ſent out.

Q. Do you know of more being aſked for by the artillery or engineers, as neceſſary for the campaign ?　36.

A. I did hear of ſome fuch intention ; but at this diſtance of time I cannot particularly anſwer that queſtion.

Q. Whether the number of artificers ſent out for that campaign were, in any degree, ſufficient for the purpoſe of carrying it on ?　37.

A Certainly not. We were under the neceſſity of collecting all the artificers that could be met with in Canada for the armament of St. John's only, moſt of the bateaux being built by private contract.

Q. Were not the operations of that campaign conſiderably retarded, for want of the number of artificers that were aſked for and not granted ?　38.

A. Had the number of artificers been greater, there can be no doubt but the work would have gone on much faſter. With reſpect to the artificers being demanded, I have already ſaid I do not recollect the number.

Q. Were there not horſes neceſſary for conveying the ſtores and ammunition neceſſary for the field train ; and how many ?　39.

A. The beſt anſwer to that queſtion will, I apprehend, be a ſtate of the number of horſes actually attached to the ſeveral brigades of artillery, ſince the allotment of ſtores and ammunition were exactly proportioned to the number of pieces which they accompanied.——

[The brigade attached to the advanced corps of light artillery conſiſted of eighty-five——]

Anſwer interrupted going into the detail.

Q. How many horſes might have been ſpared, if the heavy park of artillery had not attended the army ?　40.

A. It would have made a difference of two hundred and thirty-ſeven horſes.

Q. Was the army furniſhed with carts to have employed thoſe two hundred and thirty-ſeven horſes ?　41.

A. I really cannot anſwer that queſtion of my own knowledge.

[Withdrew.

Jovis

Jovis 3° *die Junii*, 1779.

LIEUTENANT COLONEL KINGSTON called in, and examined by General Burgoyne.

1.   Q. IN what capacity did you act in the campaign of 1777?
      A. As deputy adjutant general of the province of Quebec; I acted as adjutant general of the army under General Burgoyne, and also as secretary to General Burgoyne.

2.   Q. Did not that double capacity, and the confidence with which General Burgoyne treated you, lead you to the knowledge of the material circumstances attending that campaign?
      A. I looked on myself to be in the entire confidence of the general.

3.   Q. Did General Burgoyne give any orders for the augmentation of artillery destined for this expedition, after his arrival in Canada?
      A. There was no such order went through me; nor did I hear of any such order being given.

4.   Q. Have you reason to believe that the proportion of artillery employed was according to the opinion and recommendation of Major General Phillips?
      A. I believe General Burgoyne had the greatest confidence in General Phillips's knowledge and abilities; and I believe the proportion of artillery to have been arranged between General Phillips and Sir Guy Carleton, because I don't know of any directions given by General Burgoyne upon that head.

5.   Q. What were the orders given, at the opening of the campaign, respecting the incumbrances of baggage?

      [*The witness refers to the orderly book, which he had with him.*

      Read the orders.

      They are the original orders, written by myself at the time.

      [*Reads.*] " Extracts from orders issued by Lieutenant General Burgoyne at Montreal,
                       dated 30th May, 1777.
      ". The regiments destined for the expedition under General Burgoyne are to
      " leave in their respective stores their blanket coats, legging, and all baggage
      " that can be spared during the summer months; the officers are depended on
      " not to encumber the service with more baggage than shall be absolutely ne-
      " cessary for a campaign where the movements may be expected to be sudden
      " and alert; the portion of bateaux to each regiment will be regulated on those
      " principles."

6.   Q. Were those orders afterwards enforced?

                                                                      A. Orders

A. Orders were iſſued again to the ſame purport, dated Skeneſborough Houſe, July 12.

[*Reads.*] " It is obſerved that the injunction given, before the army took the field,
" relative to the baggage of officers, has not been complied with ; and that the regi-
" ments in general are encumbered with much more baggage than they can poſſibly be
" ſupplied with means of conveying,· when they quit the lake and rivers ; warning is
" therefore again given to the officers, to convey by the bateaux, which will ſoon
" return to Ticonderoga, the baggage that is not indiſpenſibly neceſſary to them ;
" or upon the firſt ſudden movement, it muſt inevitably be left upon the ground.
" Such gentlemen as ſerved in America the laſt war may remember that the officers
" took up with ſoldiers' tents, and often confined their baggage to a knapſack for
" months together."

Q. Have you a letter from General Burgoyne to General Reideſel, on the ſubject 8.
of the incumbrance of baggage ?

A. I have an extract of it, taken from the original letter in the letter-book. It is
as follows :

*Extract of a Letter from Lieut. Gen. Burgoyne to Major General Reideſel, dated Head
Quarters at Skeneſborough, the 18th July,* 1777.

" Je vous ſupplie de faire en ſorte, que l'eſprit de l'ordre par rapport
" à le renvoye des baggages des officiers à Ticonderoga aye lieu.
" Les baggages des officiers Britanniques ſont deja renvoyés, et il n'en
" reſte à pluſieurs qu'une petite tente, et un valiſe. C'eſt réelement pour
" l'intereſt de l'officier à la fin, que je ſuis ſi porté à cet article."

T R A N S L A T I O N.

" I requeſt you to take meaſures that the ſpirit of the order reſpecting
" the ſending back officers' baggage to Ticonderoga may have due force.
" The baggage of the Britiſh officers is already gone, and many of them
" have only retained a ſmall tent and one cloak bag. It is really for the in-
" tereſt of the officers, in the end, that I am ſo preſſing upon this ſubject."

Q. When the contract was made for horſes and carts at Montreal, was it the 9.
general opinion of the perſons of beſt intelligence conſulted, that the number was
more or leſs than neceſſary for the ſervice on which we were going ?

A. In general converſation on that ſubject I remember to have heard it ſaid, that
though they were inſufficient, we might expect to find additional ſupplies in the
country. I have extracts of letters here that paſſed between General Burgoyne and See Appen-
General Phillips on that ſubject. They are extracted from the original letter copy- dix.
book.

Q. Have y u the returns, or extracts of the returns, of the ſtrength of the army 10.
at all the different periods of the campaign ?

A. I have extracts from the returns.

11.   Q. What was the strength of the regular troops, at the highest, at the opening of the campaign, rank and file, fit for duty?

A. The first returns I received on the first of July,

                    The British were   3576 fit for duty.
                    Germans   2919 do.
                                           ‾‾‾‾‾‾
                                            6489

I speak solely of the army under Lieut. General Burgoyne.

12.   Q. What were the numbers of the artillery, and the corps under Lieutenant Nutt, attached to the service of the artillery?

                    British artillery   257
                    Germans   100
                    Recruits under Lieut. Nutt   154

13.   Q. Were there any other troops in the army that could be called regulars?

A. There were Canadians, Provincials, and Indians; but I never considered them as regulars, because they were not disciplined.

14.   Q. Can you state about what was the number of the Canadians?

A. The Canadians were 148 the highest number.

15.   Q. The Provincials?

A. I would be understood to speak to the opening of the campaign the first of July. They were low then, and encreased afterwards. They were then 83.

16.   Q. The Indians?

A. Between three and four hundred. It was very difficult to collect what their number was exactly.

17.   Q. Was the army ever so high in numbers, Provincials and Indians excepted, as at that period?

A. I believe it never was. On the 3d of September additional companies joined the British, to the amount of about 300 men; but from killed and wounded, and the garrison left at Ticonderoga, the army was at no time equal to its first number.

18.   Q. What was the force left at Ticonderoga?

A. The first garrison consisted of 462 British, rank and file, 448 Germans, rank and file; making 910 in the whole.

19.   Q. Do you remember the difficulties which attended moving the wounded to Ticonderoga, after the action at Huberton?

A. I remember to have heard they were very great. Different propositions were made for the removing them, such as biers and hand-barrows, which were so very incommodious, that I remember to have been told that the wounded would rather be left where they were than move in the then state of their wounds by such conveyances.

20.   Q. Do you know what were General Burgoyne's motives for detaching General Reidesel with a large corps of troops to the country in the neighbourhood of Castleton?

A. I don't remember to have been present when General Reidesel received his orders or instructions; but I understood it was to create an alarm towards the Connecticut, to give encouragement to the loyal inhabitants, if any such there were, and to protect those that were wounded at Huberton or thereabouts.

Q. Was

Q. Was the removal of thoſe wounded effected long before General Reideſel was 21.
recalled from Caſtleton?

A. I believe not; for I am not quite certain that the whole were moved when General Reideſel returned to the army at Skeneſborough, a day or two before the firſt
diviſion of the army moved towards Fort Anne.

Q. Have you any papers written by General Burgoyne between the time he was 22.
at Montreal and the time he left Skeneſborough, explanatory of the motives on
which he acted?   See Appen-
A. I have. They are extracts from the original letter-book.   dix.

Q. Are you acquainted with any facts that will aſcertain whether, on the army's 23.
arriving at Fort Edward, it was forwarder in its progreſs towards Albany, in point
of time, than it would have been had it taken the route by Ticonderoga and Lake
George?

A. In anſwer to that queſtion I have to ſay, the army, by taking that route, was
a-head of the tranſport of proviſions, which, for the greater part, went from Ticonderoga by the route of Lake George.

Q. At our firſt arrival at Fort Edward, and previous to the roads being mended, 24.
in what proportion did proviſions arrive at our camp?

A. Very little more than for the immediate conſumption.

Q. Have you the memorandum-books of Sir Francis Clarke?   25.
A. Yes.

Q. Do you know them to be his hand-writing?   26.
A. I am fully convinced of it, having ſeen him enter many of the articles in theſe
books.

Q. Has there been any alteration or addition ſince you had them?   27.
A. None.

Q. What was the character of Sir Francis Clarke reſpecting his accuracy? 28.
A. I never ſaw an officer more attentive to the duties of his ſtation than Sir Francis
Clarke, and always found him exceedingly accurate in the remarks he made.

Q. Are there any memorandums reſpecting the arrival of proviſions at that 29.
time?

A. There are ſeveral.

Q. You will read two or three?   30.
A. [Reads.]—" Fifth Auguſt. Victualling of the army out this day. and from
" difficulties of the roads and tranſports, no proviſion came in this night."

" Sixth Auguſt.—At ten o'clock this morning, not quite enough proviſions arrived
" for the conſumption of two days."

Q. Was it in general underſtood, from the combined intelligence received by 31.
General Reideſel, while he was detached to Caſtletown, and that received by General Burgoyne from the Provincials in his camp, that there were many well affected
inhabitants towards Bennington, who would ſhew themſelves on the approach of
troops; and that there was dejection and ſubmiſſion among the party attached to the
congreſs in that country?

A. I did hear ſeveral reports to that purpoſe.

Q. Have

32. Q. Have you the original rough draft of the expedition to Bennington, as preſented to General Burgoyne from General Reideſel; with General Burgoyne's alterations and additions?

A. I have the original rough draft of the propoſals for the expedition to Bennington; but not being preſent at the time, I can't ſay whether thoſe propoſals were delivered by General Reideſel or not; but I know of alterations made in thoſe propoſals by General Burgoyne, from a knowledge of his hand-writing.

See Appendix. *Note,* The witneſs delivered in to the Committee the original rough draft of the Inſtructions, with a fair copy.

33. Q. Whether you have reaſon to know that all the eraſures and alterations in that plan were made before the expedition took place?

A. I believe they were, from the reading of it.

34. Q. Do you remember taking this plan to General Phillips the day General Burgoyne went to Fort George to inſpect the tranſport of proviſions?

A. I do remember it very well; it was the rough draft I took.

35. Q. What were General Phillips's ſentiments upon it?

A. I remember General Phillips and I had a long converſation on the ſlowneſs of the arrival of the tranſport of proviſions; and he ſaid he looked on this as a very good idea; that he ſaw no objection, and aſked me if I knew of any.

36. Q. Do you remember ſhewing the plan to General Fraſer?

A. I do very well.

37. Q. What did he expreſs on the ſubject?

A. He deſired me to leave it with him till the afternoon for his conſideration. He came himſelf to my tent the next morning early; he expreſſed himſelf to me in a manner that conveyed a diſapprobation of the Germans being employed in it. I think I obſerved to him that ſince the honour gained by the advanced corps at Huberton, I believed General Reideſel was deſirous of having the Germans employed. I mentioned to General Fraſer my ideas of proviſions being obtained by that expedition, and the army thereby enabled to get quicker on to Albany than waiting for the ſlow tranſport from Fort George. General Fraſer ſaid ſomething about Germans, which I don't recollect; which brought this remark from me. I deſired General Fraſer, from the friendſhip he had for General Burgoyne, if he ſaw any real objection to this plan, to expreſs himſelf fully and freely to General Burgoyne himſelf; that the ſcouts of the army and the guides were attached to his the advanced corps, and he might, through them, perhaps know more of the nature of the country than I did; and therefore I preſſed him to mention his objections, if he had any, to General Burgoyne. I think he ſaid, but am not quite certain, " the Germans are " not a very active people; but it may do." I preſſed him at parting to go to General Burgoyne, if he thought it would not do. He ſaid No, and went off.

38. Q. Were not many of the Provincials in the army of the country about Bennington, and towards the Connecticut?

A. I can't pretend to ſay they were from that country; but I underſtood many of them were well acquainted with that country.

Q. Do

Q. Do you remember Captain Sherwood in particular?　39.
A. I do very well.
Q. Was he of that country?　40.
A. I underſtood he was of that neighbourhood.
Q. Did you ever hear Colonel Skene, or any other Provincial, conſulted on an　41.
expedition into that country, expreſs any apprehenſion of its ſucceſs?
A. I never did.　Sir Francis Clarke told me he had received favourable accounts
from Colonel Skeene; and I believe after part of the expedition had taken
place.
Q. Are there any memorandums of Sir Francis Clarke's, reſpecting the expedi-　42.
tion to Bennington?
A. Yes.
Q. Is there any that marks the diſtance between Batten Kill and Bennington?　43.
A. Yes; it is his hand-writing.
[Reads.] " From the mouth of Batten Kill, Eaſt, for two miles; then ſtrike off
" South Eaſt for about fifteen miles to Cambridge; and ſo on about twelve miles
" to Bennington."　44.
Q. Have you the original letters, written from Colonel Baume to General Bur-
goyne, while he was on the expedition?　See the Ap-
A. They are here.　[He delivered them in to the Committee.　pendix.
Q. Is there any memorandum of Sir Francis Clarke's marking the time when　45.
Colonel Breyman was ordered to march to ſupport Colonel Baume?
A. [Reads.] " 15th Auguſt.　Expreſs arrived from Sancoick; at five in the morn-
" ing; corps de reſerve ordered to march.
" 16th Auguſt.　During the night, expreſs arrived from Sancoick with an account
" of the repulſe this evening of a detachment of ours on an expedition.
" Sunday, 17th Auguſt.　The general went up to the twentieth regiment, ad-
" vanced on the road to Sancoick, and met the corps de reſerve, the men of that
" expedition returning all day."
Q. Do you recollect what time of the day it was General Burgoyne met Colo-　46.
nel Breyman on his return on the 17th?
A. I think it was ſometime between one and three o'clock.
Q. Have you the inſtructions given by General Burgoyne to Colonel Skeene on　47.
that expedition?
A. Here is a copy of them.　See the A;—
Q. Is there any memorandum of Sir Francis Clarke's, of any intelligence received　pendix.
from Colonel St. Leger about this time?
A. There is of the 12th of Auguſt.
[Reads.] " This morning received intelligence of an action near Fort Stanwix."
Q. After the failure of the expedition to Bennington, can you ſpeak to the ef-　49.
forts made for forwarding proviſions?
A. I know that very great efforts were made both before and after.　I underſtood that General Burgoyne and General Phillips had been both at different times
at Fort George to forward the proviſions, and I believe ſubſequent to the ill news
from Bennington.　The quarter-maſter-general (I mean Captain Money,) was ſent
by

by General Burgoyne to Fort Edward, and I believe to Fort George, to collect all horses and teams possible, and to make every exertion to bring forward the provisions.

50. Q. Have you the calculation, made by the commissary-general, of the carriages and horses necessary for different given quantities of provisions?

See the Appendix. A. It is here. I believe it is the original.

51. Q. Did the march of the artillery from Fort George to the bridge of boats over Hudson's River, interfere with the transport of provisions?

A. I have had many conversations with General Phillips and the quarter-master-general about the transport of provisions, and never remember to have heard from them, or any other person, that the march of the artillery interfered in any manner with the transport of provisions.

52. Q. About what time did the additional companies arrive?
A. The 3d of September.

53. Q. What was the state of the army when we passed the Hudson's River?
A. My return goes to the 1st of September.
       British, fit for duty under arms, 2635 rank and file.
       Germans   —   1711
The 300 additional did not join the army till the 3d of September, so that this return is exclusive of them.

54. Q. What was the strength of the artillery and Lieutenant Nutt's corps at that time?
A. I believe there was very little variation in either of them from the former return.

55. Q. Have you General Burgoyne's application to Sir Guy Carleton for a garrison from Canada for Ticonderoga, before he passed the Hudson's River?

See the Appendix. A. I have extracts from letters of General Burgoyne to Sir Guy Carleton, the 11th of July, 1777, and the 29th of July, 1777.

56. Q. Was there any considerable alteration in the strength of the army between the return of the 1st of September, and the action on the 19th?
A. There was a skirmish or two, but the loss was not material in that interval.

57. Q. In the course of the service, did you ever know any instance of a day of action, where there was not some deductions from the effective strength upon paper, for baggage guards, bat-men, care of the sick, and other indispensible regimental contingencies?
A. I apprehend there must always be deductions of that sort.

58. Q. In the service of our campaign, was there not a considerable additional deduction for the care and defence of the bateaux and movable magazines?
A. It must of course make an additional drain from the army.

59. Q. Was not all we had of the forty-seventh regiment appropriated to that particular service?

60. A. It generally was; I believe always so.
Q. These deductions considered, about what number do you compute the British line to have consisted of on the day of the action of the 19th.

A. I

A. I believe the four regiments of the line engaged that day amounted to little more than one thouſand one hundred men on the ſpot under arms in the action.

Q. What loſs did the Britiſh ſuſtain in that action? 61.

A. Killed, wounded, and priſoners, rather more than leſs than five hundred.

Q. Can you ſpeak particularly to the loſs of the line? 62.

A. I believe about ſeventy-ſix killed rank and file, and between two hundred and forty and two hundred and fifty wounded, and about twenty-eight or thirty miſſing and priſoners.

Q. Do you recollect the ſtrength of the 20th regiment when they made their 63. laſt charge on the enemy?

A. I do very well. I was by General Phillips when the orders were given for that charge; he was then in the front of the line: the ranks appeared to be very thin, the regiment were much fatigued with the length of the action, but moved on to the charge with ſpirit.

Q. Do you remember General Burgoyne going up to the ſixty-ſecond regiment 64. immediately after the firing ceaſed, and the report that was made to him by the commanding officer of the ſtate of that regiment?

A. I remember it, and the officer reporting the great loſs they had ſuſtained in the action; I ſaw them, and they appeared to be very conſiderably reduced in number.

Q. Do you remember the officer mentioning that they had not above fifty or ſixty 65. men in the regiment?

A. I can't ſpeak poſitively to that; but in my own judgment they did not exceed that number.

Q. Were not both the field-officers wounded? 66.

A. Colonel Anſtruther and Major Harnage were both wounded, and a great many other officers were killed and wounded, and the regiment ſuffered greatly.

Q. To what degree did the men of the artillery ſuffer in that action? 67.

A. I think, but am not quite certain, that the number that were with four guns amounted to forty-eight. I ſaw Captain Jones, who was a very gallant man, and commanded thoſe four guns, killed, and ſome other officers wounded, and I believe about thirty-ſix of the men were killed and wounded. I ſhould in juſtice to the artillery ſay, that I think it is not in the power of men to keep a better fire, both of round and grape-ſhot, than was ſucceſſively maintained for ſeveral hours that day.

Q. From your experience in the ſervice, do you conceive it would have oc- 68. curred to any officer, to engage troops, if he could poſſibly avoid it, in the ſituation in which the Britiſh line was the day after that action?

A. The experience of an officer of my inferior rank does not lead to much; but I ſhould have been ſorry to have given orders to thoſe regiments, after the gallant ſufferings of that day, to have attacked an army reported, both from our ſpies and our priſoners, to be very near if not more than four times the number of our whole force: add to this, the country was a very thick wood, and
the

the fituation of the rebel camp, I believe, could not by any means be reconnoitred within that fpace of time.

69.   Q. Do you remember General Burgoyne receiving a letter from Sir Henry
Clinton the day but one after that action, informing him, that he intended about
that time an attack on Fort Montgomery ?

A. I do remember his receiving a letter from Sir Henry Clinton about that time;
it was the 22d of September.

70.   Q. Do you imagine that any officer knowing of that letter would have entertained thoughts of immediately renewing an attack upon the enemy ?

A. As far as an opinion of an officer of my inferior rank goes, I fhould not
have thought of it, nor did I hear any officer of any rank exprefs fuch an idea
at that time.

71.   Q. From what you knew of the country, did you not believe that a fuc-
cefsful attack from Sir Henry Clinton during the time we lay at that camp,
would either have diflodged General Gates entirely, or have obliged him to detach confiderably from his army ?

A. I remember our fcouts giving information, that a bridge was laid over
the Hudfon's River, very near the enemy's camp ; and it was the opinion of
fome very confidential men that were employed in that army in that capacity,
and were much under the direction of General Frafer, that on the approach of
Sir Henry Clinton's army, the army of Mr. Gates could not ftand us, but would
crofs the river, and go towards New England. Whether the idea was right or
wrong, I can't tell.

72.   Q. Did you ever hear fuch perfons, or any others, exprefs an idea, that the
enemy would have taken the fame meafure on our advancing to attack them
without that co-operation ?

A. I don't remember to have heard any fuch thing.

73.   Q. Do you imagine that any officer knowing of Sir Henry Clinton's letters,
would have thought it proper to retreat after the action of the 19th of September ?

A. I never heard any officer exprefs an idea of that fort. I don't know what
officers might be within the knowledge of fuch a letter; but I lived intimate-
ly with General Phillips, General Frafer, and with Mr. Twifs, the engineer ;
whether the letter was in their knowledge or not, I don't know : but I never
heard them exprefs fuch an idea.

74.   Q. Did you ever hear any officer of that army, though unacquainted with
the letter, before or fince the time, exprefs a difapprobation of the meafure of
remaining in that camp without either attacking or retreating ?

A. Neither then or at any time while I remained in America, and of courfe
not fince.

75.   Q. From your converfation with the chief engineer, and from other circumftances, have you reafon to know, that every poffible means were ufed after
the action of the 19th, to obtain a knowledge of the ground on the enemy's
left ?

A .I

A. I had frequent converfations with the chief engineer on that fubjeft. I believe his attention was given to that point almoft every day, and a knowledge of that ground I underftood to be very difficult to be obtained.

Q. Was not the right of the enemy deemed impracticable.   76.

A. I had no opportunity myfelf of feeing the right of the enemy; but I underftood from others, that the pofition was too ftrong to be attacked with any profpeft of fuccefs.

Q. Were there not frequent confultations held between General Burgoyne, Ge- 77: neral Phillips and General Frafer, previous to the movement up to the enemy on the 7th of October?

A. I underftood there was fcarce a day paffed without fuch confultation; I believe no day after the action of the 19th.

Q. Did you conceive that the chief purpofe of that movement was to attain 78. a knowledge of the left of the enemy's pofition, and if expedient to attack them there?

A. I underftood it was.

Q. Did it appear to you, that the force left in camp, under General Hamil- 79. ton, was more than fufficient to keep the enemy in check?

A. I don't think it was.

Q. From the intimacy and confidence in which you lived with General Bur- 80. goyne and General Frafer, do you imagine any difagreement of opinion could have fubfifted between them without your knowledge?

A. I think I muft have heard of it.

Q. Do you know any inftance, but more efpecially refpecting the periods of 81. paffing the Hudfon's River, the action of the 19th of September, and that of the 7th of October, wherein General Frafer expreffed a difapprobation of General Burgoyne's meafures?

A. I do not: but I would beg leave to obferve, that upon the plan to Bennington, General Frafer had expreffed a different opinion, with refpect to employing the Germans. At the time of paffing the Hudfon's River, and after it was croffed, I had a great deal of converfation with General Frafer: he feemed to exprefs fatisfaction in the manner in which the troops had paffed.

Q. In the action of the 7th of October, after the German troops on the left 82. of the artillery had given way, did you obferve General Phillips and General Reidefel in perfon?

A. I was with General Phillips at different times, and I faw General Reidefel more than once; they were both very active, and exerted themfelves very much to form the broken troops, and to make the retreat as regular as the circumftances would permit.

Q. What was the laft time you faw Sir Francis Clarke in that action, and do you 83. know what orders he was carrying?

A. It was after the retreat was become very general. Sir Francis Clarke afked me, if I had given any orders to the artillery to retreat? I told him, that as there was a major-general of the artillery in the field, who was confeffed by the army to be a very excellent officer, I would not take on myfelf, as ad-

M   jutant-

jutant-general, to give orders to any part of the artillery. Sir Francis Clarke told me, that a diſpoſition had been made for a general retreat, and that he was going with orders from General Burgoyne to bring off the artillery. About the inſtant we were parting, a very heavy fire came upon us from the enemy, and I have ſince had reaſon to believe, that Sir Francis Clarke received his wound at that time.

84.   Q. On the day of the 8th, do you remember the enemy forming a line in the meadows, and making a demonſtration of attacking us?

A. I do remember it very well, and that there was a great deal of cannonading from the enemy.

85.   Q. Do you remember alſo a cannonading in the afternoon, about the time of General Fraſer's funeral?

A. I think I ſhall never forget that circumſtance. General Fraſer, I under-ſtood had deſired to be buried privately, in one of the redoubts that had been raiſed for the protection of our magazines and ſtores; as the corpſe was paſſing by, General Burgoyne, General Phillips, and I believe General Reideſel, and ſeveral other officers, out of reſpect to General Fraſer's memory, and to do him honour in the eyes of the army, notwithſtanding his requeſt, attended his fune-ral into the redoubt. The enemy were in this inſtance, I thought, very defec-tive in point of humanity; they pointed a gun or two at that very redoubt, and kept up a briſk cannonade during the whole of the funeral ſervice, which was performed with great ſolemnity and very deliberately by Mr. Brudenel, the chaplain. I never ſaw ſo affecting a ſight.

86.   Q. Do you remember on the march to Saratoga ſeeing a corps of the enemy at work on the plain of Saratoga?

A. I do very well; a working party, and what appeared to be a battalion or more drawn up as a covering party.

87.   Q. Was that the corps that afterwards took poſt on the oppoſite ſide of the river?

A. I believe it was the ſame corps I ſaw afterwards paſſing the ford.

88.   Q. After the arrival of the army at Saratoga, was Lieutenant Colonel Suther-land detached with a command to cover a party of workmen to repair bridges and roads, in order to continue the retreat on the weſt ſide of the river?

A. He was ordered with a party to repair bridges and roads on the weſt ſide.

89.   Q. Do you remember on what account Colonel Sutherland and the party were recalled?

A. I believe it was on information given by our ſcouts, that the enemy were preparing to attack us in great force.

90.   Q. Have you further reaſon to know that a geneaal attack on that day was really intended by the enemy?

A. There was particular caution ſent round to all the troops to be prepared for that attack, as it was expected it would be attempted under cover of a very thick fog then prevailing. After the convention had taken place, a gene-ral officer in the rebel ſervice acquainted me, that ſuch an attack was intended,

           and

and from information, I believe from deferters, or from their own fcouts, that our army was exceedingly well prepared to receive them, that they would be very much expofed when they came on the plain to our artillery, he not only retreated with his command, but fent word to another general officer to retreat alfo. The other general officer was his fenior; but he had taken that upon him, from the fear of the confequences of fuch an attack, of which he fent word to General Gates, who approved and confirmed his order.

Q. Previous to the council of war to which the field officers were called, do you remember it being determined in the council of the generals, to try a night march, abandoning the carriages and baggage, and orders being given for the delivery of as much provifions as the men could carry?   91.

A. I do remember fuch a determination very well.

Q. What prevented the execution of it?   92.

A. I underftood there were fuch difficulties in getting out the provifions, that the delivery of the neceffary provifions could not be accomplifhed.

Q. Had we intelligence the next day from different fcouts, that the enemy was in poffeffion of the country in force, on both fides the Hudfon's River, between us and Fort Edward?   93.

A. I underftood, from fome of the fcouts that we had been accuftomed moft to depend on, that the enemy were fo pofted.

Q. Have you reafon to know that the intelligence General Burgoyne ftated to the council of war on this fubject was true?   94.

A. I was affured by one of the general officers who conducted us towards Bofton that troops of theirs were in the pofition that our fcouts had given us information of.

Q. Did you learn at the fame time at what period thofe pofts were taken up by the enemy, whether before or after our arrival at Saratoga?   95.

A. I have extracts of minutes made at that time, from the mouth of the general officer I mentioned.

[Reads.]—" When the king's army was returning to Saratoga, a brigade of " fifteen hundred men were pofted on the eaft fide of the Hudfon's River, to difpute " the ford, and two thoufand men more were pofted between us and Fort Edward, " on the fame fide of the river."—Fourteen hundred more alfo were pofted oppofite to Saratoga, a little above the other party I mentioned before, to prevent our paffing the Hudfon's River. Fifteen hundred of thofe I have mentioned were pofted on or before the 5th of October. The others, I remember very well now to have heard, were pofted previous to the 7th of October.

Q. Have you an extract of the laft council of war at which the field officers affifted?   96.

A. The extract is true, excepting the names of the officers, and the votes they gave. I have the original paper, with the names of the officers that compofed the council; and I believe their opinions.   [The extract produced. See Appendix.]

Q. Did you ever hear of a propofal made by General Phillips, to make a way from Saratoga to Ticonderoga with a body of troops?   97.

M 2   Never

A. Never with a body of troops; but I remember to have heard General Phillips make an offer, which I thought a very ſpirited one, to riſk his life in attempting with one or two of our beſt guides, to find a paſſage to Ticonderoga, and do his utmoſt for the defence of that garriſon, as an artillery officer, ſhould the enemy attack that fortreſs after the convention ſhould take place.

98.   Q. Have you the return of General Gates's army, ſigned by himſelf?
A. I have; but I have forgot to bring the original. I have the extract.

For the original return, ſee the Appendix, No. XVI.

[*Reads.*] " Copy from General Gates's return, from his camp at Saratoga; 16th October, 1777.

" Brigadiers	— —	12
" Colonels	— —	44
" Lieutenant Colonels	— —	45
" Majors	— —	49
" Captains	— —	344
" Firſt Lieutenants	·	332
" Second Lieutenants	— —	326
" Enſigns	— —	345
" Chaplains	— —	5
" Adjutants	—	42
" Quarter-maſters	— —	44
" Paymaſters	— —	30
" Surgeons	— —	37
" Mates	— —	43
" Serjeants	— —	1392
" Drummers	— —	636
" Preſent fit for duty	—	13,216."

I underſtand theſe laſt are rank and file, becauſe the others are mentioned before.

" Sick preſent	— —	622
" Sick abſent	— —	731
" On command	— —	3875
" On furlow	— —	180."

I believe that the men on command were explained to me by General Gates to have been detached from his army, in the rear and upon the flanks of the king's troops, previous to the convention.

99.   Q. Do you apprehend that that return includes the corps that were on the other ſide of the Hudſon's River, immediately oppoſite to Saratoga?

A. I do recollect the name of one of the general officers who was on the other ſide of the Hudſon's River, included in Mr. Gates's return, and therefore I imagine the men under his command are included alſo. When I ſay one, I do not mean to have underſtood that the other two general officers, the one who was ſtationed with a party oppoſite to Saratoga, and the one who was ſtationed on the ſame ſide of the water, between us and Fort Edward, are not alſo included in General Gates's return.

Q. Do

Q. Do the returns to which you referred of our army ſtate the effective ſtrength, 100. at the time of ſigning the convention ?

A. They do ſtate the rough number, collected at that time, of men preſent and under arms.

State the numbers. 101.

The Britiſh appeared to have been	1905
Germans —	1594

I can't be anſwerable for the correctneſs of thoſe numbers, as they were taken in a great hurry.

Q. Can there poſſibly be a miſtake of many hundreds ? 102.

A. I can ſtate from a monthly return of the firſt of November, fit for duty,

$$\left.\begin{array}{l}\text{Britiſh} — — — \quad 2086 \\ \text{Germans} — — \quad 1633 \end{array}\right\} \text{Rank and file.}$$

There might be people recovered from their wounds who were diſcharged from the hoſpital, and had joined the corps ; or there might have been a miſtake in the return, juſt before the convention, in the confuſion of the army at that time.

Q. Do you remember what paſſed reſpecting the military cheſt, while the treaty 103. of Saratoga was depending ?

A. I do remember that it was ſtrongly recommended to the commanding officers of corps to take ſums of money from the paymaſter general, on account of ſubſiſtence then due to their regiments ; and I believe a great deal of money was ſo diſtributed, and regularly accounted for to the paymaſter general on the ſubſequent ſettlement of the pay of the army.

Q. What became of the reſt of the money in the military cheſt ? 104.

A. It was taken by the paymaſter general to Albany.

Q. Did any part of it fall into the hands of the enemy ? 105.

A. Not a ſhilling that I ever heard of.

Q. Was any proportion of it loſt, embezzled, or ſecreted ? 106.

A. If any ſuch thing had happened, I think the paymaſter general would have applied to me immediately. Never having heard, then or at any time after, of any loſs having been ſuſtained, I do not believe there was any loſs ſuffered in the retreat or after it.

Q. Was the ſecret ſervice account, during the campaign, kept by you ? 107.

A. It was.

Q. Could you produce the ſeveral articles of that account, if called on for 108. it ?

A. I have either a copy of it at home of my own, or from the paymaſter general.

Q. Did General Burgoyne ever appropriate any part of that expenditure to the 109. extraordinaries of his own expences, or to any other purpoſe for his own uſe ?

A. Never that I know of.

Q. Muſt not you have known it if it had been ſo ? 110.

A. Certainly.

Q. Were there not occaſions where General Burgoyne paid, from his own purſe, 111. expences that, in the opinion of others, he might have been juſtified in placing to the public account ?

A. I

A. I remember to have been told by other gentlemen, that expences of that ſort General Burgoyne had been at, ought to have been charged in that manner.

112. Q. What was the nature of thoſe expences?

A. They were preſents to people who had diſtinguiſhed themſelves, and in acts of charity to women who had loſt their huſbands, and other occaſions which it was very proper for a general officer to give, and very proper to put into a public account.

113. Q. Had not General Burgoyne, from his ſituation, all the expences attending a Commander in Chief?

A. He certainly had, from being obliged to keep a public table for the entertainment and refreſhment of officers and others coming to head quarters, on duty or buſineſs; and I know thoſe expences to have been very great, from the exceeding high price of all the articles of life in that part of the world.

114. Q. Did General Burgoyne ever receive more than the appointment of a lieutenant general?

A. Never.

115. Q. Was there not a board of general officers appointed at Cambridge, to inſpect all the accounts of the campaign; and did not General Burgoyne regulate the payment of the battalions by the report of that board?

A. There was ſuch a board, and the payments were regulated according to the report of that board.

116. Q. Upon the whole of what you know of General Burgoyne's receipts and expences, do you believe he was, in his own purſe, a gainer or a ſufferer in the campaign 1777?

A. I really believe his appointments were not equal to his expences in that campaign.

Examined by other Members of the Committee and by General Burgoyne occaſionally.

117. Q. What were the numbers of the effective British, at the opening of the campaign 1777, including officers and non-commiſſioned officers?

A. I have not thoſe returns; but they were ſent to the Commander in Chief, and my extracts are for the rank and file.

118. Q. Can you anſwer that queſtion with reſpect to the Germans?

A. My extracts are the ſame both for the Britiſh and the Germans.

119. Q. What was the greateſt number of Provincials in the army at any time in the campaign?

A. I believe the only queſtion that has been aſked reſpecting them was at the beginning of the campaign; they were then eighty-three. On the firſt of September they amounted to about ſix hundred and eighty, which was the greateſt number they ever amounted to.

120. Q. What do you mean by Provincials?

A. I

A. I underſtand them to be inhabitants of that country, aſſembled under officers who were to·have had different commiſſions, provided they had ever amounted to certain numbers.

Q. Do you include Canadians under the name of Provincials?   121.

A. I believe, in the former part of my evidence, the Canadians were ſtated to be one hundred and forty-eight, and diſtinguiſhed from the Provincials.

Q. Was General·Burgoyne's ſecond order of the twelfth of July, relating to the baggage, ſtrictly complied with?   122.

A. I conceive it was the duty of the commanding officers of regiments to enforce an obſervance and obedience to the general orders.

Q. Was it actually enforced in ſuch a manner to the degree you thought it ſhould have been?   123.

A. I am not quite poſitive whether there was not another order iſſued afterwards.

[*Queſtion repeated.*]   124.

A. I never had any report made to me by a commanding officer of any corps, of that order not being complied with.

Q. What was your own ocular obſervation of the quantity of baggage carried with the army; and did it appear to you that that order could have been fairly complied with?   125.

A. I own I don't recollect, not hearing any complaint nor attending to it. The quarter maſter general of the army muſt naturally know more of the baggage than the adjutant general.

Q. Do you know what allowance of waggons was made to a regiment?   126.

A. I don't recollect any waggons that we had to allow.

Q. Was none of the baggage brought down in wheeled carriages?   127.

A. Several officers, I believe, bought waggons and carts of the country people for their own uſe; but I do not remember any of the king's carts or waggons being appropriated to the carriage of officers' baggage. It might be, but I don't recollect it.

Q. Can you ſay, in a general way, how many horſes might be employed in carrying the baggage of the army, including officers' horſes?   128.

A. I never had any information upon that ſubject; it did not belong to my department, and I had much buſineſs on my hands.   129.

Q. How was the regimental baggage carried?

A. I believe chiefly in bateaux.

Q. How was it carried when there was no water-carriage?   130.

A. I can't ſpeak to that point, having had no information on that ſubject; and when I ſpeak of bateaux, I ſpeak generally, having *had* no information on the ſubject.   131.

Q. Can you ſay, in a general way, how many women attended the army?

A. I had really ſo much to do that I had not much leiſure to pay much attention to the ladies; and I know very little of their beauty or their numbers.

Q. Would not the feeding of two thouſand women be a conſiderable object with reſpect to the proviſions of the army?   132.

A. I

A. I fhould have been very forry to have had two thoufand women to have experienced that.

133. Q. How many women were there, if not two thoufand?

A. I would wifh to give the houfe every information in my power, w hencan fpeak with any degree of accuracy or tolerable guefs. I have feen the commif-fary of provifions return, and I think the number of women returned, as victualled from the ftores, were very very few.

134. Q. Do you think that a corps of dragoons mounted would have been of great ufe to the army?

A. I own, I very much wifhed thofe few dragoons we had could have been mounted, becaufe, though in that part of America that I faw they might not have been neceffary or ufeful to have made a charge, I think thofe light dragoons might be always applied to very ufeful fervices.

135. Q. How many had you of thofe dragoons?

A. They are included in the ftrength of the Germans, and I really do not re-member their particular number.

136. Q. If none or lefs of the park of artillery had been brought forward, would there not have been horfes to have mounted thofe dragoons?

A. I believe there might have been horfes enough taken from the artillery, or from the provifion train, to have mounted thofe dragoons, if it had been thought more expedient to have employed the horfes in that manner; but they were hired or contracted for, for the fpecial purpofes of carrying provifions, and bringing on the artillery, and never meant by the perfons who furnifhed the contract for the dra-goon fervice.

137. Q. If a fmaller quantity of baggage had been carried, might not the officers have fpared fome of their baggage horfes for mounting the dragoons?

A. I never met with an officer who had horfes to fpare. I know Sir Francis Clarke and myfelf wifhed to buy horfes to carry our own fervants; cared very little what expence we were at, and yet I could not obtain any.

138. Q. Do you know of any corps or party finding their way back to Ca-nada?

A. I never heard of any corps finding its way there; and I underftood from the guides who were with us, previous to the convention's taking place, that if that was attempted, we muft break into fmall parties, and go by what is called Indian paths.

139. Q. Suppofing there was a fmall party that found its way to Canada by In-dian paths, do you think it would have been poffible for an army to have done the fame?

A. My idea of that muft be founded upon the report of thofe guides who had ferved us very faithfully as fcouts upon former occafions, and who inform-ed me that we muft break into very fmall parties, to have any chance of mak-ing our way through the woods to Canada; and I remember that when General Phillips offered to attempt to find his way to Ticonderoga, it was talked of and looked on to be as defperate as gallant.

140. Q. If any party did make its way to Canada, do you not fuppofe it muft

be

be that party of provincials that ran away while they were employed to repair roads. and that were never heard of afterwards?

A. I remember fome were reported to have run away who were making roads, and it is likely to have been that party.

Q. When you mentioned the higheft number of provincials, did you mean 141. that they were all armed?

A. I know that they were not all armed. We had not arms for them.

Q. Of thofe that were armed, fome refpectable perfons excepted, were they 142. much to be depended upon?

A. A very great part of them were fuch as I fhould have placed very little dependence upon.

Q. Before the army left Canada, was there not a ftrict order, that not more than 143. three women a company fhould be fuffered to embark?

A. I do know there was fuch an order iffued, and I never heard any complaint of its having been broke through. I don't recollect the date of that order, or I would have turned to my book, and ftated to the houfe, upon the firft queftion relative to the number of women that were employed on our expedition.

Q. Is it not the cuftom in all armies victualled from the king's ftores, to prohibit the delivery of provifions to any women over and above the number allowed 144. by order?

A. It was cuftomary in all places where I ferved in the laft war, and very ftrong and peremptory orders were given on that fubject to the commiffaries in our army.

Q. Do you not then believe, that all women who followed your army were 145. fed from the ration of the men they followed, or found their provifion in the country?

A. I remember, upon afking the commiffaries how there came to be fo few women in the provincial returns, I was told, it was the cuftom for them to be fupplied out of the men's rations.

Q. Were the women conveyed on baggage carts or horfes, or did they walk 146. a-foot?

A. I never heard of the women's being conveyed on baggage carts or the king's horfes.

Q. If the women neither employed the king's horfes, nor confumed his pro- 147. vifions, do you think they were more of impediment, or of comfort to the king's troops?

A. I never underftood from my converfation with the commanding officers, or others, that the women were any impediment.

Q. If after the taking of Ticonderoga there was any doubt in the army in which 148. you ferved, of their being able to reach Albany?

A. I don't remember to have heard any doubts expreffed upon that fubject, meaning foon after the taking Ticonderoga.

Q. Was it generally underftood in the army, that it was was well fupplied with 149. all the neceffaries, appointments for war, and articles proper for forwarding the expedition to Albany?

N.   A. I

A. I always underſtood that the army had been very well ſupplied with every thing.

150.   Q. Do you believe, if the ſecretary of ſtate had ordered the army under General Howe to co-operate with the army under General Burgoyne for the North River, with a view to have formed the junction of the two armies, that the diſaſter which befel General Burgoyne's army could have happened ?

A. If a junction could have been formed, I ſhould apprehend that Mr. Gates's army might have been diſlodged, and that the misfortune at Saratoga would not have happened. This is only matter of opinion.

151.   Q. Do you apprehend, that if the army under Sir William Howe had operated on the North River, with a view to effect a junction, that ſuch a junction would have taken place ?

A. I had an opinion while in America, that if the expedition which came up the Hudſon's River under General Vaughan, could have have been there about the time of our action of the 19th of September, that Mr. Gates would have found it difficult to have kept his army together, if he had not croſſed over the Hudſon's River towards New England. But this is mere matter of private opinion.

152.   Q. If you are of opinion, that the troops under General Vaughan would have had ſo powerful an effect, even ſo late as September, what effect do you think Sir William Howe's army, aſſiſted by all the fleet and craft, would have had as early as the beginning of July, immediately after the impreſſion which took place among the enemy after the defeat at Ticonderoga ?

A. I did not know what force there was under the command of General Vaughan, nor do I even now know ; but I ſhould think moſt certainly, that a great army upon the Hudſon's River near Albany, would have contributed very much to our making our way to Albany.

153.   Q. Have you ever conſidered what were the cauſes of the failure of the expedition under General Burgoyne, and to what do you impute it ?

A. I looked upon our force not to be equal to the forcing our way to Albany without ſome co-operation.

154.   Q. Where then did you expect that co-operation ?

A. I had no where to expect it from, but up the Hudſon's River from New York ; and the ſucceſs of Colonel St. Leger's expedition would have been of uſe certainly.

155.   Q. If General Waſhington's army had not been diverted, would it not have impeded, or ſtopped the progreſs of any army up the Hudſon's River.

A. I don't know the ſtrength of General Waſhington's army, nor the nature of the country between Albany and New York ; and therefore I cannot form any judgment of what would have happened.

156.   Q. Are you not of opinion that there are very ſtrong paſſes or poſts on that river ?

A. I found them very ſtrong between Ticonderoga and Albany, and from reports of military men of high reputation in the ſervice, I have underſtood there were many very ſttong poſts between New York and Albany.

157.   Q. From whence is the account of the ſtrength of Mr. Gates's army taken ?

A. From

A. From a return voluntarily given by General Gates to me for my own fatis-faction when at Albany, and that return was figned by General Gartes.

Q. Have you that return ?   158.

A. I gave it to General Burgoyne ; I faw it to-day ; he has it.

Q. Was it by confent of General Gates that the foldiers after the convention re- 159.
tained their cartouch-boxes ?

A. They retained their belts, and I really don't recollect whether their car-touch boxes were in general retained or not : but talking with Mr. Gates when the king's troops marched by with the accoutrements on, Mr Gates afked me (we had been old acquaintance formerly) whether it was not cuftomary on field days for arms and accoutrements to go together ? I told him, there was nothing faid in the convention that I had agreed to with him relating to the accou-trements, and that he could have no right to any thing but what was ftipulated in that treaty. He replied, " You are perfectly right;" and turned to fome of the officers in their fervice by, and faid, " If we meant to have had them, we ought " to have inferted them in the convention."   [*Withdrew.*

R E M A R K.

Review of the Evidence; its several Parts compared with the prefatory Speech and Narrative; and additional Remarks and Explanations.

T H E noble Lord who is at issue with me upon this occasion has, in a great measure, deprived me of the benefit of a reply, properly so called, because he has produced no defence. His Lordship certainly has been accused by me in many instances of a very serious nature. If he is really willing that his political, and my military conduct should be tried by facts alone, I certainly have not shewn less inclination than his Lordship for that test; but, taxed as I avow he has been by me, with proceedings derogatory to the obligations which ought to subsist between man and man, I really expected, as I believe did the House of Commons and the public, to have heard from him some justification in those respects. Instead of that, the noble Lord, in opening the subjects to which he proposed to call evidence, touched so slightly upon the branch of the enquiry in which we are parties, that a stranger would hardly have thought there subsisted a dispute between us. His Lordship contradicted nothing that I have alledged respecting his conduct or my own; he stated no circumstance of blame against me, except he meant as such the enterprize of Bennington, which he qualified with the epithet "fatal," and pronounced to be the cause of all the subsequent misfortunes. He passed entirely over the transactions at Saratoga. Of forty officers or more, belonging to the Convention troops, then in England, one only was proposed to be called on his Lordship's part, *viz.* Lieutenant Colonel Sutherland, of the 47th regiment, upon parole from the Congress, and acting with a corps of the Fencible Men in North Britain; but, upon further reflection, his Lordship thought proper to dispense with the attendance of this officer; and the only witness under order of the House was Mr. Skene. No man was better qualified to give an account of the proceedings at Bennington; and I heartily lament that the public is deprived of his testimony.

But although I am thus left in possession of the evidence, uncontroverted by the noble Lord, I avail myself of my right of closing the cause, for the following purposes: first, to collect from the minutes (which, in an enquiry of this nature, are unavoidably prolix and disarranged) the scattered parts, and apply them to facts, under distinct and separate heads. Next, to examine whether the facts (which, from the silence of the noble Lord, I am to assume as admitted by him) are in any respect invalidated by the cross examination of the witnesses by other gentlemen. And

lastly,

The conduct of Lord G. Germain, during the enquiry.

Claim of G. Burgoyne to close the cause.

Mode of proceeding.

laftly, to explain fuch circumftances, and anfwer fuch new and collateral objections, as have been pointed at in the fame crofs examination, and were omitted, or only flightly noticed in my opening, becaufe they did not exift, or were not deemed poffible objects of blame or cavil. In purfuing thefe purpofes, I fhall confider the proofs precifely in the order of the facts to which they are produced.

Infinuation of having acted unfairly by Sir Guy Carleton, overthrown by his own evidence.

Though the firft circumftance I took notice of in my opening, viz. my conduct refpecting Sir Guy Carleton, was rather an infinuation than an allegation againft me, I thought it right that it fhould be the firft overthrown by evidence; for while it remained in any degree of force, it gave a general tinge, as it was meant to do, to my whole caufe. I could not but expect even the virtuous prejudices of the human heart to be againft me, whilft it was poffible to be conceived that in abfence of the commander in chief, to whom I had acted fecond; whofe attention I had conftantly experienced; and with whofe confidence I was then honoured; I had practifed unmanly and adulatory intrigue to fuperfede him in a favourite object of command.— There are few worfe modes of betraying a fuperior officer to be found upon the records of difhonour; and whoever reflects upon the degree of odium with which the moft palliated acts of that fpecies have been received by mankind, will not wonder at or condemn my impatience, in applying my firft queftions to Sir Guy Carleton to that particular object. Clear as my juftification ftood by the letter formerly referred to,

See Sir Guy Carleton's evidence, qu. 1, 2, 3.

(No. II.) I fhall be forgiven for obtaining, though with fome redundancy, a full and fatisfactory confirmation of my innocence, from the verbal teftimony of the party whom I was fuppofed to have injured.

It may be proper here to obferve, that the abovementioned afperfion, to which I have fo often adverted, and at which I have ftrove in vain for due terms to exprefs my indignation, was not the only one caft upon me refpecting Sir Guy Carleton. When impartial and candid men revolted at the infinuation of my treachery, my prefumption and infolence (a leffer but ftill a calumnious charge) was pointed out in that part of the

Afperfion from the paper, No. III.

paper (No. III.) that treats of the force to be left in Canada, and the difpofition of it. I am pleafed with the queftions in the crofs examination of Sir Guy Carleton, marking the prefcribed diftribution of the troops, &c. (38, 39, 40, 41, 42, 43.) becaufe that enquiry affords me an opportunity of juftifying myfelf in a point which I have not taken notice of before. The pofts, and the troops which I imagined would be ne-

refuted.

ceffary to occupy them, were fpecified merely to fhew that the number of 3000 was indifpenfibly requifite for the defence of the province. The whole of that detail concurred with General Carleton's requifitions for reinforcement, and with my reafoning upon thofe requifitions; and when I affert, as I now do, that I never prefumed to fuggeft the neceffity or propriety of forming a detail of pofts, (thus given for informa-

tion)

information) into precife orders for the general upon the fpot, I am fure the fecretary of ftate will no more contradict that affertion than he has done any other I have made.

When in the fame paper I confidentially communicated my reafons for preferring certain corps to others, I was actuated by the fame principle of offering every opinion that could conduce to make the intended fervice effectual. I thought it a juft claim in an arduous undertaking, to have my own choice of the troops; and I am perfuaded Sir Guy Carleton never took ill of me, either that claim, or a fubfequent one in the fame paper, of being held free from any imputation of delay, till I fhould be clear of the province of Quebec. With an unfeigned confidence in Sir Guy Carleton, I thought it a precaution fully juftifiable, to fecure myfelf againft others, in the numerous and complicated departments under him, who might be found lefs equitable than he is.

No. III.

Apology for fpecifying corps.

I know I have before complained of the production of thefe fecret communications; but after fo many precedents as the laft Seffion furnifhed, of withholding parts of correfpondences from Parliament, upon the plea that they might affect individuals, the noble Lord's filence upon thofe complaints, gives me a right ftill to comment upon the finifter purpofes that are to be afcribed to the production of that paper at length, rather than by extract. Thofe purpofes were various; but it muft be confeffed one, and only one, good effect may refult from a review of them, viz. It may ferve as a falutary caution to any officer, who fhall for the future be admitted into confultation with the fame minifter, how he commits himfelf by an opinion of men and things.

The next point that I entered upon previoufly to my narrative, was the tenor of my orders, and I believe it was generally expected that the noble Lord would have taken fome notice of the fact I alledged, *that every difcretionary latitude which I had propofed was erafed, while the plan was in his hand.* As his Lordfhip had fo much commented upon the nature of peremptory orders, as a *general* queftion, in my abfence, it would have been fair in him to have reafoned upon them after that important and decifive circumftance was laid open.

Remarkable circumftance refpecting the conftruction to be put upon my orders.

The general idea *of forcing a way to Albany*, which the army at its outfet conceived, by reafoning upon the apparent principles of the campaign, without participation of the letter of the orders is clear, from the general tenor of the evidence. I wifhed, it is true, to have heard more copioufly the fentiments of Sir Guy Carleton, becaufe he had full participation of the orders. From the temper and judgment that always direct his conduct, he declined giving an opinion at the bar upon what might become a queftion in the Houfe. But I have fince (upon requeft) received his permiffion to publifh a letter from him to me, dated foon after the Convention of Sara-

The general opinion of the army upon forcing a way to Albany.

 toga,

toga, which is in the Appendix No. X. and with this reference I close my review of the prefatory matter which I laid before the Committee.

Review of the first Period.

Most of the circumstances stated in my Narrative respecting the first period of the
campaign, were, from their nature, to be established by written testimony; and the
papers, No. VII. and VIII. in the Appendix, were added to those before produced for that purpose; but the returns of the troops, No. XI. are moreover au-
Strength of thenticated by the proper official authority, the adjutant general, and the detail of
the army. the artillery, by the Major of brigade in that department.

From the evidence of the latter, is also confirmed all that I advanced respecting the
Proportion opinion and recommendation of Major General Philips, for the proportion of artille-
of artillery. ry employed; for the moderate quantity of it, comparatively with the principles and
Evidence of practice of other services, and for the great expected use of artillery in the country
Capt. Blom-
field, from where we were to act.
quest. 4. to 9.

Had these opinions been merely speculative, the intelligence of the persons from
whom they came would have given them sufficient authority. But fortunately they
The uses of are verified by facts; for it appears from a multitude of evidence, that the enemy
it. Captain made the true use of local advantages: they fortified every pass or proper post: the
Blomfield
from question nature of the country, and the necessity of keeping the banks of rivers, made it
10 to 17. impossible to turn those posts: had I wanted therefore artillery, I could not have
Evidence of
Lord Balcar- proceeded any given ten miles, but at a heavy expence of my best troops. When it
ras, from was found that I was provided with that forcible arm, the enemy invariably quit-
question 14.
to 19. ted their entrenchments, either to retreat, or fight upon ground where they supposed
Lord Balcar- artillery could be least effectually employed. I am to thank the honourable member,
ras's cross
examination, whatever his intentions might have been, who by his cross examination placed the
quest. 93, 94. expediency of carrying the train I did, in so clear a view.

The only remaining fact of the first period to which verbal evidence is applicable, viz. The impossibility of following the enemy further than they were follow-
Lord Balcar- ed in their precipitate retreat from Ticonderoga, is established by Lord Balcarras, and
ras, quest. 8. by Lord Harrington.
Lord Har-
rington,
question 4.

Review of the second Period.

In entering upon the evidence which respects the first transaction of the se-
March from cond period, viz. the march from Skenesborough to Fort Edward, I cannot help
Skenesbo-
rough to Fort   4   observing
Edward.

obferving how much of the blame imputed to me has been occafioned by mifreprefentation from perfons whofe bufinefs it was to decry my actions ; and by uncommon miftakes in the geography of the country by thofe to whom my actions were mifreprefented. By the crofs examination of Lord Balcarras it muft be fuppofed, that the perfons who fufpected I erred in not taking the route by *South Bay* after the fuccefs at Ticonderoga, did not know where *South Bay* was. They feem equally ignorant of the fituation of *Pitch-pine Plains*, by the queftion immediately following the former one ; and it muft have been a furprife to the enquirers to find that the route which they were inclined to approve, was precifely that which the main body of the army took under me in perfon, and with fuch effect, as to come up with the rear of the enemy and drive them from their fortified poft at Skenefborough, with the lofs on their part of five armed veffels and all the reft of their water-craft.

But it may be faid, this part of the crofs-examination, though incomprehenfible in point of geography, ftill applied to the queftion taken notice of in my narrative, viz. " Whether it would not have been more expedient to return to Ticonderago, and " take the route by Lake George, than to proceed, as I did, by the Pitch Pine Plains " to Fort Edward ?"

I fhall not recapitulate the various motives I have before ftated in fupport of that preference, having publickly in my favour the opinion of an officer fo enlightened in military fcience, and fo well acquainted with the country as Sir Guy Carleton ;* and never having heard a difference of opinion in any other officer of a like defcription, to reft much more upon a fubject fo fupported by reafoning and by fuccefs, might be conftrued an attempt to divert the attention of my examiners from points lefs defenfible. I therefore fhall only add two fhort remarks ; the one, that the fact of gaining confiderable time by allotting the whole fervice of the water-craft to the tranfport of provifion and ftores over Lake George, inftead of employing great part of it for the tranfport of the troops is inconteftably proved by the evidence of Captain Money and Lieutenant Colonel Kingfton : the other, that to have reached Fort Edward with the troops fooner than the 29th of July (the day that the firft embarkation of provifions arrived at Fort George) would not only have been ufelefs, but alfo highly impolitic ; becaufe the fubfiftence of the troops at Fort Edward, before the arrival of that embarkation, muft have been brought by land carriage through much difficult road all the way from Fort Anne, when, on the contrary, by remaining in the neighbourhood of Skenefborough till the paffage of Lake George was effected, exclufively of the confiderations of covering the removal of the hofpital of Huberton, and alarming the Connecticut by the pofition of General Reidefel's corps, the army was commodioufly fupplied by water-carriage.

*See alfo the map of country.

The

Side notes (right margin):

Miftakes in geography.

Lord Balcarras, queft. 90.

Queftion 91.

Sir Guy Carleton, queft. 9, 10.

Confiderable time gained by the army taking the route to Fort Edward by land.

Captain Money, queft. 4 to queft. 11. Lieut. Col. Kingfton, queft. 23.

The next circumſtance for examination, according to the order of the Narrative, is the tranſport of the magazines of proviſions, &c. from Fort George ; and it is highly incumbent upon me to ſhew the difficulties of that operation, becauſe, if they were avoidable, it muſt be acknowledged one of the principal grounds upon which I vindicate the plan of the expedition to Bennington will fail me.

But I am perſuaded, every candid examiner will firſt indulge me in a ſhort pauſe.

The charges brought againſt the Lt. General's conduct at this part of the campaign.

It will be recollected, that this is the only part of the campaign upon which the noble Lord has laid his finger, as judging it productive of the ſubſequent events. The croſs-examination had already been preſſed upon the ſame ideas. Such want of knowledge of the nature of tranſport in that country has been betrayed ; ſo much prepoſſeſſion of unneceſſary delays has appeared ; ſuch emphaſis of queſtion has attended every circumſtance of my conduct at this period, that I ſhall ſtand acquitted of prolixity, if I preface the application of the ſubſequent evidence by a more comprehen-

Survey of his difficulties and anxieties

five and complete ſurvey of the difficulties and anxieties of my ſituation than I thought was neceſſary before.

Feeding the army.

The combination of arrangement for feeding the army might, in fact, be ſtated to have extended even to Ireland ; for ſome part of the ſupply depended upon the victualling fleet which was prepared in that country, according to my requiſition before I left London, and had not reached Quebec when the army took the field. The tediouſneſs of the navigation from Quebec to the mouth of the Sorel need not be again deſcribed. The next embarraſſment was to manage the conveyance for that part of the ſupply which came from Montreal, and which was much the greateſt, without interfering with the tranſport which with equal neceſſity was to be expedited up the Saint Lawrence to Lake Ontario, for the ſervice of Colonel St. Leger's expedition, and the immenſe ſtores (then neceſſarily upon the move alſo) for the winter maintenance of the upper country. To theſe might be added a liſt of chances and inconveniences, incident to the carrying places between Chamblée and Saint John's ; the uncertaintainty afterwards of the paſſage over Lake Champlain, and Lake George; the laborious and ſlow operations of drawing the boats over the iſthmus which divides the two Lakes. Theſe together make a ſyſtem of embarraſſments and diſappointments hardly to be conceived by thoſe who have not experienced them.

But although the whole of this arrangement (the furniſhing the upper country excepted) was made under my direction, I have been content to date my difficulties from the lodgement of the ſupplies at Fort George ; and I have touched the other parts only to ſhew more perſpicuouſly the unfairneſs of judging of an American campaign upon European ideas. How zealouſly ſoever a general, in ſuch an undertaking as mine, may be ſerved by the chiefs of departments (and much praiſe is due

from

from me upon that fcore) for one hour he can find to contemplate *how he fhall fight his army, he muft allot twenty to contrive how to feed it.*

The behaviour of the Indians is a circumftance too material to be paffed over in a review of the anxieties in this part of the campaign. I had difcerned the caprice, the fuperftition, the felf-intereftednefs of the Indian character from my firft intercourfe, even with thofe nations which are fuppofed to have made the greateft progrefs towards civilization: I mean with thofe called the domiciliated nations near Montreal. I had been taught to look upon the remote tribes who joined me at Skenefboroug, as more warlike ; but a very little time proved that, with equal depravity in general principle, their only pre-eminence confifted in ferocity. The hopes I had placed in their wild honour, and in the controul of their conductors, which, as I ftated before, at firft had been promifing, were foon at an end ; and their ill-humour and mutinous difpofition were manifeft foon after my arrival at Fort Edward. The apparent caufes of their change of temper were the refentment I had fhewn upon the murder of Mifs Macrea, and the reftraints I had laid on their difpofition to commit other enormities ; but I never doubted that their evil paffions were fomented, and their defection completed by the cabals of the Canadian interpreters. Rapacity, felf-intereft, and prefumption are the characteriftics of thefe men, with fome few exceptions. The acquifition of the Indian language has ufually been a certain fortune to a man with an artful head and a convenient confcience.

To check the old practices of peculation in thefe men, Sir Guy Carleton, with great judgment, had given the fuperintendency of the Indian department to Major Campbell and Captain Frazer, gentlemen of the higheft integrity. The Britifh officers employed folely in the military conduct of that department, were alfo felected with equal propriety. The interpreters had from the firft regarded with a jealous eye a fyftem which took out of their hands the diftribution of Indian neceffaries and prefents ; but when they found the plunder of the country, as well as that of the government, was controuled, the profligate policy of many was employed to promote diffention, revolt, and defertion.

I take this occafion to acquit Monfieur St. Luc of any fufpicion of his being concerned in thefe factions ; but I believe he difcerned them. He certainly knew that the Indians pined after a renewal of their accuftomed horrors ; and that they were become as impatient of his controul as of all other, though the pride and intereft of authority, and the affection he bore to his old affociates, induced him to cover the real caufes under various frivolous pretences of difcontent, with which I was daily tormented, but to which I conftantly attended : and though I differed totally with Saint Luc in opinion upon the efficacy of thefe allies, I invariably took his advice in the

management

Behaviour of the Indians.

Lord Harrington from queft.6 to 23.

St. Luc.

management of them, even to an indulgence of their moſt capricious fancies, when they did not involve the diſhonour of the King's ſervice and the diſgrace of huma‑ nity. The council of the 4th of Auguſt was held at his preſſing inſtance; and in that council, to my great aſtoniſhment (for he had given me no intimation of the de‑ ſign) the tribes with which he was moſt particularly connected, and for whom he in‑ terpreted, declared their intention of returning home, and demanded my concurrence and aſſiſtance. The embarraſſment of this event was extreme. By acquieſcing, I voluntary relinquiſhed part of my force that had been obtained with immenſe charge to government, that had created high expectation at home and abroad, and that in‑ deed my own army was by no means in condition to diſpenſe with; becauſe, depend‑ ing upon the ſuppoſed aſſiſtance of this much over‑valued race for ſcouts and out‑ poſts, and all the leſſer, but neceſſary ſervices, for giving due repoſe to the camp, the Britiſh light‑infantry had been trained to higher purpoſes: they were deſtined to lead in the general and deciſive combats I expected in the woods, and could not be ſpared, or riſked, or harraſſed, without palpable conſequences of the moſt diſagree‑ able kind.

On the contrary, I was convinced a cordial reconciliation with the Indians was only to be effected by a renunciation of all my former prohibitions and an indulgence in blood and rapine: I had not a friend in the department in whom I could confide except Major Campbell, Captain Frazer, and the other Britiſh officers: their ignorance of the languages, and the very probity of their characters, rendered them of no weight in Indian councils. An anſwer, neverthelefs, was to be made upon the moment; and the part I took was to give a firm refuſal to their propoſition, and to adhere to the controuls I had before eſtabliſhed; but, with a temperate repreſentation of the ties of faith, of generoſity, and honour, to join every other argument conſiſtent with thoſe principles which I could deviſe, to perſuade and encourage them to continue their ſervices.

This ſpeech appeared to have the deſired effect. The tribes neareſt home affected to ſeparate from the others, and only preſſed for permiſſion to return in parties to gather in their harveſt, propoſing to relieve each other; which was granted. Some of the remote tribes alſo ſeemed to retract their propoſitions, and profeſſed a zeal for the ſervice; but the deſertion took place the next day by ſcores, loaded with ſuch plunder as they had collected; and it continued from day to day, till ſcarce a man that had joined at Skeneſborough remained. This whole tranſaction, I aver, was before the plan of Bennington was formed. It appears ſo from the evidence produced upon the croſs examination by the gentlemen to whom I am obliged upon ſo many occaſions, for elucidating different ſubjects; and the preciſe date could have been

further

Lord Har‑ rington's qu. laſt re‑ ferred to.

Lord Har‑ rington's qu. laſt referred to. & ib. qu. 87.

further fupported by a memorandum of Sir Francis Clerke; but I thought that reference fuperfluous in a matter fo notorious.

That Monfieur St. Luc, anxious for the credit of his favourite troops, and invited
by the propenfity he found in the minifter to liften to any whifpered intelligence, in
contradiction to that he received from the General himfelf; that, under thefe tempta-
tions, that wily partizan fhould mifplace dates, and confound caufes, neither furprifes
nor offends me. With this expofition of fact, I leave him in full poffeffion of his
petulancy refpecting my military talents; and am concerned at no effect of his comments or communications, in the minifter's clofet or in the news-papers,* except as
they may have tended to fupport the general fyftem of deception which has fo long
and fo fatally influenced his Majefty's advifers. The Indian principle of war is at
once odious and unavailing; and if encouraged, I will venture to pronounce, its confequences will be feverely repented by the prefent age, and univerfally abhorred by
pofterity.

But to proceed to the furvey of other difficulties of the time. Great attention was
due to the management of the German troops.

German troops.

The mode of war in which they were engaged was entirely new to them; tempta-
tions to defert were in themfelves great, and had been enhanced and circulated among
them by emiffaries of the enemy with much art and induftry. Jealoufy of predilection
in the allotment of pofts and feparate commands ever fubfifts among troops of different
ftates; and a folid preference of judgment in the commander in chief often appears a
narrow national partiality.

I confefs I was much affifted in maintaining cordiality in an army thus compofed,
by the frank, fpirited, and honourable character I had to deal with in Major General
Reidefel;—a character which was very early impreffed upon my mind, and which
no trials of intricacy, danger, and diftrefs, has fince effaced; but addrefs was ftill
requifite to fecond his zeal, and to diffufe it through the German ranks; and I
ftudied to throw them into fituations that might give them confidence in themfelves, credit with their prince, and alacrity in the purfuit of an enterprife, which,
when its difficulties were confidered, in fact required enthufiafm.

Character of M.G. Reide-fel.

Other parts of the alliance, though not liable to fufpicion of treachery, like the
Indians, nor of confequence to be fo much attended to as the Germans, neverthelefs had their perplexities. The Canadians, were officered by gentlemen of great

The Cana-dian troops.

* One of thofe comments Lord George Germain thought proper to ftate, in a fpeech in the Houfe
of Commons. His Lordfhip gave me a character in the words ufed by Mr. St. Luc, in a converfation
between them.—" Il eft brave, mais lourd comme un Allemand."
The letter alluded to was addreffed to me from Canada, after Mr. St. Luc's voyage from England.
I do not know to whom the duplicate was addreffed, but he certainly was a perfon of diligence; for it
appeared in the news-papers the fame day I received the original.

condition in their country, but were not to be depended upon. Inftead of the enterprifing and daring fpirit which diftinguifhed the character of that people under the
French government, was fubftituted a longing after home, the effect of difufe of
arms and long habits of domeftic enjoyments; and this difeafe *(mal de payz)* is
carried in them to a greater proverbial extreme than in any other people to whom
the term is more commonly applied.

It was neither eafy to keep thefe people together, nor to fupport the ideas of refpect which the enemy entertained of them from the remembrance of the former war.
The only manner of effecting the latter purpofe was to fhew them occafionally at a
diftance, but rarely to commit them upon parties where they were likely to fall in
with the beft claffes of the Rangers oppofed to us: perhaps there are few better in
the world than the corps of Virginia Riflemen, which acted under Colonel Morgan.

Provincial
corps.
The Provincial Corps, of which I had two in embryo, and feveral detached parties, were yet a heavier tax upon time and patience. They were compofed of profeffed Loyalifts, many of whom had taken refuge in Canada the preceding winter,
and others had joined as we advanced. The various interefts which influenced
their actions rendered all arrangement of them impracticable. One man's views went
to the profit which he was to enjoy when his corps fhould be complete; another's,
to the protection of the diftrict in which he refided; a third was wholly intent upon
revenge againft his perfonal enemies; and all of them were repugnant even to an idea
of fubordination. Hence the fettlement who fhould act as a private man, and who
as an officer, or in whofe corps either fhould be, was feldom fatisfactorily made
among themfelves; and as furely as it failed, fucceeded a reference to the Commander in Chief, which could not be put by, or delegated to another hand, without diffatisfaction, encreafe of confufion, and generally a lofs of fuch fervices as they
were really fit for, *viz.* fearching for cattle, afcertaining the practicability of routes,
clearing roads, and guiding detachments or columns upon the march.*

Other critical
embarraff-
ments.
Such were the embarraffments of my mind, added to the many neceffary avoca-
tions of command purely military. It will likewife be remembered that Lieutenant
Colonel St. Leger was, at this time, before Fort Stanwix: every hour was pregnant
with critical events. The candid and unprejudiced, reflecting upon fuch a fituation, will check the readinefs of their cenfure: far be it from me to contend that I
did not commit many errors: I only hope to have proved, that they are not thofe

---

* I would not be underftood to infer, that none of the Provincials with me were fincere in their
loyalty; perhaps many were fo. A few were of diftinguifhed bravery, among which it would be unjuft
not to particularize Mr. Fiftar, who fell at Bennington, and Capt. Sherwood, who was forward in
every fervice of danger to the end of the campaign. I only maintain that the interefts and the paffions
of the revolted Americans concenter in the caufe of the Congrefs; and thofe of the Loyalifts break
and fubdivide into various purfuits, with which the caufe of the King has little or nothing to do.

which

which have yet been fpecifically pointed at, and whatever blame may be imputable to me in other inftances, my late examiners are not juftly intitled to triumph on any of their difcoveries.

And now for the expedition to Bennington as it ftands upon evidence. Expedition to Benning-ton.

The queftions upon the crofs examination are fo explanatory of the hints which fell from the noble Lord afterwards, that one would almoft imagine the hints were originally defigned to precede. It will be regular for me, therefore, to confider them in that manner, and, from the whole I am to collect, that the faults meant to be eftablifhed are, that I employed Germans to found the difpofition of a country in which no Germans refided : that the mounting dragoons was unneceffary : that the range given to the expedition was too great : that it was not originally defigned for Bennington : that the force was inadequate. Faults fup-pofed.

In regard to the firft of thefe charges, relative to the employment of Germans, it would be wafte of time to add to the full anfwer given by Lord Harrington. Colonel Kingfton has anfwered the queftion refpecting the mounting the dragoons ; and moreover it will be remembered, that the collecting horfes was by no means confined to that fervice. They were requifite for carrying the baggage of the army, as expreffed in the inftructions to Colonel Baume, to the amount of 1500. This circumftance may have ftruck fome gentlemen, as confirming the idea that the baggage attending the army was of enormous bulk. I requeft a fufpence of judgment upon this article, till I come to the proper place of explanation ; and I revert to the part of the charge which feems of moft importance, viz. the extent of the march, as defcribed in the Inftructions, compared with the ftrength of the detachment, &c. Fault of em-ploying Ger-mans, Lord Harrington, queft. 90 91. Lieut. Col. Kingfton, q. 134 to 137.

It can hardly efcape obfervation, what ftrength to my defence upon this point may be derived from advocates who were not expected to appear in my behalf. For I take fupport from the noble Lord himfelf, and all who have believed in his late affertions, or adhered to his favourite doctrines, by pleading that I undertook the expedition to Bennington upon report, ftrengthened by the fuggeftion of *perfons of long experience and refidence in America ; who had been prefent on the fpot when the rebellion broke out ;* and whofe information had been much refpected by the adminiftration in England ; *that the friends to the Britifh caufe were as five to one,* and that they *wanted only the appearance of a protecting force to fhew themfelves.* Some criticifers upon the adequacy of the force I employed, may defert the caufe of the noble Lord ; but will *He* maintain, that a recruit of force from the enemy's country was a wild expectation, when the recruiters, provincial colonels, governors, land proprietors, and popular leaders of the party who glory in the defignation of Tory, were upon the fpot, and perfonally interefted in the levies ? *He* muft furely ftand forth my advocate in this point, or entirely forget the reafoning he held to Sir William See the In-ftructions and all other papers re-fpecting Ben-nington. No. IV.

The ground of the under-taking to Bennington fupported by the doctrine of Lord G. Germain.

liam Howe, when without the advantages of such recruiters; against the belief of the General himself; unprepared to repair the disappointment, if disappointment ensued, in a measure of so much more magnitude, and so much less real encouragement, *He* referred to that expedient of recruiting from the enemy, what he had not strength to supply from the national troops.*

This I must insist is an unanswerable defence, with respect to the noble Lord, and those who think with him; for it is strict and positive coincidence with their opinions, past and present—and if I said it will be so with those to come, my prophecy would be authorized by the conviction and triumph which Mr. Galway's evidence, respecting the loyalty of the Americans, seemed to produce in the parties to whom I allude.

But in due respect to other judges, it is incumbent upon me to state a more serious defence.

As Lieutenant Colonel Kingston cannot prove juridically that the rough draft of the design which ended the affair of Bennington was the same which was delivered by General Reidesel, and I am unwilling upon memory to incur a possibility of mistake, even in an immaterial circumstance that respects an absent friend, I am content it should be considered as an uncertaintainty, and I drop all use that could be drawn from the original composition. It will fully answer my purpose to adhere to the bare assertion which I am sure will never be contradicted, that Major General Reidesel originally conceived an expedition for the purpose of mounting his dragoons, and supplying the troops in general with baggage-horses; that I thought his idea might be extended to much greater use, and that the plan was considered, amended, and enlarged, in concert with him. Therefore upon the abstract ground and reason of the measure, I might urge, that it was supported by naked military principle, according to the sentiments of a general of great natural talents, and long service under the first masters of the age. It is proved, that the same sentiments were ratified by the full approbation of Major General Phillips, an officer of similar description, to whom the plan was communicated; and if a single part of the same plan, mentioned to be at first disapproved by Brigadier General Frazer, continued to be so after explanation, that disapprobation did not appear. Indeed the utmost that can be drawn from the evidence of Lieutenant Colonel

Lieut. Col. Kingston's quest.

* In a letter from Lord George Germain to Sir William Howe, dated May 28, 1777, after acknowledging that the force for the campaign would be short of the General's requisitions, is the following paragraph.
  " If we may credit the accounts which arrive from all quarters, relative to the good inclinations of " the inhabitants, there is every reason to expect that your success in Pensylvania will enable you to, " raise from among them such a force as may be sufficient for the interior defence of the province, " and leave the army at liberty to proceed to offensive operations."
  The whole of the letter, from which the above is an extract, is curious, and may be seen in the Parliamentary Register, No. 68.

King-

Kingſton, or any other witneſs, amounts to no more than an implied wiſh in the Brigadier to have conducted the expedition at the head of his diſtinct corps. It was the fact. Devoted to glory and prodigal of life ; earneſt for the general ſucceſs of the campaign, and particularly anxious for every plan adopted by the man he loved, he grudged a danger or care in other hands than his own. It was not envy or diſparagement of the German troops, but zeal and impatience for employment, that influenced his predilection for the Britiſh. I honoured the principle, while I reſtrained it ; and I reſerved his ardour and judgment for a ſecond movement, which required thoſe qualities much more than the expedition to Bennington did, according to any intelligence or appearance of things at the time. It will be obſerved from the evidence, that the whole of Brigadier Fraſer's corps was thrown over the river, and actually poſted at the opening of the plain near Saratoga, when Col. Baume marched ; and the deſign was, upon the firſt news of Baume's ſucceſs, to have puſhed that corps to take poſſeſſion of the heights near Stillwater, and to have intrenched there, till the army and the proviſion could have joined, by which means the whole country on the weſt ſide the river, to the banks of the Mohawk, would have been our own.

But moreover it is to be obſerved, that Major General Reideſel was far from being ignorant, as has been ſuggeſted, of the nature of the country, or the profeſſions of the inhabitants. He was juſt returned from commanding a detached corps at a conſiderable diſtance from the main army, in the very heart of the country from which the enemy's force at Bennington was afterwards ſupplied. He ſpoke the Engliſh language well ; he was aſſiſted by many natives of the beſt information.

It is evident, that the brave but deceived officer who commanded the detachment, was induced to deviate from the cautions preſcribed in the inſtructions. A plan drawn by an engineer upon the ſpot is added to the evidence produced to the committee, to ſhew more clearly where that deviation happened. It appears alſo in proof, that the meaſures taken to relieve Colonel Baume, upon the news of his difficulty, were the moſt ſpeedy that could be uſed, and would have been timely, had not Colonel Brieman's march been more tardy than could have been ſuppoſed poſſible. I take the fact as ſtated in his own account, without impeaching his credit with regard to the obſtacles he deſcribes. But as a farther vindication of the intelligence and principle upon which the original ſtrength of the detachment was framed, and the mere accident which made even error poſſible, I requeſt admiſſion for the proof of a new fact which I did not know it was in my power to bring, till after Captain Money had left the bar of the Houſe of Commons ; and as I was precluded from calling him a ſecond time, by the abrupt cloſe of the proceedings, I had no other way of laying it before the public, than by ſtating the queſtion in writing,

Lord Harrington's q. 28 to 31.

writing, and requiring his authority to publiſh the anſwer, which I obtained, and
they are as follows :

Q. Do you know any circumſtance reſpecting an unexpected reinforcement received by the rebels at Bennington near the time of the action ?

A. " A few days after I was priſoner in the rebel camp, ſome of their officers
" told me, that it was a providential circumſtance, that General Starks was coming
" through Bennington with 1200 militia of the New-Hampſhire Grants, to join
" their main army near Albany, for the guard on the proviſion at Bennington did
" not amount to more than 400 men ; and that on his hearing of a detachment of
" our army being only four or five miles from him, he with the guard, and what
" militia could be collected in the neighbourhood, attacked and defeated the de-
" tachment, as well as the reinforcement that were on their march to join them.
" The rebel officers alſo informed me, and I have ſeen accounts that agree with
" what I then heard, that during the action General Starks was ' luckily.' joined
" by Colonel Warner with a conſiderable body of men. I have frequently heard
" our officers ſay that were, in this action, that had Colonel Baume retreated four
" miles, and recroſſed the river he paſſed the day before, and taken poſt there,
" when he found by information he could not proceed, and had wrote for a rein-
" forcement, he would have met Colonel Breiman coming to his aſſiſtance, and
" would not have riſqued the loſs of his corps, which by his inſtructions were ſo
" ſtrongly recommended, as not even to riſque a conſiderable loſs. This, Sir, is
" as nearly as poſſible the anſwer I ſhould have given had the queſtion been aſked
" me in the Houſe of Commons.—J. Money."

This piece of evidence will ſerve to ſhew that it was not the ſucceſs of the rebels
at Bennington that animated the militia to aſſemble, and march in the cauſe of the
Congreſs ; and he muſt be of ſteady faith indeed in American loyalty who can ſuppoſe
much of it really exiſted in the country of the Hampſhire Grants (howſoever it had
been affected and profeſſed) when he reflects, not only that General Starks and Colonel
Warner were not oppoſed in collecting their men, though my army, then in a tide of
ſucceſs, were near at hand ; but alſo that not a loyaliſt was found earneſt enough to
convey me intelligence.

It will likewiſe appear, from this piece of evidence, when compared with the map
of the country and the diſpoſition of the troops, that had not the accidental paſſage of
the detachments under Starks and Warner been exceedingly critical, it could not
have availed.—Forty-eight hours ſooner, they would have joined General Gates ; and
he would hardly have detached them, or any other part of his force, back to Bennington, even though he had heard of a movement to my left ; becauſe he muſt have
known that the whole of Fraſer's corps lay ready to march rapidly upon him from my
right.

right.—Forty-eight hours later, the blow would have been ftruck; and the ftores, confifting of live cattle, and flower, with abundant carriages to convey it, would have been out of reach.

Another reflection will be apt to arife in fpeculative minds upon this fubject, viz. on what nice chances depends the reputation of an officer who acts under felfifh and ungenerous employers! Such men not only with-hold the fair protection that would arife from an explanation of his motives, but are the firft to join the cry of the uninformed multitude, who always judge by events. Thus every plan receives a colouring in the extreme; and is denominated (often with equal injuftice) a fatal error or a brilliant enterprize.

But it ftill may be faid, the expedition was not originally defigned againft Bennington. I really do not fee to what it could tend againft me, if that fuppofition were in a great degree admitted. That fome part of the force was defigned to act there, will not be difputed by any who read Colonel Baume's inftructions, and confult the map. The blame or merit of the defign altogether, muft reft upon the motives of expediency; and it is of little confequence whether the firft and principal direction was againft Bennington, or Arlington, or any other diftrict, as my intelligence might have varied refpecting the depofits of corn and cattle of the enemy. At the fame time I muft obferve it is begging the queftion, to argue that Bennington was not the real, original object, becaufe Bennington was not mentioned in the draft of inftructions. A man muft indeed be void of military and political addrefs, to put upon paper a critical defign, where furprize was in queftion, and every thing depended upon fecrefy. Though it were true, that I meant only Bennington, and thought of nothing lefs than the progrefs of the expedition, in the extent of the order, I certainly would not now affirm it, becaufe I could not prove it; and becaufe it would feem, that I fearched for remote and obfcure juftification, not relying upon that which was manifeft; but furely there is nothing new or improbable in the idea, that a general fhould difguife his real intentions at the outfet of an expedition, even from the officer whom he appointed to execute them, provided a communication with that officer was certain and not remote.

Crofs-examination of Lord Harrington, q. 89.

This review of the affair of Bennington, tho' long, I truft will not be deemed mifplaced; and from the different parts of it, I think, will clearly be eftablifhed the few following affertions.

1ft. That the defign upon Bennington was juftified by the circumftances of the time.

2d. That there was no reafon to fuppofe the force of the enemy there greater than what the detachment was adequate to defeat.

3d. That when the force was difcovered to be greater, the ill confequences would have been avoided had not Colonel Baume deviated from his inftructions, by commit-

4.   ting

ting his regular force in the woods inftead of fortifying a poft in the open conntry, and exploring the woods only with the Indians, Canadians, and Provincials, fupported by Captain Frafer's corps, who were complete mafters of fuch bufinefs.

4th. That after Colonel Baume had committed that error, it would have been re-trieved had Colonel Brieman's reinforcement accomplifhed their march in the time they ought to have done.

5th. That the ftrength of the enemy was merely accidental.

And, as a final obfervation, I will add, that when a minifter ftates a common acci-dent of war, independent of any general action, unattended with any lofs that could affect the main ftrength of the army, and little more than the mifcarriage of a forag-ing party, to have been fatal to a whole campaign, of which he had directed the pro-grefs and apportioned the force, he makes but an ill compliment to his own judgment:

Difficulty of forming a magazine af-ter the difap-pointment at Bennington. Lieut. Col. Kingfton, q. 24 to 31.

The next clafs of proofs in regular progreffion, applies to the difficulty of bringing forward a magazine of provifion, after the difappointment of obtaining live ftock and flower at Bennington. It has been fhewn, by the evidence of Captain Money, Lieu-tenant Colonel Kingfton, and the authentic memorandums of Sir Francis Clarke, that early in the month of Auguft it was no eafy tafk to fupply the daily confumpfion of the army. Our powers were afterwards, in fome degree, encreafed by the arrival of more contract horfes, acquifitions of more ox-teams from the country, and the great vigilance exerted in the departments of the quarter-mafter-general and infpector, whofe affiftants had been augmented.

A minute inveftigation of this operation I am fenfible will be thought dry, and perhaps unneceffary, by general readers—they will pafs it over—but there are thofe who have laid much ftrefs upon a wafte of time, and who take delight in tracing the fmall parts of a fubject with fcrupulous exactnefs. With fuch it is my duty, as a per-fon on my defence, to enter into detail, and I will lay my ground in the queftion put to Captain Money in his crofs-examination and his anfwer.

Q. Why did the Army remain from the 16th of Auguft to the 13th of September, " before they croffed the Hudfon's-River to engage the Rebels at Stillwater ?"

A. " To bring forward a fufficient quantity of provifions and artillery, to enable the " General to give up his communication."

Capt. Mo-ney, q. 20; and for the general ac-count of the efforts ufed fee the fame evidence from q. 12 to 25.

With all the powers of conveyance poffible to be muftered, Captain Money computes, (and his computation tallies nearly with the table formed by the Commiffary-General) that five days provifion, viz. four for forming the magazine and one for daily confump-tion, was the moft that could be conveyed at once.

To bring this to an average I will affume only two days for accidents of weather, roads, fatigue of cattle, breaking of carriages, and other common difappointments : this is much lefs time than according to the evidence might be allowed, and upon This computation it would take ten days to convey the magazine to Fort Edward only.

The stage from thence to the encampment and intended depofitary muft not be computed by diftance but by impediments. The rapids of the river and the different carrying-places have been defcribed by the witueffes, and it refults that this ftage was much longer in point of time than the former one. It was not poffible to keep the tranfports going at both ftages together for the ten days mentioned, becaufe there were not boats in the river fufficient for more than the daily fupply; nor could they have been conveyed there in that time by any poffible means, for thefe reafons; the boat carriages, which were of a conftruction fimilar to timber carriages ufed in England, were only twelve in number, and each carriage employed fix horfes or four oxen to draw it; and could any other means of draft for boats over land have been contrived, or cattle have been fupplied from the artillery, or any other department, all would have been ufelefs; becaufe the boats themfelves, to a greater amount than thofe above fpecified, were wanting till after the whole of the provifion tranfport between Ticonderoga and Fort George, upon which they were employed, was finifhed, and it had barely kept pace fo as to fupply the land tranfport between Fort George and Fort Edward.

I defire only an allowance of fifteen days for the carriage over the fecond ftage, and it will thus take, in the whole, twenty-five days to form the magazine alone.

I claim no additional allowance of time for conveying one hundred boats, at leaft, through the difficulties of land and water, in the two ftages, but comprife that labour among the reft of the laft fifteen days. It muft be neverthelefs obferved, that even this number was fhort of what was wanting, and, to fave time, all the artificers were employed in building fcouls (fourteen of which were finifhed during the tranfport) to make water craft, in the whole fufficient to carry the magazine forward, after the communication fhould be at an end: The new caulking the boats, though indifpenfibly neceffary to great part of them, after paffing the lakes loaded, and afterwards being fhaken and damaged by land carriage, is another work which I throw into the laft fifteen days of the tranfport, or into the fubfequent four days, which muft at the leaft be allotted for loading the magazine, and arranging the order of its proceeding both in refpect to navigation and defence. This was committed to very expert naval officers, and was matter of no trivial concern, or eafy execution.

The whole bufinefs, according to the above reprefentation and calculation, both which are founded upon evidence, would have taken twenty-nine days: twenty-feven only were employed, viz. from Auguft the 16th to September the 13th. The exertions in fact, outwent the calculation; and I challenge the moft minute fpeculatifts, to try the time and the powers we poffeffed, by every poffible diftribution of carriages and cattle, different from that which was practifed, and I will venture to fay none will be found lefs dilatory.

It appears clearly in proof, that no impediment to this tranfport was occafioned by the interference of the artillery; but it has been implied by fome queftions in the crofs

Q examina-

examinations, that if the artillery did not interfere with the transport, the transport ought to have interfered with the artillery, and that by appropriating their horses to the provision train, much time might have been saved.

It might be a sufficient answer, that the artillery, for the reasons I have before assigned, was not to be dispensed with, and consequently the horses were to be preserved: but I besides have shewn, that they could not have been of use to the transport of the boats; and to satisfy every scruple, and to shew how mistaken they are who suppose an advantage was to be obtained by the employment of artillery horses to convey provisions, I now offer to their reflection the additional fact, that they could have been of no avail, because we had neither carts nor pack-saddles, more than were in use already.

Lieut. Col. Kingston, q. 5 to 8 inclusive, and from 122 to 130.

That the baggage of the army was an impediment to the transport, is another accusation clearly confuted by the united evidence of Lieutenant Colonel Kingston and Captain Money.*

Having thus shewn that the transport of provision and other stores, for about thirty days, was effected in the shortest time possible, it now becomes necessary to examine

the

---

* In justice to the officers who are supposed to have disobeyed orders, in respect to the bulk of it, it may be necessary to take some notice, (and this is the proper place) of the error of making that supposition upon the directions given to Colonel Baume for procuring 1300 horses for that specific use. I believe the lowest allowance of but horses ever made to an army was as follows :

To a field officer	3 per battalion	6
A captain	2 do.	12
A subaltern	1 do.	16
A surgeon and mate	2 do.	2
A chaplain	1 do.	1
A quartermaster	1 do.	1
For carrying the company's tents, two horses to each company	do.	16
	Total per battalion	54

N. B. This calculation was made upon eight companies to a battalion, in which two field officers companies are included.

The horses for the five British battalions of the line, upon calculation, amount to	270
General Fraser's corps, reckoned to be equal to four battalions	216
Five German battalions at 70 horses per battalion, that being the difference in proportion to their strength	350
Breyman's corps	100
Total for the regiments of the regulars	936

STAFF.

Two major generals	12
Four brigadiers	16
British quarter master general, and his assistants	12
German ditto	12
The hospital	30
Total of staff	82

IRREGU-

the queftion, which has been very much canvaffed in print, and by the crofs examination, appears to have made impreffion upon fome gentlemen ; whether this preparation might not have been difpenfed with, and the army have reached Albany by a rapid march, the foldiers carrying upon their backs a fufficiency of provifion to fupport them during the time.

Queftion made, whether the army might not have proceeded to Albany without ftores ? Idea of a rapid march.

It is very natural for men of all defcriptions, to apply the idea of a rapid march to a diftance of fifty miles, for it is not more meafuring in a ftreight line from Fort Edward to Albany, and it will be proper to confider the principle and practibility of fuch march, with refpect to two diftinct periods, the one before, the other after the attempt upon Bennington.

With refpect to the firft, it will be remembered, that in the ftate the roads then were, and with the refources then to be employed, no provifion before-hand was attainable. Therefore, to have brought the plan of a rapid advance within the compafs of a poffibility, the operation muft have begun by marching the whole rapidly backward, in order to load the men with their packs of provifions. How the troops, zealous as they were, would have relifhed a ftep fo uncommon in its nature, and productive of fo much unexpected fatigue, particularly how the Germans would have been fo perfuaded of the neceffity as to have undertaken it with good will, cannot be afcertained.

But thefe doubts apart, it remains to be confidered, how the troops were to pafs two very large rivers, the Hudfon and the Mohawk, without previous provifion for a bridge, or water-craft for conveying large bodies at once. Every conceffion a fanguine projector can defire fhall be made upon this point alfo ; the contrivance of rafts, bound together by twigs and ftrips of bark, as in fact was practifed at this very period for the paffage of Frafer's corps over Hudfon's River, fhall be admitted equally practicable for the whole army ; and in argument be it trufted to chance to pafs the Mohawk in the fame way ; or fhould it fail, let recourfe be had to the ford,' which is known to be practicable, *except after heavy rains*, near Schenectady, about fifteen miles from the mouth of the river.

Thefe conceffions granted, we will fuppofe the army on the bank of the Hudfon's River, where they afterwards paffed it.

The idea of a rapid march will of courfe be exempt from all thought of perfonal incumbrances (provifion exempted) and the foldier will ftand reprefented in the imagination, trim and nimble as he is feen at an exercife in an Englifh encamp-

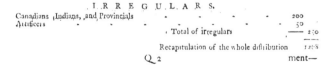

I R R E G U L A R S.

Canadians, Indians, and Provincials	-	-	-	-	200
Artificers	-	-	-	-	50
		Total of irregulars			—— 250

Recapitulation of the whole diftribution   1268

ment—

ment—Indeed it is neceſſary he ſhould be conſidered in that form ; for nothing can be more repugnant to a projeĉt of rapidity, than the ſoldier's load, were he to carry all the articles belonging to him in a campaign.*

But it may be ſaid, and with truth, that troops are uſually relieved from a conſiderable part of this burthen, and many examples of this relief may be brought from the general cuſtom of ſervice, and from many movements of General Howe's army in particular—nay more, it was a frequent practice of the very army in queſtion, to march free from knapſacks and camp equipage. The Wigwam, or hut conſtructed of boughs, may be made a very wholſome ſubſtitute for a tent ; and when victual can be cooked before-hand, even the camp kettle for an expeditious march may be laid aſide. All theſe examples are admitted : but they all imply conveniencies for the ſeveral articles to follow, and to be brought up in due time. In our caſe they muſt have been loſt irrecoverably.

Will it be argued, that ſome medium might have been deviſed ? And although it were impoſſible, conſiſtently with the idea of rapidity, to carry forward more proviſion than for bare ſuſtenance during the march, yet carts might have been found ſufficient to carry the men's knapſacks, and camp kettles, and other indiſpenſible articles ? This ſuppoſition would betray a great ignorance of the country. From Saratoga to Albany there is only one road practicable for wheel carriage. There are many places where by deſtroying the bridges over deep gullies which diſcharge themſelves into the main river, a paſſage would be rendered impoſſible, not only for a wheel carriage, but a horſe. There are others where the road is bounded by the river on one ſide, and by almoſt perpendicular aſcents covered with wood on the other. Here the very ſhort work of felling a few trees would ſtop all paſſage. The expence of time to remove theſe obſtructions, or to make new roads, would have brought famine. All notion, therefore, of conveying any articles more than could be carried upon men's ſhoulders muſt ecaſe. The notion of artillery, even the ſmalleſt pieces, muſt alſo ceaſe of courſe, not even a little ammunition-tumbril could have found its way.—An eaſy ſacrifice to the theoriſts, who have maintained the inutility of artillery : but any officer who has ſeen the ground of this ſuppoſed march, would point out a dozen paſſes, not to ſpeak of the paſſage of the Mohawk, where, ſtrengthened with abattis and ſuch other works as the rebels are expert in making in a very few hours, five hundred militia would ſtop for a time, ten times their number of the beſt troops in the world who had not artillery to aſſiſt them.

---

* They conſiſt of a knapſack, containing his bodily neceſſaries, a blanket, a haverſack with proviſions, a carteen, a hatchet, and a fifth ſhare of the general camp equipage belonging to his tent. Theſe articles (reckoning the proviſion to be for four days) added to his accoutrements, arms, and ſixty rounds of ammunition, make a bulk totally incompatible with combat, and a weight of about ſixty pounds.

Having

Having stated these objections to the principle of a rapid march, let us now, from the knowledge that has been since obtained of circumstances, consider what would have been the certain consequences of the attempt.

Those who are acquainted with the capricious workings of the tempers of men, will not wonder at the difficulty of prevailing upon a common soldier in any exigency to husband his provisions. In a settled camp, the young soldier has very short fare on the fourth day after delivery: but upon a march in bad weather and bad roads, when the weary foot slips back at every step, and a general curse is provoked at the weight that causes the retardment, he must be a patient veteran, and of much experience in scarcity, who is not tempted to throw the whole contents of the haverfack into the mire. He feels the present incumbrance grievous—Want is a day remote.—" Let the General find a supply: it is the King's cause and the General's interest—he will never let the soldier be starved."

This is common reasoning in the ranks. I state it for those who have not seen fatiguing service, and may have a judgment to form upon it. It need not be applied to the present consideration; for had the march taken place at the time it ought to have done, upon the principle of the defenders of that scheme, the time that Frafer's corps first past the river upon the bridge of rafts, waste would only have conspired to accomplish in *three days* a ruin that with the best husbandry would have been inevitable in *six:* for the same fall of rain which it has been shewn in evidence actually carried away the bridge a very few days after it was constructed, necessarily made the ford of the Mohawk for an advance, and every ford of the Hudson's River for a return, impassable. It hardly need be noticed, that a flood must have made any use of rafts, could they have been timely obtained, equally impracticable. The army, therefore, would have become victims to famine, without a blow, or a single effort of the enemy. Saratoga must have been the anticipated scene of surrender, without other conditions than the mercy of sustenance; the whole force of Mr. Gates would have been loose to co-operate with Mr. Washington, with the finest season of the campaign before them; and the General of the northern army, without a shadow of professional defence, and precluded from the plea usually so persuasive, that he fought hard before he failed, must have met the censure of his Sovereign and a justly offended country, with none to support him but the present advocates of a rapid march. Could his dependence have been sure even upon them? Would they not rather have adhered to their opposite and original system (for strange as it is, the same men have supported both) and have asserted, that it was extreme rashness to cross the Hudson's River at all?

If what I have said in objection to the principle and practicability of a rapid march to Albany, previous to the attempt upon Bennington, has weight, very little need be added on the subject afterwards, because every objection will multiply up-

4   on

on the mind of the most cursory observer. I shall only call the attention to a very few essential circumstances. The enemy was in force; a proof of his being so is, that Mr. Gates quitted his position behind the Mohawk, which was his strongest, and advanced to Stillwater. The force found at Bennington upon the march from the Hampshire Grants to the main army, proved the vigour and alacrity of the enemy in that country. The circumstances of the action at Bennington established a yet more melancholy conviction of the fallacy of any dependence upon supposed friends. The noble Lord has said, that "I never despaired of the campaign before the affair of Bennington; that I had no doubt of gaining Albany in as short a time as the army (in due condition of supply) could accomplish the march." I acknowledge the truth of the assertions in their fullest extent; all my letters at the time shew it. I will go further, and in one sense apply with the noble Lord the epithet "fatal" to the affair of Bennington. The knowledge I acquired of the professors of loyalty was "fatal," and put an end to every expectation from enterprize unsustained by dint of force. It would have been excess of frenzy to have trusted for sustenance to the plentiful region of Albany. Had the march thither been practicable in all respects, and even unopposed, (which nobody will think would have been the case) the enemy finding the British army unsupplied, would only have had to compel the Tories to drive the cattle and destroy the corn or the corn mills, and the convention of Albany instead of Saratoga must have followed. Would the Tories have risen? Why did they not rise round Albany and below it, at the time they found Mr. Gates's army increasing by separate and distinct parties from remote distances? They were better qualified by their situation to catch the favourable moment than I was to advise it. Why did they not rise in that populous and as supposed well affected district, the German Flats, at the time St. Leger was before Fort Stanwix? A critical insurrection from any one point of the compass within distance to create diversion, would probably have secured the success of the campaign.

But to revert to the encrease of reasons against a rapid march after the affair of Bennington. It was then also known, that by the false intelligence respecting the strength of Fort Stanwix, the infamous behaviour of the Indians, and the want of the promised co-operation of the loyal inhabitants, Lieut. Col. St. Leger had been obliged to retreat. The first plausible motive in favour of hazardous haste, the facilitating his descent of the Mohawk, was thus at an end. The prospect of finding the enemy dispersed it has before been shewn was over.

The impossibility of preserving a communication was also evident. Was the army to have proceeded to action without hospital stores, as well as without victual? The general who carries troops into fire without precautions to alleviate the certain consequences, takes a sure step to alienate the affections, and destroy the ardour of the

Col. St. Leger's letter. No. V.

the foldier—he exacts more than human fpirit can furnifh. Men need not be habituated to fields of battle to be convinced of this truth. Let the mind reft for a
moment on the objects which will rife within it after the mention of action, and then
reflect, there is not a mattrafs for broken bones, nor a cordial for agony and faint-
nefs. They who talk of thefe rapid marches, fuppofe no oppofition, or no fuffering
in confequence of oppofition. The hundreds of wounded men to be cruelly abandoned (if the reft could be prevailed upon to abandon thofe whofe cafe might the
next day be their own) make no part of the confideration of thefe gentlemen of
precipitate imaginations. But officers who are refponfible to God and their country for the armies they conduct, cannot fo eafily overlook fuch objects ; and muft be
patient at leaft till a few hundred beds, and a proper proportion of medicine and
chirurgical materials, can be brought up for troops that are to fight as well as to
march.

The confideration of rapid movement has run into much length : the ftrefs laid
upon it in the crofs-examination, was the caufe. I beg leave very fhortly to recapitulate the principal points, and fhall then difmifs it to the public judgment, without great apprehenfion of having it renewed even in fpeculation.

Had a proper ftore of live cattle been obtained by the expedition to Bennington,
(and by the bye it will be remembered, that had the loyalifts of the country been
really of the number and defcription reprefented, that acquifition might have been
made without an action) all the carriages might have been appropriated folely
to the conveyance of flour, hofpital accommodations, entrenching tools, and other
abfolute neceffaries ; and a rapid march to Albany might have been hazarded.

After the expedition to Bennington had failed of that great purpofe, had a garrifon for Ticonderoga been attainable from Canada, and the force then at Ticonderoga been brought forward, to eftablifh a poft of communication, and fecure a
paffage of the river by a fortified bridge, and redoubts upon the heights which
every where command the river, on one fhore or the other, a forced march might
ftill have been juftifiable, becaufe a retreat was fecure : but, divefted of both thefe
refources, a rapid movement muft inevitably have led to rapid ruin.

Having gone through all the material points previous to the 13th of September,
and fhewn, I truft, by diftinct evidence, as well as reafoning, the expediency of
the march from Skenefborough to Fort Edward ; the principle of the expedition to
Bennington ; the caufe of its failure ; the efforts ufed to bring forwards the provi- Review of the
fion and neceffary ftores, and the impracticability of proceeding without thofe meafure of
ftores ; the attention of the reader will now be carried to a review of the meafure paffing the Hudfon's
of paffing the Hudfon's River on that day. River.

I entered pretty fully, in my Narrative, into the principles which then actuated
me ; and I fhall not enlarge upon them. I have only to requeft every man who
has

has been led to doubt whether I was required by duty, situation, the voice of the army, and the voice of reason, to advance and fight, to follow the consideration of those principles, with a revisal of the applicable part of the verbal evidence, and I will then venture further to appeal to their judgment, whether, instead of being required, I was not compelled, by the state of things, to act as I did; even independently of the peremptory tenor of my orders, which, confident in the strength of my case, I have purposely omitted, upon this occasion, to reconsider.

Lord Balcar-
ras's quest. 3
and 4, 21 to
28, 30 to 32.
Lord Har-
rington's, 32
to 37.
Capt. Mo-
ney, 56, 61,
and 65 to 68.
Brigadier
Frafer's fen-
timents.

In regard to the point so much agitated in this country, though with no foundation whatever from any thing that happened in America, Brigadier Frafer's sentiments upon this measure of passing the Hudson's River, it would be trifling with the patience of the reader to recapitulate and point the evidence to a matter which I do not believe there is a man so prejudiced as now to dispute, viz. that that officer joined in opinion and impatience with the rest of the army. But though the falsehoods so grossly and so long imposed upon the public, respecting this matter, are no more, it may not be unworthy curiosity to explore their origin and trace their progress.

Progress of
the falfe-
hoods propa-
gated.

It is not difficult to discern that the suspicion of difference of opinion in the army, upon the measure of passing the Hudson's River, arose from the paragraph in my public letter from Albany to the Secretary of State, wherein I say that I had called no council upon that subject, but had acted upon my own judgment of the peremptory tenor of my orders.

That a man, chief in authority, should take entirely upon himself a measure of doubtful consequence, and upon mere principle preclude himself from any future means of shifting or dividing the blame that might ensue, appeared incredible at Whitehall: the greater part of that political school concluded the profession of such candour must be a finesse, and that, in fact, the General had not communicated with his officers, because he knew opinions would have been against him.

When little minds think they have got a clue of littleness it is wonderful with what zeal and dexterity they pursue and improve it. Correspondence and intelligence were not wanting; disappointed jobbers, discarded servants, dissatisfied fugitives of every fort, spies, tale-bearers, and sycophants, whom it is to the honour of a General to have his enemies, and a disgrace to Office to encourage, abounded in town; and the primary idea once given, it was carried forward by very ready assistance, and even logical deduction.——As thus:

The General declares in his dispatch, he called no man into council upon the measure of passing the Hudson's River: *Therefore*, his officers differed in opinion upon the expediency of advancing.

To differ in opinion upon that expediency, they must construe his orders not to be peremptory: *Therefore*, he stands single in the interpretation he put upon his orders.

If

If his officers faw that he was unadvifedly and defparately leading his army to death, they would certainly remonftrate: *Therefore*, they remonftrated.

The remonftrance would naturally be made to him by fuperior officers: *Therefore*, the conclufion follows; Major General Phillips and Brigadier General Frafer actually made a remonftrance againft paffing the Hudfon's River.

General Reidefel, who was next in rank to General Phillips, feems to have been forgotten. He was probably overlooked in the eagernefs to get at General Frafer, on whofe name the important ftrefs was laid, and for two palpable reafons; the one, that his name ftood high in the public eftimation, and greatly as it deferved fo to ftand, perhaps it acquired, upon this intended ufe, more juftice from fome quarters than it would otherwife have received.

The fecond and more prevalent reafon was, that Brigadier General Frafer was dead.

Thus then ftood the affertion when I arrived in England: " *Major General Phillips and Brigadier General Frafer remonftrated againft paffing the Hudfon's River, which movement was the caufe of all the fubfequent misfortunes.*" And having traced this falfehood to its maturity, it now may be equally curious to follow its decline.

After my arrival in England, the friendfhip, and general conformity of fentiment between General Phillips and me became more known. He was alive, and might poffibly foon return. His name was therefore withdrawn from the remonftrance, and referved, in cafe he did not return, to give colour to a fecond falfehood, * then kept back, but fince produced as one of the laft efforts of malignity in the courfe of the late enquiry.

The firft public occafion that offered was feized by me to pledge my honour upon the whole ftory of difagreement of opinion being falfe; and I dared any man to produce a letter or a fentence, from Brigadier Frafer or any other officer, to authorife a fufpicion of its being true. Lieutenant General Frafer, upon the fame occafion in the Houfe of Commons, voluntarily and generoufly entered into my juftification, upon the authority of his correfpondence with his late relation, and the knowledge of his general fentiments.

The falfehood was immediately fo far weakened, that the word *Remonftrance* was changed into *Opinion*. " *Brigadier Frafer's opinion was againft paffing the Hudfon's River*;" and thus it remained, now and then affifted and cherifhed, when it was very languid, by a whifper, " *that there were ftill letters to be produced*," till the late enquiry took place; and the evidence of Lord Balcarras, Lord Harrington,

---

* That General Phillips offered to conduct a part of the army from Saratoga to Ticonderoga. See this falfehood refuted, in the evidence of Lord Balcarras, Col. Kingfton, &c.

Colonel

Colonel Kingſton, &c. gave the death blow to the laſt ſtruggling efforts of that calumny. The raſhneſs of paſſing the Hudſon's River was obliterated; every com. ment upon that *fatal* ſtep was ſuddenly dropt, as if the river had funk under ground; the charge, with the full accompaniment of General Fraſer's diſapprobation, re. monſtrance, &c. &c. was ſhifted; the miniſter was as nimble as his confederates, and exclaimed upon the *fatality* of the expedition to Bennington.

And here I ſhall finally reſt the ſupport I have been ſo anxious to derive from that grave which has been ranſacked by my adverſaries for evidence againſt me. As a ſoldier I avow a pride in having poſſeſſed Brigadier Fraſer's eſteem. As a de-fendant I am ſenſible I have dwelt upon it to a fault. The precedent of a Chief in Command ſuffering the comments of an inferior to be a teſt of his actions, requires an apology to my profeſſion. It lies in the eminence of my friend's cha-racter. His approbation gave a grace to my defence, and I was impatient to confute the calumny that would have robbed me of it; but to admit that it was neceſſary for my acquittal would be to countenance and forward the moſt pernicious and pre-poſterous doctrine that ever was practiſed to miſlead the public, and to betray the ſervice.

The comments of an inferior offi-cer no pro-per teſt of a ſuperior's conduct.

When a miniſter or his confederates lean upon private report, table talk, and half ſentences, to depreciate an officer they dare not themſelves accuſe, it is a feebleneſs of vengeance that, in its firſt aſpect, is contemptible in the extreme; but it calls for our indignation when we extend our view to its principle and effects. They operate to the very inverſion of due patronage, and the abſolute extinction of every idea upon which command ought to be beſtowed, or can efficaciouſly be exer-ciſed; they tend to encourage officers to be ſpies and informers; to render camps and fleets, properly the reſidence of harmony and honour, the ſeats of ſuſpicion, diſcord, faction, treachery, and mutiny.

The diverſity and importance of the matter brought to review in the period of the campaign I am now cloſing, has led to greater length than I was aware of; but I cannot diſmiſs it without one reference, addreſſed to ſuch of the examiners of my conduct as have inſiſted upon the tardineſs of the northern army.

Comparative view of the campaigns in 1759 and 1777.

The reference I would plead is to a campaign in the ſame country, memorable for having been conducted by an officer whoſe example muſt be acknowledged, at this juncture, to be of ſplendid and peculiar authority; I mean the campaign of Lord Amherſt, in the year 1759.

The great points of the war in America that year were to divide the enemy's force, and at the ſame time to direct the ſeveral operations with ſuch concurrence, that, though ſeparate and remote, they ſhould aſſiſt each other. The firſt objects of the

4

army

army to which I allude were to reduce Ticonderoga and Crown Point, and the ultimate and moft important one was to effect a junction with Mr. Wolfe before Quebec.

Thus far there is great fimilarity between the plans of the two campaigns, except that the points from which the armies marched, and to which they were deftined, were exactly reverfed.

In the Spring, 1759, the army, then affembled at Albany, took the field as early as the feafon would admit : but fuch were the natural impediments of the country, that though fupported by the unanimous zeal of the inhabitants, and furnifhed with abundant fupplies of draft cattle, carriages, water-craft, and every other neceffary ; the feveral departments well directed, and no enemy to oppofe the march, the General (Lord Amherft) was not able to commence the attack of Ticonderoga till the 7th of July, when the enemy abandoned that poft, and retreated to Crown Point.

The diftance from Albany to Fort George is between fixty and feventy miles, the paffage over Lake George to Ticonderoga about forty miles.

The General had reafon to believe that Crown Point would be given up at his approach as precipitately as Ticonderoga had been. He did not, however, reach it, a diftance of thirteen miles, and water-carriage at will, till the 14th of Auguft.

Was it at that time afked by the minifter or his adherents, what was the army doing not to purfue a flying enemy ?——Not to purfue when the whole country behind was their own, and magazines, baggage, hofpitals, and every other neceffary, might follow at leifure, and in fecurity ! When it was forefeen an encreafe of fleet was to be conftructed at Crown Point, to obtain the fuperiority over the enemy upon Lake Champlain, and confequently that every day's delay, in becoming mafter of that poft, rifked the campaign !

Although thefe enquiries were not then fuggefted to the public, an anfwer to them has been given, greatly to the honour of the General, in a very impartial hiftory of that time. "The army was employed in repairing the fortifications at "Ticonderoga; and the General took his meafures with the fame care as if he ex-"pected an obftinate defence, and attempt to furprife him on his march."

The enemy actually did abandon Crown Point on the approach of the General, the 14th of Auguft ; and, as foon as in poffeffion of that poft, he fet about fortifying it as he had done Ticonderoga. The time confumed in that operation, and in building new veffels, brought it to the middle of October before the General could embark upon the Lake. A fufpence, undoubtedly, of great anxiety ; for the great end of the campaign, the junction of the two armies, upon which the reduction of all Canada was thought to depend, was unattained.

But did the minifter or his adherents *then* cavil at the tardinefs of that army ?— Enterprifing, fanguine, and impetuous, as was the character of that minifter's

R 2

coun-

councils, there was not lefs energy in his profection. The nation, not a party, were his adherents; and his word was a *fiat* of fame. He beftowed emphatic pralfes on his General; and a failing campaign became part of that balis, from which he has afcended to the high honours he now defervedly poffeffes.

It would be great prefumption, and it is far from being intended, to draw any parallels or inferences from the campaigns of 1759 and 1777, except fuch as merely apply to confumption of time under fimilar circumftances. In other points the pretenfions of the refpective Generals may be as different as their fortunes; or, to make a much clearer diftinction, and a yet ftronger contraft, as wide afunder as the aufpices under which they ferved, thofe of Mr. Pitt and of Lord George Germain.

Obfervations, &c. refpecting the third Period.

" A feries of hard toil, inceffant effort, ftubborn action, till difabled in the col-
" lateral branches of the army, by the total defection of the Indians, and the defer-
" tion or timidity of the Canadians and Provincials, fome individuals excepted;
" difappointed in the laft hope of any timely co-operation from other armies; the
" regular troops reduced, by loffes from the beft parts, to 3500 fighting men, not
" 2000 of which were Britifh; only three days provifions, upon fhort allowance,
" in ftore; invefted by an army of 16,000 men, and no apparent means of retreat
" remaining, I called into council all the generals, field officers, and captains com-
" manding corps, and by their unanimous concurrence and advice, I was induced
" to open a treaty with Major General Gates, &c."

Appenix,
No. XIV.
Such was the fummary of affairs given in my letter from Albany to the fecretary of ftate. At the time it was written, I little expected to have occafion for any other teftimony of my actions; and it has therefore been fuppofed, that I gave them a colouring more fpecious than exact. This is the ftage of my defence in which I am defirous to bring that matter to judgment; and I have quoted the above paf-fage, exprefsly to lead the attention of every examiner to the whole of that letter. Let it now be confidered, unitedly with my late narrative, and both be compared in detail with the evidence—I am bold to ftake my caufe upon the iffue—And reft-ing upon thefe references, my comments upon this period, though it is the moft im-portant, will be fhorter than upon either of the former: the proofs alfo are more collected, and the matters controverted or ftarted in crofs-examination are fewer.

The firft remark I have to make is, that while the managers of the minifter's caufe have never admitted a doubt of the reality of thofe movements in the cam-paign, with the propriety of which their ingenuity promifed them even a coloura-ble caufe of cavil, they have had the addrefs, when any little fkill and conduct were generally acknowledged, to call the exiftence of fuch movements into queftion. I cannot make this remark more pertinently than at prefent, when the march of the

army,

army, preceding the action of the 19th of September, is in its due place the object of notice—" A pretty combination of columns and deployments compofed at Al- " bany, and very fit for a Gazette." This fort of language I believe moft perfons have heard, who have converfed with the dependents or runners of office, and it will be my excufe for fubmitting to the judgment of my profeffion a plan of the movement. It will fhew in fome degree the difficulties that the nature of the country oppofed to a combined march of columns; and at the fame time the difadvantage (I might fay the certain defeat) that muft have been fuftained, had the army been only in one column upon the ground where it was attacked, or had the combination of the other columns, thofe of General Prafer in particular, been lefs exact to the point of time in which it was expedient they fhould arrive and form.

March to the enemy on the 19th of Sept. Plan IV.

To prove that this march was not *compofed* at Albany, I refer to feveral witneffes, but particularly to the Earl of Harrington. His fituation, as my aid-de-camp, gave him a general knowledge of a movement, that an officer employed in the execution of a fingle part of it could not have acquired. It will be confidered by all who know the qualities of my noble friend, as very honourable to the difpofitions of that day, that they are fo circumftantially retained in fo diftinguifhing a mind; and for my own part, I cannot commit them to military judgment under a better truft than the accuracy of his defcription.

Lord Balcarras, queft. 33, 34. Maj. Forbes, quefl. 3 to 7. Lord Harrington's quefl. 38 to 42 inclufive..

I fhall not therefore detain the reader an inftant longer from a fubject fo worthy his attention, as the evidence refpecting the behaviour of the troops in the enfuing events of that day.

Few actions have been characterized by more obftinacy in attack or defence. The Britifh bayonet was repeatedly tried ineffectually. Eleven hundred Britifh foldiers, foiled in thefe trials, bore inceffant fire from a fucceffion of frefh troops in fuperior numbers, for above four hours; and after a lofs of above a third of their numbers (and in one of the regiments above two thirds) forced the enemy at laft. Of a detachment of a captain and forty-eight artillery men, the captain and thirty-fix were killed or wounded. Thefe facts are marked by a concurrence of evidence that no man will difpute. The tribute of praife due to fuch troops will not be wanting in this generous nation; and it will as certainly be accompanied with a juft portion of fhame to thofe who have dared to depreciate or fully valour fo confpicuous— who have their ears open only to the prejudice of American cowardice, and having been always loud upon that courtly topic, ftifle the glory of their countrymen to maintain a bafe confiftency.

Action of 19th Sept.. Lord Harrington's queft. 43 to 49 inclufive. Lord Balcarras, 35 to 39. Capt. Money, 26 to 30. Maj Forbes, 8 to 10. Lieut. Col. Kingfton, 57 to 67.

It will be obfervable from the accounts of the killed and wounded, that the lofs of officers in all the actions of the campaign was proportionably much greater than that of the private men: and as this obfervation applies particularly to the action we are confidering, it may not be improper to account for it in this place.

The

Reafon of the
difpropor-
tion of killed
and wound-
ed.

The enemy had with their army great numbers of markfmen, armed with rifle-barrel pieces: thefe, during an engagement, hovered upon the flanks in fmall detachments, and were very expert in fecuring themfelves, and in fhifting their ground. In this action, many placed themfelves in high trees in the rear of their own line, and there was feldom a minute's interval of fmoke in any part of our line without officers being taken off by fingle fhot. *

It will naturally be fuppofed, that the Indians would be of great ufe againft this mode of fighting. The example of thofe that remained after the great defertion proved the contrary, for not a man of them was to be brought within the found of a rifle fhot. The Canadians were formerly very expert in fervice of this nature; but befides the change in their military character, which I noticed before, their beft officer was killed early in the action, which event caft a general damp upon the corps. A few of the Provincials were ferviceable: but the beft men I had to oppofe as markfmen, were the German chaffeurs, though their number was fo fmall, as not to be one to twenty of the enemy.

Proceedings
of the army
after the ac-
tion.

The crofs-examination upon the proceedings of the army after this action will fhew the folly there would be in bringing a military caufe to a parliamentary enquiry, upon the prefumption that any parts of it would be left unexamined. The very want of practical knowledge in the enquirers renders them more inquifitive, and much more tenacious of doubts and furmifes, than they would otherwife be: for in-

Crofs-exa-
mination of
Lord Balcar-
ras, queft. 98
to 100.
Ditto of Lord
Harrington,
50 and 106.
Lieut. Col.
Kingfton, 68.
Maj. Forbes,
19.
Capt. Mo-
ncy, 32.
Lieut. Col.
Kingfton, 69
to 76.
Lord Har-
rington, 56.
Lord Balcar-
ras, queft.
100.

ftance; I do not believe that with an army exhaufted by a long and fevere action, and deprived of an uncommon portion of officers, the queftion of attacking the enemy next morning would have occurred to any man of profeffional judgment: that enemy too in a pofition of which no further knowledge could be obtained than that it was covered by an intrenchment and abattis, and the approach to be made through a thick wood, without any avenue cut, or a fingle poft fortified to fecure a retreat, or to cover the magazine, which afforded the only poffible means of fubfiftence.

Equally remote would be the thoughts of military men from attacking a few days after, when it appeared I had received a letter from Sir Henry Clinton, informing me of a diverfion fo powerful as an attack upon Fort Montgomery to be undertaken as at that very time.

The queftions relating to the enemy having their baggage packed, if that circumftance was meant as an indication that they meant to retreat, is another proof how

* Capt. Green, aid de camp to Major General Phillips, was fhot through the arm by one of thefe markfmen as he was delivering me a meffage. I learned, after the convention, from the commanding officer of the rifle-men, that the fhot was meant for me; and as the captain was feen to fall from his horfe, it was for fome hours believed in the enemy's army that I was killed. My efcape was owing to the captain happening to have a laced furniture to his faddle, which made him miftaken for the general.

little

little the queftioners knew of fervice. It does not appear in evidence how the fact was: but no officer will difpute, that if the enemy had not only packed their baggage, but actually conveyed it to the other fide the river, they would have acted conformably to the general practice of fervice when action is expected; and to no circumftance of fervice more than to that when it is refolved to difpute a poft to the laft extremity.

Upon the whole of my fituation at that time, I am fo confident that it was the part of an officer to fortify and wait events, that I am only further intent to prove that I fortified properly, the nature of the ground and my feveral purpofes confidered. Upon this principle I fubmit the plan annexed. It will alfo fhew the na- Plan.No. V. ture of the ground between the two armies, and ferve to explain the difficulties the witneffes exprefs of taking a view of the enemy's left: but it will be confidered, that befides thefe apparent obftacles to a near approach, the enemy abounded in militia, which fupplied out-pofts and fcouts, that could by no means be driven in without making the army liable to a general action.

As for any other intelligence than what could be obtained by eye-fight it was generally contradictory, always imperfect; the deferters were often fufpicious, the prifoners very few. I never faw any inftance of fervice where it was fo difficult to obtain information. Among people fpeaking the fame language with ourfelves, and many of them profeffing the moft favourable difpofitions, fcarcely any could be prevailed upon, by rewards or principle, to rifk his perfon for the purpofe of intelligence.

In regard to the crofs-examination, refpecting the time neceffary for the conftruction of the redoubts and other works, I neither thought it worth while to conteft it at the time, nor fhall I conteft it now, though nothing would be more eafy than to fhew that there was a great deal of neceffary labour which the queftions did not lead to, and confequently the witneffes could not with propriety enter into the explanation of them. But what makes the confumption of time to me immaterial is, that I place my juftification upon the expediency of waiting the co-operation from Sir Henry Clinton. It is in proof, that I received a letter from him the day after the action of the 19th, * informing me that he meditated an attack upon Fort Montgomery as at that very time. And as I have already faid, that I fhould have thought it the part of madnefs to have rifked an attack upon the enemy, in the weak ftate of my army, for fome time after the late action, and under the expectation of fo powerful a diverfion; fo fhould I have deferred it longer, even after being recruited from the hofpital, on account of the fame expectation, and the further chance of the reinforcement of Colonel St. Leger's corps, and perhaps a convoy of provi-

---

* The original letter is in my poffeffion, but could not be produced without difcovering a fecret mode of conveying intelligence that it might be improper to make public.

fions from Ticonderoga : fo far am I from conceiving the paft delay blameable, that I acknowledge the meafure of the 7th of October was precipitated by fome days, by the forage being become fo fcarce, that a fupply could only be obtained by a movement of the army.

If any perfons have fuppofed, that what has been called the inactive ftate of the army at this period was a ftate of reft, they are as much miftaken as they would be if they fuppofed it in any other circumftance comfortable. From the 20th of September to the 7th of October, the armies were fo near, that not a night paffed without firing, and fometimes concerted attacks upon our advanced picquets; no foraging party could be made without great detachments to cover it; it was the plan of the enemy to harrafs the army by conftant alarms, and their fuperiority of numbers enabled them to attempt it without fatigue to themfelves.

Alert fituation of the army from 20th Sept. to 7th Oct.

By being habituated to fire, our foldiers became indifferent to it, and were capable of eating or fleeping when it was very near them : but I do not believe either officer or foldier ever flept during that interval without his cloaths, or that any general officer, or commander of a regiment, paffed a fingle night without being upon his legs occafionally at different hours, and conftantly an hour before day-light.

The circumftances in general of the action of the 7th of October ftand in that arragement in the evidence of the Earl of Balcarras, Earl of Harrington, Lieut. Col. Kingfton, and Captain Money, and have been fo little controverted by crofs-examination, that any length of comment upon them is unneceffary. I will only obferve, that the movement of the enemy under General Arnold, mentioned in my Narrative, is confirmed as far as circumftantial teftimony can confirm it, by Captain Money. And if there can be any perfons, who, after confidering that circumftance, and the pofitive proof of the fubfequent obftinacy, in the attack upon the poft of Lord Balcarras, and various other actions of that day, continue to doubt, that the Americans poffefs the *quality* and *faculty* of fighting (call it by whatever term they pleafe) they are of a prejudice that it would be very abfurd longer to contend with.

Lord Balcarras, 46, &c. Lord Harrington, 57, &c. Lieut. Col. Kingfton, 77, &c. Capt. Money, 35 to 48
See alfo Plan V.

But though comments upon this part of the evidence may be fpared, the remembrance of what I perfonally underwent cannot fo eafily be fuppreffed; and I am fure I fhall not outgo the indulgence of the candid, if in delineating fituations fo affecting, I add feelings to juftification. The defence of military conduct is an interefting point of profeffional honour; but to vindicate the heart, is a duty to God and to fociety at large.

Few conjunctures in the campaign I have been defcribing, few, perhaps, upon military record, can be found fo diftinguifhed by exigencies, or productive of fuch critical and anxious calls upon public character, and private affection, as that which now took place.

At

In the firſt place, the poſition of the army, was untenable, and yet an immediate Lord Balcar-ras, 52. retreat was impoſſible ; not only from the fatigue of the troops, but from the neceſſity of delivering freſh ammunition and proviſions.

The loſſes in the action were uncommonly ſevere. Sir Francis Clarke, my aid-de-camp, had originally recommended himſelf to my attention by his talents and dili-gence : as ſervice and intimacy opened his character more, he became endeared to me by every quality that can create eſteem, I loſt in him an uſeful aſſiſtant, an amia-ble companion, an attached ftiend : the ſtate was deprived by his death, of one of the faireſt promiſes of an able general.

The fate of Colonel Ackland, taken priſoner, and then ſuppoſed to be mortally wounded, was a ſecond ſource of anxiety—General Fraſer was expiring.

In the courſe of the action, a ſhot had paſſed through my hat, and another had torn my waiſtcoat. I ſhould be ſorry to be thought at any time inſenſible to the protect-ing hand of Providence ; but I ever more particularly conſidered (and I hope not ſuperſtitiouſly) a ſoldier's hair-breadth eſcapes as incentives to duty, *a marked renewal of the truſt of Being*, for the due purpoſes of a public ſtation ; and under that reflection to loſe our fortitude, by giving way to our affections ; to be diverted by any poſſible ſelf-emotion from meeting a preſent exigency with our beſt faculties, were at once diſhonour and impiety.

Having therefore put aſide for a time my private ſenſations, it has been ſhewn that Lord Balcar-ras, 53. I effected an entire change in the poſition of the army before day-light. The plan will Lord Har-rington, 66. ſhew the new ground taken up. Early in the morning of the 8th, General Fraſer Plan, No. VI. breathed his laſt—and with the kindeſt expreſſions of his affection, his laſt requeſt was State of things on the 8th. brought me, that he might be carried without parade by the ſoldiers of his corps to the great redoubt, and buried there. The whole day of the 8th of October was cor-reſpondent to this inauſpicious beginning. The hours were meaſured by a ſucceſſion of immediate cares, encreaſing doubts, and melancholy objects. The enemy were formed in two lines. Every part of their diſpoſition, as well as the repeated attacks Lord Har-rington, 67, &c. upon Lord Balcarras's corps, and the cannonade from the plain, kept the troops in momentary expectation of a general action. During this ſuſpenſe, wounded officers, ſome upon crutches, and others even carried upon hand-barrows by their ſervants, were occaſionally aſcending the hill from the hoſpital tents, to take their ſhare in the action, or follow the march of the army. The generals were employed in exhorting the troops.

About ſun-ſet the corpſe of General Fraſer was brought up the hill, attended only Gen. Fraſer's funeral. by the officers who had lived in his family. To arrive at the redoubt, it paſſed with-in view of the greateſt part of both armies. General Phillips, General Reideſel, and myſelf, who were ſtanding together, were ſtruck with the humility of the proceſſion :

S

They

They who were ignorant that privacy had been requested, might conftrue it neglect. We could neither endure that reflection, nor indeed reftrain our natural propenfity to pay our laft attention to his remains. The circumftances that enfued cannot be better defcribed than they have been by different witneffes.* The inceffant cannonade during the folemnity ; the fteady attitude and unaltered voice with which the chaplain officiated, though frequently covered with duft, which the fhot threw up on all fides of him ; the mute but expreffive mixture of fenfibility and indignation upon every countenance : thefe objects will remain to the laft of life upon the minds of every man who was prefent. The growing dufkinefs added to the fcenery, and the whole marked a character of that juncture that would make one of the fineft fubjects for the pencil of a mafter that the field ever exhibited—To the canvas and to the faithful page of a more important hiftorian, gallant friend ! I confign thy memory. There may thy talents, thy manly virtues, their progrefs and their period, find due diftinction ; and long may they furvive ;——long after the frail record of my pen fhall be forgotten.

Night march of the 8th. The reflections arifing from thefe fcenes gave place to the perplexities of the night. A defeated army was to retreat from an enemy flufhed with fuccefs, much fuperior in front, and occupying ftrong pofts in the country behind. We were equally liable upon that march to be attacked in front, in flank, or rear. The difpofition of march had been concerted as much as circumftances would admit ; and it was executed by the officers and the troops in general with a precifion that experience in critical fituations can only teach. The baggage, which could only move in one column, and in a narrow road, fell into the confufion which it is impoffible for caution to guard againft in the dark, becaufe a fingle accident of an overturn or a broken wheel, or even the ftupidity or drunkennefs of a driver, may ftop and often

Lord Harrington, 70, and from 112 to 118. confufe the motion of the whole line. Care was taken that no fuch accident fhould break the order of the troops, and orders were fent to Major General Phillips, who commanded the rear guard, in cafe he was attacked, to pay attention only to the main object of covering the troops ; or, if occafion were, of taking a pofition to give them time to form.

Continuance of the march on the 9th. At day-break the next morning the army had reached very advantageous ground, and took a pofition in which it would have been very defirable to receive the enemy. A halt was neceffary to refrefh the troops, and to give time to the bateaux, loaded with provifions, which had not been able to keep pace with the troops, to come a-breaft. A portion of provifions was delivered alfo from the bateaux, not without apprehenfion that that delivery might be the laft : for there were parts of the river in which the boats might be attacked from the other fide to great advantage, notwithftanding the correfpondent movement of the army.

* Particularly Lieutenant Colonel Kingfton, 85.

The

The above purpofes being effected, the army proceeded in very fevere weather, and through exceeding bad roads.

Befides the continuation of difficulties and general fatigue, this day was remarkable for a circumftance of private diftrefs too peculiar and affecting to be omitted. The circumftance to which I allude is Lady Harriet Ackland's paffage through the enemy's army, to attend her wounded bufband, then their prifoner.

The progrefs of this lady with the army could hardly be thought abruptly or fuperfluoufly introduced, were it only fo for the purpofe of authenticating a wonderful ftory.—It would exhibit, if well delineated, an interefting picture of the fpirit, the enterprize, and the diftrefs of romance, realized and regulated upon the chafte and fober principles of rational love and connubial duty. *(margin: Extraordinary occurrence of private diftrefs.)*

But I beg leave to obferve befides, that it has direct reference to my fubject, to fbew what the luxuries were with which (as the world has been taught to believe) the army was encumbered ; what were the accommodations prepared for the *two thoufand women* that are gravely fuppofed, in the crofs examination, to have followed with the baggage. An idea fo prepofterous, as well as falfe, would have been a fitter fubject for derifion than refutation, but that it was malicioufly intended ; not, I am confident, by the member who afked the queftions, but by the perfons who impofed upon him, to effect by prejudice what they defpaired of effecting by fact.—Not content with cavilling at our pretenfions of having *fought* hard, they would not allow the army even the claim upon the good-nature of the nation, of having *fared* hard for its fervice. *(margin: Lieut. Col. Kingfton, 131 to 133.)*

I fhall however confider part of this ftory as fo far unconnected with the immediate bufinefs I was upon (purfuing the line of evidence upon the retreat to Saratoga) as to give it in the margin. It may well ftand by itfelf; and I venture to think that this one example of patience, fuffering, and fortitude, will be permitted to pafs without cenfure or obloquy. *

When

---

* Lady Harriet Ackland had accompanied her hufband to Canada in the beginning of the year 1776. In the courfe of that campaign fhe had traverfed a vaft fpace of country, in different extremities of feafon, and with difficulties that an European traveller will not eafily conceive, to attend, in a poor hut at Chamblée, upon his fick bed.

In the opening of the campaign of 1777 fhe was reftrained from offering herfelf to a fhare of the fatigue and hazard expected before Ticonderoga, by the pofitive injunctions of her hufband. The day after the conqueft of that place, he was badly wounded, and fhe croffed the Lake Champlain to join him.

As foon as he recovered, Lady Harriet proceeded to follow his fortunes through the campaign, and at Fort Edward, or at the next camp, fhe acquired a two-wheel tumbril, which had been conftructed by the artificers of the artillery, fomething fimilar to the carriage ufed for the mail upon the great roads of England. Major Ackland commanded the Britifh grenadiers, which were attached to General Frafer's corps ; and confequently were always the moft advanced poft of the army. Their fituations were often fo alert, that no perfon flept out of their cloaths. In one of thefe fituations a

S 2   tent,

When the army was upon the point of moving after the halt described, I received a meſſage from Lady Harriet, ſubmitting to my deciſion a propoſal (and expreſſing an earneſt ſolicitude to execute it, if not interfering with my deſigns) of paſſing to the camp of the enemy, and requeſting General Gates's permiſſion to attend her huſband.

Though I was ready to believe (for I had experienced) that patience and fortitude, in a ſupreme degree, were to be found, as well as every other virtue, under the moſt tender forms, I was aſtoniſhed at this propoſal. After ſo long an agitation of the ſpirits, exhauſted not only for want of reſt, but abſolutely want of food, drenched in rains for twelve hours together, that a woman ſhould be capable of ſuch an undertaking as delivering herſelf to the enemy, probably in the night, and uncertain of what hands ſhe might firſt fall into, appeared an effort above human nature. The aſſiſtance I was enabled to give was ſmall indeed; I had not even a cup of wine to offer her; but I was told ſhe had found, from ſome kind and fortunate hand, a little rum and dirty water. All I could furniſh to her was an open boat and a few lines, written upon dirty and wet paper, to General Gates, recommending her to his protection.

tent, in which the major and Lady Harriet were aſleep, ſuddenly took fire. An orderly ſerjeant of grenadiers, with great hazard of ſuffocation, dragged out the firſt perſon he caught hold of. It proved to be the major. It happened, that in the ſame inſtant ſhe had, unknowing what ſhe did, and perhaps not perfectly awake, providentially made her eſcape, by creeping under the walls of the back part of the tent. The firſt object ſhe ſaw, upon the recovery of her ſenſes, was the major on the other ſide, and in the ſame inſtant again in the fire, in ſearch of her. The ſerjeant again ſaved him, but not without the major being very ſeverely burned in his face and different parts of the body. Every thing they had with them in the tent was conſumed.

This accident happened a little time before the army paſſed the Hudſon's River. It neither altered the reſolution nor the chearfulneſs of Lady Harriet; and ſhe continued her progreſs, a partaker of the fatigues of the advanced corps. The next call upon her fortitude was of a different nature, and more diſtreſsful, as of longer ſuſpenſe. On the march of the 19th, the grenadiers being liable to action at every ſtep, ſhe had been directed by the major to follow the route of the artillery and baggage, which was not expoſed. At the time the action began ſhe found herſelf near a ſmall uninhabited hut, where ſhe alighted. When it was found the action was becoming general and bloody, the ſurgeons of the hoſpital took poſſeſſion of the ſame place, as the moſt convenient for the firſt care of the wounded. Thus was this lady in hearing of one continued fire of cannon and muſketry, for four hours together, with the preſumption, from the poſt of her huſband at the head of the grenadiers, that he was in the moſt expoſed part of the action. She had three female companions, the Baroneſs of Reideſel and the wives of two Britiſh officers, Major Harnage and Lieutenant Reynell; but in the event their preſence ſerved but little for comfort. Major Harnage was ſoon brought to the ſurgeons, very badly wounded; and a little time after came intelligence that Lieutenant Reynell was ſhot dead. Imagination will want no helps to figure the ſtate of the whole groupe.

From the date of that action to the 7th of October, Lady Harriet, prepared for new trials! and it was her lot that their ſeverity encreaſed with their numbers. She was again expoſed to the hearing of the whole action, and at laſt received the ſhock of her individual misfortune, mixed with the intelligence of the general calamity, the troops were defeated, and Major Ackland, deſperately wounded, was a priſoner.

The day of the 8th was paſſed by Lady Harriet and her companions in common anxiety, not a tent, nor a ſhed being ſtanding, except what belonged to the Hoſpital, their refuge was among the wounded and the dying.

Mr.

Mr. Brudenell, the chaplain to the artillery (the fame gentleman who had officiated fo fignally at General Frafer's funeral) readily undertook to accompany her, and with one female fervant, and the major's valet-de-chambre (who had a ball which he had received in the late action then in his fhoulder) fhe rowed down the river to meet the enemy. But her diftreffes were not yet to end. The night was advanced before the boat reached the enemy's out-pofts, and the centinel would not let it pafs, nor even come on fhore. In vain Mr. Brudenell offered the flag of truce, and reprefented the ftate of the extraordinary paffenger. The guard, apprehenfive of treachery, and punctilious to their orders, threatened to fire into the boat if it ftirted before day-light. Her anxiety and fuffering were thus protracted through feven or eight dark and cold hours ; and her reflections upon that firft reception could not give her very encouraging ideas of the treatment fhe was afterwards to expect. But it is due to juftice at the clofe of this adventure to fay, that fhe was received and accommodated by General Gates with all the humanity and refpect that her rank, her merits and her fortunes deferved.

Let fuch as are affected by thefe circumftances of alarm, hardfhip and danger, recollect, that the fubject of them was a woman ; of the moft tender and delicate frame ; of the gentleft manners ; habituated to all the foft elegancies, and refined enjoyments, that attend high birth and fortune ; and far advanced in a ftate in which the tender cares, always due to the fex, become indifpenfibly neceffary. Her mind alone was formed for fuch trials.

I now return to the army, which arrived in the night at Saratoga, in fuch a ftate of fatigue, that the men for the moft part had not ftrength or inclination to cut wood and make fires, but rather fought fleep in their wet cloaths upon the wet ground under the continuing rain, and it was not till after day-light that the artillery and the laft of the troops paft the Fifh Kill, and took a pofition upon the heights and in the redoubts formerly conftructed.

Arrival of the army at Saratoga. Lord Harrington, 71, &c. Lord Balcarras, 57, &c.

The interval between taking that pofition, and the conclufion of the treaty, is the folemn crifis in which I confider myfelf as peculiarly accountable to my country. And if all the circumftances mentioned by me, in my own vindication, in my Letters, or my Narrative, are not eftablifhed, and many of them ftrengthened by pofitive proof; if every furmife of a furrender on my part, while there was a poffibility of avoiding it by fight, by manœuvre, or by retreat, is not done away ; if even in the laft extremity, it does not appear I was ready and forward to prefer death to difhonour ; if the evidence I have adduced is not clear, diftinct, and direct to thefe points, the public odium, piercingly as it affects a fenfible breaft, would be far fhort of the punifhment I deferve.

Interval between the arrival at Saratoga and figning the convention.

I cannot but confider it as one encouragement under this appeal, and it is no fmall one, that though very few parts of my preceding conduct have efcaped the fcrutiny of

crofs-croſs-examination, not a material tranſaction of this criſis has been controverted or glanced at. I beg leave to recapitulate the tranſactions upon which I rely.

Lord Har-
rington, 74
to 76.
Lieut. Col.
Kingſton, 86.
See the plan.
Lieut. Col.
Kingſton, 91
92.

It is proved by the evidence of the Earl of Harrington and Colonel Kingſton, that the enemy was poſted on the eaſt lide the river to guard the ford.

It is further proved by the evidence of Lieut. Col. Kingſton, that in concert with the general officers, it was determined to try a night march on the eaſt ſide the river, abandoning the baggage; and that the attempt was prevented by the impoſſibility attending the delivery of neceſſary proviſion. The ſame witneſs goes on to ſhew, that the next day it was evident, that had the delivery been poſſible, the attempt would ſtill have failed, for we then received intelligence of the enemy being pre-

Lieut. Col.
Kingſton, 93,
94, 95.

viouſly in poſſeſſion, in force, of the country on both ſides the river between us and Fort Edward.*

Lieut. Col.
Kingſton, 88,
89, 92.
See the plan.
No. VII.

While the army was lying day and night upon their arms, " in anxious hope of " ſuccour from our friends, or as the next deſirable expectation, an attack from " the enemy,"† I cannot omit obſerving from the ſame evidence (that of Colonel Kingſton) how near the laſt expectation was being accompliſhed. It would be im-proper to pronounce poſitively what would have been the iſſue : but I requeſt the attention of my military readers to the plan of the ground, as an argument of the probability of ſucceſs. The diſpoſition of the enemy being to paſs the Fiſh-Kill in different columns, and to make their great effort upon the plain, they muſt have formed under the fire of all our park artillery, within reach of grape-ſhot, a croſs fire from the artillery and muſketry of the intrenched corps upon the hill, and the muſketry of the 20th regiment, which was at eaſy diſtance to be ſupported by the Germans, in front; added to this would have been the advantage, which though always wiſhed for we never had attained, of a charge upon an open plain. I am perſuaded the general judgment will go with me when I lament the accident that prevented the enemy's deſign (when ſo far advanced in it, as actually to have paſſed the river with one column) as one of the moſt adverſe ſtrokes of fortune in the whole campaign.

Lord Har-
rington, 84,
85, 86.
Lord Balcar-
ras, from 60
to the end.
Maj. Forbes,
22 to 29.
Lord Balcar-
ras, 64.

The ſtate of things after this diſappointment is given by the Earl of Harrington : " It was as bad as poſſible; the numbers of the army were few, their proviſions " ſhort, their poſition not a good one, owing to the nature of the country." This ſtate is corroborated by the evidence of the Earl of Balcarras and Major Forbes, with the additional circumſtance, that there was not a ſpot to be found in the whole poſition which was not expoſed to cannon or rifle ſhot.

---

* It was alſo in contemplation to force a way back to Albany, had the enemy in the diſtribution of their poſts weakened their right, ſo as to have made the effort poſſible. See Lord Harrington's evi-dence.

† Letter from Albany to the ſecretary of ſtate.

The

The minutes of the first council of war prove the unaninity of opinion for opening the treaty ; and it is proved by the evidence of Colonel Kingston, that the force of the enemy was actually greater, and their position stronger, than the intelligence I had received and laid before the council of war represented them. Appendix, No. XV. Lieut. Col. Kingston, 91, &c.

It is proved by the fullest evidence, that the terms first proposed by the enemy were instantly and unanimously rejected by the council of war as dishonourable. Maj. Forbes, 31 to 34. Lord Balcarras, 65 to 73.

The same unanimity in approving the terms I proposed and obtained, is equally incontestably established.

And lastly, two papers are produced, and authenticated beyond a possibility of cavil, the one General Gates's return signed by himself, shewing the effective strength present of the rebel army ; the other, the minutes of the last council of war, shewing, that even supported as I was by the unanimity of the former councils, in opening and conducting the treaty, I was repugnant to the signing of it, upon a flight hope entertained of a remote relief—(a hope arising from some intelligence received in the night of Sir Henry Clinton's moving up the North River) and gave my voice against a majority accordingly ; that I at last thought myself compelled to yield to the majority upon " the uncertainty of the intelligence, and the improbability " of General Clinton's motions being effectual if true ; upon the doubts entertained " of some part of the troops, if the negotiation of the treaty ceased, and of a greater " part for want of bodily strength, if desperate enterprizes were to be afterwards " undertaken ; and lastly, upon the reflection that a miscarriage of such enterprises " must be fatal to the whole army, and that even a victory could not save it." Appendix, Nᵒ. XVI. Appendix, No. XVII. See also Lord Balcarras, 130, 131, 132.

To this mass of evidence, apposite and direct to every fact essential to my justification, I beg leave to add the opinion of the army, that the terms obtained were better than the situation of things gave us a right to expect. For a proof that such was their opinion, I refer to the testimony of Lord Balcarras. Lord Balcarras. Lord Harrington.

A fair judgment upon recent events is hardly to be expected, especially while many prejudices are alive. It will be allowed me to assume, what no one has ever ventured to deny, that there may be a combination of circumstances under which an army may be justified in treating with an enemy. That the army under my command was under such circumstances at Saratoga is also generally acknowledged : but what is not denied to me from my own situation, is attempted to be withheld, by some, on account of the quality of the enemy. They suggest that there should be no treaty with rebels. It is unnecessary in answer to have recourse to history. I will not take defence from treaties between Spain, the haughtiest power of the world, and the arch-rebel the great Prince of Orange ; nor between Charles the First and the arch-rebels the English Parliament (for such in both instances they were called) I need only refer to the examples existing at that time in America, Reflections upon the convention.

2   and

and fince much improved on at home. My fuperior officer in America, with the approbation of government, had treated upon different occafions with General Wafhington. The Britifh government in its higheft collective authority, the King in Parliament, has fince commiffioned five members of that Parliament, the one a peer, the others of eminent ftation in military and civil capacities, to *treat with* rebels, I had almoft faid to *fue* to rebels for peace, by the furrender of almoft every principle for the maintenance of which they had profecuted the war.

Thus highly juftified in treating with rebels, I am at a lofs to difcover by what poffible mode of defence I could have acquitted myfelf to God or my country, when the brave and intelligent officers of my army unanimoufly refolved, upon military principle, precedent and reafon, that the treaty was expedient, and the terms honourable, if I had delivered them up to certain deftruction, or even to be prifoners at difcretion.

If the informed and difpaffionate part of mankind fhould agree in fentiment with the unanimous voice of the army, upon the convention of Saratoga, furely. to impute to it the final lofs of the army is too palpable an injuftice long to remain upon the minds of the moft prejudiced. The convention exprefsly preferved the army for the fervice of the ftate. According to that convention a truce was made during the war, between that army and the enemy, in America, and it now might have been acting againft the Houfe of Bourbon in any other part of the world. The army was loft by the non-compliance with the treaty on the part of the Congrefs; and that violation of faith no man will ever be found to juftify.

I will not decide how far it was encouraged in America, by the perfuafion that the miniftry of Britain had neither power nor fpirit to redrefs the wrong; and that they had funk the nation fo low, in point of refpect, that the world would over-look, where fhe was concerned, an action that would have excited, in any other cafe, univerfal cenfure and indignation. But whatever motives the Congrefs may have had, the tamenefs and filence with which the Britifh minifters have borne this outrage, is aftonifhing. That men fo conftant and fo prodigal in their anger againft the Congrefs, as never before to have failed in expreffing it, even in cafes where it bordered upon being ridiculous, fhould on a fudden become cold and mute, and dead to feeling, in a cafe where refentment was juftly founded, can hardly be accounted for, except upon the principle that it was better to fupprefs the jufteft cenfure upon a power they detefted, than that even a particle of unme-rited odium fhould be wanting to load the man whom they were refolved to deprefs.

APPEN-

CONCLUSION.

I AM not aware that in the preceding Review of Evidence I have neglected any part essential to my defence. I do not reckon as such, that part which applies to the management of the public purse. The calumny designed to wound me upon that head was too gross to succeed: it perished in its birth, and scorn is the only sentiment excited by the remembrance of its momentary existence. In regard to the more plausible objections pointed against my conduct, I have not only endeavoured to meet them in the cross-examination, but have searched for them in every place where I could suppose them to originate or be entertained. If some have escaped, I shall stand excused, when it is recollected how they have grown and changed from one shape to another, and that it has never been my fortune to be confronted with an avowed and regular accuser—I despair of ever being so: but I desire it to be understood, that although I am earnest in this mode of defence, I am so far from declining another, that I shall think it one very happy circumstance of the past enquiry, if any thing contained in it should have effect hereafter to produce an enquiry by court-martial.

It would not be an ungrateful task to follow the defence of the campaign with a detail of the occurrences which happened between the time of signing the convention and my leaving America. Many of them would be found curious; and the cares and perplexities in which I bore a principal and most painful part, would create a new interest in the minds of my friends: but I do not think myself at liberty, upon the plan I laid down at my outset, to enter into matter where no blame is imputed or implied. If my proceedings during that interval deserve any credit, I am content with that testimony of it, which I may assume from the silence of my enemies.

I have not the same reasons for passing over the transactions in which I have been engaged since my return to England, because blame, and of a very atrocious nature, *has* been imputed to me. But as the principal of these transactions are already before the public, I shall mention them very briefly; and merely to introduce connectedly such further thoughts upon them as could not with propriety be stated upon any former occasion.

Immediately after my arrival, a board of general officers was appointed to enquire into the causes of the failure of the expedition from Canada. This enquiry was made the foundation of an order against my appearing at court.

The board reported, that they could not take cognizance of me being under parole—the prohibition from the King's presence neverthelefs still remained in force.

I had

I had recourfe to parliament for enquiry ; and openly, and repeatedly, and ftrenuoufly called upon the minifters to join iffue with me before that tribunal. Objection was taken againft immediate enquiry, becaufe Generals Sir Guy. Carleton and
Sir William Howe who might be parties were abfent ; but it was evidently the difpofition of the houfe, that an enquiry fhould be inftituted the enfuing feffion.

I pledged myfelf zealoufly to profecute that meafure ; I accufed minifters of inju-
rious treatment towards myfelf ; and it became my duty, upon occafions with which
my own affairs had no connection, to exprefs deeper refentments of their conduct
towards the public.

In this ftate of things parliament was prorogued on the *3d of June*. On the *5th
of June*, I received the firft order to repair to Bofton as foon as I had tried the Bath
waters. The order and my anfwer, reprefenting the hardfhip of being fent back
unheard, and the fecond conditional order, with entire flight of my reprefentations,
are too well known to require repetition : but there are two circumftances attending
the dates of thefe orders with which I was not acquainted till long after, and which
have never yet been taken notice of.

The one is, that at the very time I was told that my prefence was *material*, and
(as the fecond letter from the fecretary at war expreffed) of *fo much importance to the
troops detained prifoners in New England*, that it muft not be difpenfed with—at that
very time, it was determined to ratify the convention, according to the requifition
of the Congrefs ; and to tranfmit the ratification through other hands, and without
any participation with me, or employment of me, in carrying it to a conclufion.
It was very poffible, the troops might have been failed for England before I had
reached America, had I even complied as early as the condition of either order
could poffibly be conftrued to prefcribe. But at all events, the circumftance could
not but ferve to mark *to me* the true intent and meaning of the order beyond a poffibility of miftake—*that it was an order of vindictive punifhment* ; and my prefence
with the troops, if I reached America in time, was *material* and *important* to mark
to *them* the degree of difgrace to which I was reduced. The terms are a mockery,
and an infult upon common fenfe, if applied, in the fituation in which I was placed,
to the fervice of the King, or the confolation of the troops. Such a difplay of vengeance might indeed be intended to apply to their prudence, and to act as a cau-
-tion and warning how at their return they fhould fupport a General under the extremity of the King's difpleafure.*

The other circumftance attending thefe dates is not lefs remarkable, viz.

---

* In times when the maintenance of the conftitution in its purity is the ruling principle of an adminiftration, the King's name is introduced by office only to denote an act of the executive part of the
ftate. In times when an adminiftration mean to rule by the influence of monarchy, the language of
office is to connect the royal perfon with the act, and to give him attributes of paffion and difpleafure,
from which in his political character he i. held exempt. I difclaim language and ideas fo unconftitu-
tional and difrefpectful, and never mean to allude to my Sovereign perfonally, but in acts of juftice and
mercy.

The

The determination of changing the nature of the war, as afterwards declared by the commiffioners in America, muft have been taken at this time.

· I am very much difinclined to believe, that the confideration of my perfon as a proper victim upon that occafion was ever regularly and formally debated in the cabinet: but I cannot think it uncharitable to the individual advifer of the Crown, whoever he was, who could project fuch an order, to fuppofe, that if upon the firft exercife of *the extremes of war* on the one fide, and in the ardour of retaliation on the other, it had fo happened, that an object fo well to be fpared as an obnoxious and difgraced Lieutenant General, had opportunely prefented itfelf to the enemy's rigour, and had been detained in their prifons, the order for the voyage would not have been thought, by that individual, quite thrown away. Detention, with or without the troops, of a troublefome and bold complainant, could not be immaterial or unimportant to fuch a perfon, and the order was of an import

" —To make affurance double fure—
" And take a bond of fate—
" That he might tell pale-hearted Fear it lied."

The living prefence of an injured man is, perhaps, more offenfive and infupportable to the fight of a mean injurer, that the fpectre of him would be after death.

But to return to the facts I was recapitulating.

I remained under the conditional order in England.

The enfuing feffion, the parliamentary enquiry now laid before the ·public took place. It ended, as has been ftated, in July, 1779.

In September, I received a fevere reprimand, a denial of a court-martial, and a prohibition of ferving my country in its exigence, though other officers precifely in my fituation were employed—I refigned.

The blame laid upon me for the part I took in thefe tranfactions is, that intemperately and factioufly I engaged in oppofition; that I was guilty of difobedience to the King's orders; and it has been added in a late publication, that even my defence of my conduct is a libel upon the King's government.

I think I have perceived, that the firft part of thefe charges, a rafh engagement in oppofition, is not combated by fome who wifh me well fo ftrenuoufly as other imputations have been. It may poffibly have appeared to friendly and prudential obfervers, as a palliating plea for a reftitution to favour upon fome future occafion, to have to fay, that I had acted upon the fudden impulfe of paffion; and the fequel might be, that I had repented, and would offend no more.

Without doubting the kindnefs which fuggefts thefe excufes, I have been impelled by principles too forcible, and have taken my part too decidedly, to look for a refource in thofe or any other fubterfuges. It would be inconfiftent and difhonourable in me to withhold a public declaration upon this occafion, in addition

to

to thofe I have made upon others, that I engaged in refiftance to the meafures of the court upon mature reflection; that after collecting in my mind all the lights upon men and things which my experience and obfervation could furnifh, I believed that the conftitution of England was betrayed: and neither blaming or fufpecting any men who conceived different opinions, and acted upon them, I thought it a point of time in which a man believing as I did was called upon to facrifice to his country. The teft of this motive, it is true, muft reft between God and my confcience: but let it not be fuppofed that I acted blindly—the path of intereft, a broad and beaten track, lay clearly before me from the time I arrived in England. Supple joints, and an attentive eye, always giving way to power, on one fide, and fometimes pufhing my friends into the dirt on the other, would have carried me fafely through. I even believe, that the advifer of the letters I lately alluded to would rather have feen me in that track, than in the other which he prefcribed for me acrofs the Atlantic. ·

As little would I be fuppofed to want difcernment of the path I took : for the barefaced preferences, rewards and punifhments held forth for parliamentary conduct, were among the moft glaring parts of the fyftem I had contemplated. And it was impoffible to doubt, that as a delinquent *there*, I fhould be preffed both by art and vengeance to the end the enemies I had provoked forefaw—the lofs of my profeffion and the impoverifhment of my fortune. I truft it will be an innocent revenge on my part, to fhew them I can bear my condition firmly ; and that I am incapable of redeeming what I have loft, were it ever in my option, by the difavowal of a fingle principle I have profeffed.

I come now to the fecond charge, difobedience of orders ; and in a point that fo nearly touches the very cffence of military character, I truft I fhall not trefpafs upon the patience of the reader, if I treat it a little more at large than I have done in my correfpondence with the fecretary at war.

I admit that fubordination and implicit obedience, as applied to the operation of arms, are primary principles in the military fyftem. An army is a mere name without them. The officer who hefitates to meet certain death upon command, deferves to receive it from the hand of the executioner.

But there are poffible exceptions to thefe general principles, efpecially out of the field, in the moft abfolute fervices ; and in the Britifh fervice they are known and marked, and co-exiftent with the military eftablifhment itfelf, in the mutiny act, which confines obedience to legal commands. An army muft again be garbled like the army of Cromwell (which God avert !) before an order could be executed, like that of Cromwell, for garbling the parliament.

A high fpirit will contract the limits of obedience ftill more ; with illegal, he will reject difhonourable commands ; and he will follow the reafoning I have already premifed, and ftate it as a maxim thus: *he who obeys at the expence of for-*
tune,

tune, comfort, health and life, is a soldier; he who obeys at the expence of honour is a slave.

But I may be asked by some disciplinarians, who is to be the judge in these nice definitions of obedience? It is uncommon military doctrine, I may be told, to reason upon the King's orders—I confess it is so. Since the reign of James the Second, in the British service it never has been necessary. We have been used in this age, to see the King's name give wings and inspiration to duty. Discipline, in this country, has been raised upon personal honour—a firmer basis than fear or servility ever furnished: and the minister who first shakes that happy confidence; who turns military command to political craft; who dares to use his gracious Sovereign's name as an engine of state, to glut his own anger, or to remove his own fears, he is amongst the worst enemies to that Sovereign. But should his purposes go further (a consideration of far greater magnitude to the public) and should it be seen that the royal name was brought forth for the *discipline* of parliament, the minister so using it would be not only an enemy to his Sovereign, but a traitor to the constitution of the state.

I will close the defence of my principles respecting military subordination by reference to an anecdote well authenticated and not very remote.

An officer in a neighbouring nation, for some error he had committed in a day of battle, received a blow from his prince who commanded in person. The officer drew a pistol, and his first movement was to point it at his master; but the next (and it was instantaneous) was to turn the muzzle, and discharge the ball into his own heart. Though my case differs both in the provocation and the consequence, in many circumstances my conduct may justly be supported upon the same principle. I receive an affront that a liberal spirit cannot endure; and in a name, against which no personal resentment can be pursued, nor indeed entertained: but a suicide of my professional existence (if I may be allowed the phrase) is preferable to the state in which the affront placed me. In one instance only I renounce the parallel— God forbid I should be thought, even in a burst of passion, to have pointed at my Sovereign! It was not from his hand I received the blow.

I shall solicit the reader's attention very little further: but I feel the necessity of repeating my application to the candour of the public, both as a writer and an appellant. Defence, and imputation of blame to others, are naturally interwoven in my cause: it required a more distinct conception, and an abler hand than mine, to keep them always apart, and open to separate view. In some parts my defence may be weakened by this deficiency of skill: but I have no right to offer the same excuse for suffering any blame to rest upon others beyond what I thought myself justified to support.

Upon this principle, I think it just, at taking leave of the secretary of state for the American department, briefly to enumerate the only facts and propositions re-

3. *specting*

fpecting the plan of the expedition from Canada, that I think clearly maintainable againft him.

Firft fact. It is clear that the plan of a junction of the greater part of the forces in Canada with the army of Sir William Howe, was formed in the year 1776, when Sir William Howe was in full fuccefs ; when his whole force was in the neighbourhood, of New York, or in the Jerfies, and Mr. Wafhington was beaten, and at the weakeft.

Second fact. This plan of a junction was continued (and upon juft reafoning) in the clofe of the year 1776, when Sir William Howe's firft propofal of operations for the enfuing campaign arrived. Thofe propofals were made upon the datum of a number of troops, fufficient to furnifh, befides the main army, an *offenfive* army of 10,000 men, rank and file, to act on the fide of Rhode Ifland, by taking poffeffion of Providence, and penetrating from thence into the country towards Bofton ; and another *offenfive* army, not lefs than 10,000, to move up the North River to Albany, exclufive of 5000 for the defence of New York.

In either of the above cafes, the plan of junction could hardly have failed of fuccefs.

Third fact. On the 23d of February, Sir William Howe's alteration of the firft plan was received, and he then propofed to act with the greater part of his force on the fide of Philadelphia, at the opening of the campaign, and to enable him fo to do, to defer the *offenfive plan from Rhode Ifland till the reinforcements fhould arrive*, and to deftine only 3000 men to act *defenfively* upon the lower part of the Hudfon's River.

Fourth fact. On the 3d of March, the fecretary of ftate fignified his Majefty's entire approbation of this deviation from the plan firft fuggefted.

From thefe facts arifes my firft propofition, that at the time the change of plan for Sir William Howe's operations was adopted, by which no offenfive force was to remain upon the Hudfon's River, nor a diverfion probably to take place from Rhode Ifland, the plan of my operations, the fuccefs of which would probably depend in a great degree upon co-operation and diverfion, ought to have been changed likewife : inftead of that, it was enforced and made pofitive by the refufal of the latitude I had propofed of acting upon the Connecticut, or, in cafe of exigency, embarking the troops and effecting the junction by fea.

Fifth fact. On the 19th of March, a letter from Sir William Howe, by the fecretary of ftate, acquainting him, that a brigade of Britifh and fome companies of brigadiers and light infantry had been withdrawn from Rhode Ifland, which made the force left there merely defenfive. The fame letter mentions the profpects the enemy had of bringing 50,000 men into the field.

Sixth fact. I did not leave England till the beginning of April, by which time the fecretary of ftate muft have known, or ought to have known, that no dependance could be placed upon reinforcements from England arriving at New York in time for Sir William Howe to refume the intention he had deferred, viz. a diverfion from Rhode Ifland, or of making the force upon the Hudfon's River adequate to offenfive operation.

Hence arifes my fecond propofition, that the latitude I had propofed, or other expedients of precaution, ought then at leaft to have been adopted : inftead of which, I was fuffered to fail, ignorant of Sir William Howe's plans, and ignorant of the defalcation or the delays in the reinforcements deftined for him. The confequence was, that neither his letter to Sir Guy Carleton, put into my hands after my arrival in Canada, nor his letter to me of the 17th of June, informing me of his deftination for Penfylvania, removed my expectation of co-operation, becaufe I was to fuppofe, that fubfequent to the dates of either of thofe letters, he would receive orders from the fecretary of ftate refpecting the junction, and alfo a timely reinforcement.

Seventh fact. The fecretary of ftate makes no mention of the northern expedition in any of his difpatches to Sir William Howe at the end of March, when my orders were fixed, nor in the month of April. And it is a further fact, that I am perfuaded will not be contefted, that he did not mention any orders or recommendations relative to co-operation verbally to Sir William Howe's aid-de-camp, or any other confidential perfon who failed about that time.

The firft mention made of the neceffity of co-operation was in the fecretary of ftate's letter of the 18th of May, wherein his Lordfhip " Trufts that whatever he [Sir William Howe] may meditate, it will be executed in time to co-operate with the army ordered to proceed from Canada."

The propofition clearly juftified by thefe facts is, that if the fecretary of ftate had thought proper to fignify the King's expectation of a co-operation to be made in my favour in the month of March or beginning of April, as in confiftency he ought to have done, it would have arrived before Sir William Howe embarked his army, and in time for him to have made a new difpofition : but inftead of that, this very material injunction was not difpatched till it was almoft phyfically impoffible it fhould have any effect. And fo indeed it happened, for Sir William Howe received it on the 16th of Auguft, at a diftance from Hudfon's River too great for any detachment from his own army to be made in time, could it even have been fpared ; and the reinforcement from England, upon which Sir William Howe depended to ftrengthen Sir Henry Clinton, was much later ftill—too late (as it has been fhewn) to enable that general with all his activity and zeal to give any effectual fupport.

Indeed the conduct of the fecretary of ftate, in inferting this paragraph, in his letter of the 18th of May, when it could not avail, after omitting it when certainly it would have been timely, feems fo prepofterous, that it can only be explained by one fact. It tranfpired about that time, that Sir William Howe's army was deftined for Penfylvania, and people who had confidered the force of the enemy to be collected from the northern provinces began to be alarmed for my army. It is well known

(though

(though I cannot afcertain the date) that an officer of very great ability, and a per. fect knowledge in the country through which I was to pafs, as-foon as he heard no difpofition was made for a fupport from New York, foretold to the fecretary of ftate, or his near friends, the fall of my army. Under this apprehenfion it might appear to the fecretary of ftate a proper caution, that an expectation of co-operation fhould exift under his hand.

If plans fo inconfiftently formed, and managed by the fecretary of ftate with fo much feeming confidence, as to miflead his generals, and fo much real referve as to deftroy them, fhould be defended by that infatuated belief then entertained of the inability of the enemy to refift, I fhould beg leave to ftate, as one propofition more, that after the experience of their actions at Trenton, and many other places, and the intelligence of their new levies received from Sir William Howe, fuch con. fidence was an additional fault, and perhaps a more pernicious one than any I have ftared.

Thus much for the noble Lord in his public capacity. What fhare of the perfe- cution I have fuftained (more than I have directly expreffed in different parts of my defence) are imputable to his private councils, is not within my knowledge: but if in fpeaking of my perfecutors in general, I may be thought fometimes to have ufed ftrong terms, I have only to fay, that having advanced no fact which I am not able and refolved to maintain, I have not felt myfelf called upon, in applying thofe facts for any further attention, than to preferve the language of a gentleman, which is an attention due to myfelf as well as to the public. It is open and manly enmity alone that unites refpect with refentment.

I wifh I could as eafily apologife for all the other faults with which this under- taking abounds as a compofition. At a time when fo many pens are employed, I muft not expect to be fpared. I fhall treat with filent refpect any comments that are fairly founded and delivered with liberality; and with contempt, equally filent, the common invectives of the political prefs. This appeal is not to teft upon li- terary criticifm, or party difputation, but upon the broad equity of my country. I know that prejudice and malice will vanifh before the man who dares to fubmit his actions to that teft—If acquitted *there*, I feel I am not degraded; and I have not a fenfation within my breaft which does not at the fame time affure me, I can- not be unhappy.

J. BURGOYNE.

APPEN-

A P P E N D I X.

Copy of a Letter from Lieutenant General Burgoyne *to Lord* George Germain, *dated*
Hertford-Street, *1ſt* January, 1777.

MY LORD,

MY phyſician has preſſed me to go to Bath for a ſhort time, and I find it requiſite to my health and ſpirits to follow his advice: but I think it a previous duty to
aſſure your Lordſhip, that ſhould my attendance in town become neceſſary, relatively to information upon the affairs of Canada, I ſhall be ready to obey your
ſummons upon one day's notice.

Your Lordſhip being out of town, I ſubmitted the above intentions a few days
ago perſonally to his Majeſty in his cloſet; and I added, " That as the arrangements for the next campaign might poſſibly come under his royal contemplation
before my return, I humbly laid myſelf at his Majeſty's feet for ſuch active employment as he might think me worthy of."

This was the ſubſtance of my audience, on my part. I undertook it, and I now
report it to your Lordſhip in the hope of your patronage in this purſuit; a hope,
my Lord, founded not only upon a juſt ſenſe of the honour your Lordſhip's friendſhip muſt reflect upon me, but alſo upon a feeling that I deſerve it, in as much
as a ſolid reſpect and ſincere perſonal attachment can conſtitute ſuch a claim.

I leave in the hands of Mr. D'Oyley ſuch of the memorandums confided to me
by General Carleton as require diſpatch, ſhould your Lordſhip think proper to
carry them into execution.

I alſo leave in that gentleman's hands the copy of an application relative to boats
for the artillery, and which I take the liberty to ſubmit to your Lordſhip as well
worthy of conſideration, upon the ſuppoſition that the enemy ſhould arm upon
Lake George, and that any operation ſhould be adviſeable by that route.

I likewiſe leave the diſpoſition of winter quarters, which I received by the laſt
ſhip from Canada. I find no diſpatch is come to your Lordſhip by that occaſion,
and I conceived thoſe papers might be of uſe.

I have the honour to be,
My Lord, &c.
J. BURGOYNE.

Extract of a Letter from Lord George Germain *to Sir* Guy Carleton, *dated* Whitehall, 22d Auguſt, 1776.

THE rapid ſucceſs of his Majeſty's arms, in driving the rebels out of Canada,
does great honour to your conduct, and I hope ſoon to hear that you have been
able to purſue them acroſs the lakes, and to poſſeſs thoſe poſts upon the frontiers
which may effectually ſecure your province from any future inſult.

T His

A P P E N D I X.

His Majefty, in appointing you commander in chief of his forces in Canada, was pleafed to extend your commiffion to the frontiers of his provinces bordering thereupon, wifely forefeeing, that it might be neceffary for the compleating your plan of operations, that you fhould march your army beyond the limits of your own government. I truft, before this letter reaches you, that you will, by your fpirit and activity, have cleared the frontiers of Canada of all the rebel forces, and will have taken the proper meafures for keeping poffeffion of the lakes. That fervice being performed, his Majefty commands me to acquaint you, that there ftill remains another part of your duty to be undertaken, which will require all your abilities and the ftricteft application, the reftoring peace, and the eftablifh-ing good order and legal government in Canada. It is an object of the greateft importance to this country, the difficulties attending it are immenfe; but his Majefty depends upon your zeal, and upon your experience, for carrying it into execution. His Majefty, ever anxious for the happinefs of his fubjects, com-mands me to inform you, that no time fhould be loft in beginning fo important a work, and that you do therefore return to Quebec, detaching Lieutenant-General Burgoyne, or fuch other officer as you fhall think moft proper, with that part of your forces which can be fpared from the immediate defence of your province, to carry on fuch operations as fhall be moft conducive to the fuccefs of the army acting on the fide of New-York; and that you direct the officer fo detached to commu-nicate with and put himfelf, as foon as poffible, under the command of General Howe, you will order fuch artillery as you fhall judge neceffary to proceed with this detachment; and as a great quantity of heavy cannon and military ftores were fent, upon the fuppofition that Quebec might have been in the hands of the rebels, you will, upon requifition from General Howe, fupply him with fuch cannon and ftores as may not be wanted for the protection of Canada.

No. III.   *Thoughts for conducting the War from the Side of* Canada.

By Lieutenant-General Burgoyne.

WHEN the laft fhips came from Quebec, a report prevailed in Canada, faid to have been founded upon pofitive evidence, that the rebels had laid the keels of feveral large veffels at Skenefborough and Ticonderoga, and were refolved to exert their utmoft powers, to conftruct a new and formidable fleet during the winter.

I will not, however, give credit to their exertions, in fuch a degree as to imagine the King's troops will be prevented paffing Lake Champlain early in the fummer, but will fuppofe the operations of the army to begin from Crown Point.

But as the prefent means to form effectual plans is to lay down every poffible difficulty, I will fuppofe the enemy in great force at Ticonderoga; the different works there are capable of admitting twelve thoufand men.

I will fuppofe him alfo to occupy Lake George with a confiderable naval ftrength, in order to fecure his retreat, and afterwards to retard the campaign; and it is natural to expect that he will take meafures to block up the roads from Ticonderoga to Albany by the way of Skenefborough, by fortifying the ftrong ground at different places, and thereby obliging the King's army to carry a
weight

weight of artillery with it, and by felling trees, breaking bridges, and other obvious impediments, to delay, though he fhould not have power or fpirit finally to refift, its progrefs.

The enemy thus difpofed upon the fide of Canada, it is to be confidered what troops will be neceffary, and what difpofition of them will be moft proper to profecure the campaign with vigour and effect.

I humbly conceive the operating army (I mean exclufively of the troops left for the fecurity of Canada) ought not to confift of lefs than eight thoufand regulars, rank and file. The artillery required in the memorandums of General Carleton, a corps of watermen, two thoufand Canadians, including hatchet-men and other workmen, and one thoufand or more favages.

It is to be hoped that the reinforcement and the victuallIng fhips may all be ready to fail from the Channel and from Corke on the laft day of March. I am perfuaded that to fail with a fleet of tranfports earlier, is to fubject government to lofs and difappointment. It may reafonably be expected that they will reach Quebec before the 20th of May, a period in full time for opening the campaign. The roads, and the rivers and lakes, by the melting and running off of the fnows, are in common years impracticable fooner.

But as the weather long before that time will probably have admitted of labour in the docks, I will take for granted that the fleet of laft year, as well bateaux as armed veffels, will be found repaired, augmented, and fit for immediate fervice. The magazines that remain of provifion, I believe them not to be abundant, will probably be formed at Montreal, Sorel and Chamblée.

I conceive the firft bufinefs for thofe entrufted with the chief powers, fhould be to felect and poft the troops deftined to remain in Canada; to throw up the military ftores and provifion with all poffible difpatch, in which fervice the abovementioned troops, if properly pofted, will greatly affift; and to draw the army deftined for operation to cantonments, within as few days march of St. John's as conveniently may be. I fhould prefer cantonments at that feafon of the year to encampment, as the ground is very damp, and confequently very pernicious to the men, and more efpecially as they will have been for many months before ufed to lodgings, heated with ftoves, or between decks in fhips; all thefe operations may be put in motion together, but they feverally require fome obfervation.

I fhould wifh that the troops left in Canada, fuppofing the number mentioned in my former memorandum to be approved, might be made as follows.

	Rank and File.
The 31ft regiment, Britifh, exclufive of their light company of grenadiers — — —	448
Maclean's corps — — —	300
The 29th regiment — — —	448
The ten additional companies from Great Britain —	560
Brunfwic and Heffe Hanau to be taken by detachments or complete corps, as Major General Reidefel fhall recommend, leaving the grenadiers, light infantry and dragoons compleat —	650
Detachments from the other Britifh brigades, leaving the grenadiers and light infantry complete and fquaring the battalions equally — — —	600
	3006

My reason for selecting the 31st regiment for this duty is, that when I saw it last it was not equally in order with the other regiments for services of activity.

I propose the 29th regiment as it is not at present brigaded.

I propose Maclean's corps, because I very much apprehend desertion from such parts of it as are composed of Americans, should they come near the enemy. In Canada, whatsoever may be their disposition, it is not so easy to effect it.

And I propose making up the residue by detachment, because by selecting the men least calculated for fatigue or least accustomed to it, which may be equally good soldiers in more confined movements and better provided situations, the effective strength for operation is much greater and the defensive strength not impaired.

I must beg leave to state the expeditious conveyance of provision and stores from Quebec, and the several other depositaries, in order to form ample magazines at Crown Point, as one of the most important operations of the campaign, because it is upon that which most of the rest will depend. If sailing vessels up the St. Lawrence are alone to be employed, the accident of contrary winds may delay them two months before they pass the rapids of Richelieu, and afterwards St. Peter's Lake; delays to that extent are not uncommon, and they are only to be obviated by having a quantity of small craft in readiness to work with oars. From the mouth of the Sorrel to Chamblée, rowing and tacking is a sure conveyance if sufficient hands are found. From Chamblée to St. Therese (which is just above the Rapids) land-carriage must be used, and great authority will be requisite to supply the quantity necessary.

A business thus complicated in arrangement, in some parts unusual in practice, and in others perhaps difficult, can only be carried to the desired effect by the peremptory powers, warm zeal, and consonant opinion of the governor; and though the former are not to be doubted, a failure in the latter, vindicated, or seeming to be vindicated, by the plausible obstructions that will not fail to be suggested by others, will be sufficient to crush such exertions as an officer of a sanguine temper, entrusted with the future conduct of the campaign, and whose personal interest and fame therefore consequentially depend upon a timely out-set, would be led to make.

The assembly of the savages and the Canadians will also entirely depend upon the go e o.

Under these considerations, it is presumed, that the general officer employed to proceed with the army will be held to be out of the reach of any possible blame till he is clear of the province of Canada, and furnished with the proposed supplies.

The navigation of Lake Champlain, secured by the superiority of our naval force, and the arrangements for forming proper magazines so established as to make the execution certain, I would not lose a day to take possession of Crown Point with Brigadier Fraser's corps, a large body of savages, a body of Canadians, both for scouts and works, and the best of our engineers and artificers well supplied with intrenching tools.

The brigade would be sufficient to prevent insult during the time necessary for collecting the stores, forming magazines, and fortifying the posts; all which should be done to a certain degree, previous to proceeding in force to Ticonderoga;

roga; to fuch a degree I mean as may be fuppofed to be effected in time of tranf-
porting artillery, preparing fafcines, and other neceffaries for artillery operations;
and by keeping the reft of the army back during that period, the tranfport of
provifions wil be leffened, and the foldiers made of ufe in forwarding the convoys.

But though there would be only one brigade at Crown Point at that time, it
does not follow that the enemy fhould remain in a ftate of tranquility. Corps of
favages, fupported by detachments of light regulars, fhould be continually on foot
to keep them in alarm, and within their works to cover the reconnoitering of
general officers and engineers, and to obtain the beft intelligence of their ftrength,
pofition, and defign.

If due exertion is made in the preparations ftared above, it may be hoped that
Ticonderoga will be reduced early in the fummer, and. it will then become a
more proper place for arms than Crown Point.

The next meafure muft depend upon thofe taken by the enemy, and upon the
general plan of the campaign as concerted at home. If it be determined that
General Howe's whole forces fhould act upon Hudfon's River, and to the fouthward of it, and that the only object of the Canada army be to effect a junction
with that force, the immediate poffeffion of Lake George would be of great confequence, as the moft expeditious and moft commodious route to Albany; and
fhould the enemy be in force upon that lake, which is very probable, every effort
fhould be tried, by throwing favages and light troops round it, to oblige them to
quit it without waiting for naval preparations. Should thofe efforts fail, the
route by South Bay and Skenefborough might be attempted, but confiderable difficulties may be expected, as the narrow parts of the river may be eafily choaked
up and rendered impaffable, and at beft there will be neceffity for a great deal of
of land carriage for the artillery, provifion, &c. which can only be fupplied from
Canada. In cafe of fuccefs alfo by that route, and the enemy not removed from
Lake George, it will be neceffary to leave a chain of pofts, as the army proceeds,
for the fecurities of your communication, which may too much weaken fo fmall an
army.

Left all thefe attempts fhould unavoidably fail, and it become indifpenfibly
neceffary to attack the enemy by water upon Lake George, the army at the outfet
fhould be provided with carriages, implements, and artificers, for conveying
armed veffels from Ticonderoga to the lake.

Thefe ideas are formed upon the fuppofition, that it be the fole purpofe of rhe
Canada army to effect a junction with General Howe, or after co-operating fo far
as to get poffeffion of Albany and open the communication to New-York, to
remain upon the Hudfon's River, and thereby enable that general to act with his
whole force to the fouthward.

But fhould the ftrength of the main American army be fuch as to admit of the
corps of troops now at Rhode, Ifland remaining there during the winter, and acting
feparately in the fpring, it may be highly worthy confideration, whether the moft
important purpofe to which the Canada army could be employed, fuppofing it in
poffeffion of Ticonderoga, would not be to gain the Connecticut River.

The extent of country from Ticonderoga to the inhabited country upon that
river, oppofite to Charles Town, is about fixty miles, and though to convey artillery and provifion fo far by land would be attended with difficulties, perhaps more
than

than thofe above fuggefted, upon a progrefs to Skenefborough, fhould the objeft
appear worthy, it is to be hoped refources might be found; in that cafe it would
be advifeable to fortify with one or two ftrong redoubts the heights oppofite to
Charles Town, and eftablifh pofts of favages upon the paffage from Ticonderoga
to thofe heights, to preferve the communication, and at the fame time prevent
any attempt from the country above. Charles Town, which is very populous, from
molefting the rear or interrupting the convoys of fupply, while the army proceeded
down the Connecticut. Sould the junction between the Canada and Rhode Ifland
armies be effected upon the Connecticut, it is not too fanguine an expectation that
all the New England provinces will be reduced by their operations.

To avoid breaking in upon other matter, I omitted in the beginning of thefe
papers to ftate the idea of an expedition at the outfet of the campaign by the Lake
Ontario and Ofwego to the Mohawk River, which, as a diverfion to facilitate every
propofed operation, would be highly defirable, provided the army fhould be reinforced fufficiently to afford it.

It may at firft appear, from a view of the prefent ftrength of the army, that it
may bear the fort of detachment propofed by myfelf laft year for this purpofe; but
it is to be confidered that at that time the utmoft object of the campaign, from the
advanced feafon and unavoidable delay of preparation for the lakes, being the
reduction of Crown Point and Ticonderoga, unlefs the fuccefs of my expedition
had opened the road to Albany, no greater numbers were neceffary than for thofe
firft operations. The cafe in the prefent year differs; becaufe the feafon of the
year affording a profpect of very extenfive operation, and confequently the eftablifhment of many pofts, patroles, &c. will become neceffary. The army ought
to be in a ftate of numbers to bear thofe drains, and ftill remain fufficient to attack
any thing that probably can be oppofed to it.

Nor, to argue from probability, is fo much force neceffary for this diverfion
this year, as was required for the laft; becaufe we then knew that General Schuyler
with a thoufand men, was fortified upon the Mohawk. When the different fituations of things are confidered, viz. the progrefs of General Howe, the early
invafion from Canada, the threatening of the Connecticut from Rhode Ifland, &c.
it is not to be imagined that any detachment of fuch force as that of Schulyer can be
fupplied by the enemy for the Mohawk. I would not therefore propofe it of more
(and I have great diffidence whether fo much can be prudently afforded) than Sir
John Johnfon's corps, an hundred Britifh from the fecond brigade, and an hundred
more from the 8th regiment, with four pieces of the lighteft artillery, and a body
of favages; Sir John Johnfon to be with a detachment in perfon, and an able field
officer to command it. I fhould wifh Lieutenant Colonel St. Leger for that employment.

I particularize the fecond brigade, becaufe the firft is propofed to be diminifhed
by the 31ft regiment remaining in Canada, and the reft of the regiment drafted
for the expedition being made alfo part of the Canada force, the two brigades will
be exactly fquared.

Should it appear, upon examination of the really effective numbers of the Canada
army, that the force is not fufficient for proceeding upon the above ideas with a
fair profpect of fuccefs, the alternative remains of embarking the army at Quebec,
in order to effect a junction with General Howe by fea, or to be employed feparately

rately to co-operate with the main defigns, by fuch means as fhould be within their ftrength upon other parts of the continent. And though the army, upon examination of the numbers from the returns here, and the reinforcements defigned, fhould appear adequate, it is humbly fubmitted, as a fecurity againft the poffibility of its remaining inactive, whether it might not be expedient to entruft the latitude of embarking the army by fea to the commander in chief, provided any accidents during the winter, and unknown here, fhould have diminifhed the numbers confiderably, or that the enemy, from any winter fuccefs to the fouthward, fhould have been able to draw fuch forces towards the frontiers of Canada, and take up their ground with fuch precaution, as to render the intended meafure impracticable or too hazardous. But in that cafe it muft be confidered that more force would be required to be left behind for the fecurity of Canada, than is fuppofed to be neceffary when an army is beyond the lakes; and I do not conceive any expedition from the fea can be fo formidable to the enemy, or fo effectual to clofe the war, as an invafion from Canada by Ticonderoga. This laft meafure ought not to be thought of, but upon pofitive conviction of its neceffity.

Hertford-Street, Feb. 28th, 1777.   J. BURGOYNE.

Extract of a Letter from Lord George Germain *to General* Carleton, *dated* Whitehall, 26*th* March, 1777.   No. IV.

MY letter of the 22d Auguft, 1776, was intrufted to the care of Captain Le Maitre, one of your aid-de-camps; after having been three times in the Gulph of St. Lawrence he had the mortification to find it impoffible to make his paffage to Quebec, and therefore returned to England with my difpatch; which, though it was prevented by that accident from reaching your hands in due time, I neverthelefs think proper to tranfmit to you by this earlieft opportunity.

You will be informed, by the contents thereof, that as foon as you fhould have driven the rebel forces from the frontiers of Canada, it was his Majefty's pleafure that you fhould return to Quebec, and take with you fuch part of your army as in your judgment and difcretion appeared fufficient for the defence of the province; that you fhould detach Lieutenant General Burgoyne, or fuch other officer as you fhould think moft proper, with the remainder of the troops, and direct the officer fo detached to proceed with all poffible expedition to join General Howe, and to put himfelf under his command.

With a view of quelling the rebellion as foon as poffible, it is become highly neceffary that the moft fpeedy junction of the two armies fhould be effected; and therefore, as the fecurity and good government of Canada abfolutely require your prefence there, it is the King's-determination to leave about 3000 men under your command, for the defence and duties of that province, and to employ the remainder of your army upon two expeditions, the one under the command of Lieutenant General Burgoyne, who is to force his way to Albany, and the other under the command of Lieutenant Colonel St. Leger, who is to make a diverfion on the Mohawk River.

As this plan cannot be advantageoufly executed without the affiftance of Canadians and Indians, his Majefty ftrongly recommends it to your care, to furnifh both

expe-

expeditions with good and fufficient bodies of thofe men ; and I am happy in knowing that your influence among them is fo great, that there can be no room to apprehend you will find it difficult to fulfil his Majefty's expectations.

In order that no time may be loft in entering upon thefe important undertakings,
General Burgoyne has received orders to fail forthwith for Quebec ; and that the intended operations may be maturely confidered, and afterwards carried on in fuch a
manner as is moft likely to be followed by fuccefs, he is directed to confult with you
upon the fubject, and to form and adjuft the plan as you both fhall think moft conducive to his Majefty's fervice.

I am alfo to acquaint you, that as foon as you fhall have fully regulated every
thing relative to thefe expeditions (and the King relies upon your zeal, that you will
be as expeditious as the nature of the bufinefs will admit) it is his Majefty's pleafure that you detain for the Canada fervice

The 8th regiment, deducting 100 for the expedition to the Mohawk	460
Battalion companies of the 29th and 31ft regiments — —	896
Battalion companies of the 34th, deducting 100 for the expedition to the Mohawk — — —	348
Eleven additional companies from Great Britain — —	616
Detachments from the two brigades — —	300
Detachments from the German troops — —	650
Royal Highland emigrants — —	500
	3770

You will naturally conclude that this allotment for Canada has not been made
without properly weighing the feveral duties which are likely to be required. His
Majefty has not only confidered the feveral garrifons and pofts which probably it may
be neceffary for you to take, viz. Quebec, Chaudiére, the difaffected parifhes of
Point Levi, Montreal, and pofts between that town and Ofwegatche, Trois Rivieres,
St. John's, Sele aux Noix, La Prairie, Vergere, and fome other towns upon the
fouth fhore of St. Lawrence, oppofite the ifle of Montreal, with pofts of communication to St. John's, but he hath alfo reflected that the feveral operations which will
be carrying on in different parts of America muft neceffarily confine the attention
of the rebels to the refpective fcenes of action, and fecure Canada from external attacks, and that the internal quiet which at prefent prevails is not likely to be interrupted, or if interrupted, will foon be reftored by your influence over the inhabitants ; he therefore trufts that 3000 men will be quite fufficient to anfwer every
poffible demand.

It is likewife his Majefty's pleafure that you put under the command of Lieutenant General Burgoyne

The grenadiers and light infantry of the army (except of the 8th regiment and the 24th regiment) as the advanced corps under the command of Brigadier General Frafer — —	1568
Firft brigade, battalion companies of the 9th, 21ft, and 47th regiments, de- ducting a detachment of 50 from each corps, to remain in Canada	1194
Second brigade, battalion companies of the 20th, 53d, and 62d regiments, de- ducting 50 from each corps to remain as above —	1194

Carried over	3956

Brought over   3956

All the German troops, except the Hanau chaffeurs, and a detachment of 650, 3217
The artillery, except fuch parts as fhall be neceffary for the defence of Canada.

7173

Together with as many Canadians and Indians as may be thought neceffary for this fervice; and after having furnifhed him in the fulleft and compleateft manner with artillery, ftores, provifions, and every other article neceffary for his expedition, and fecured to him every affiftance which it is in your power to afford and procure, you are to give him orders to pals Lake Champlain, and from thence, by the moft vigorous exertion of the force under his command, to proceed with all expedition to Albany, and put himfelf under the command of Sir William Howe.

From the King's knowledge of the great preparations made by you laft year to fecure the command of the lakes, and your attention to this part of the fervice during the winter, his Majefty is led to expect that every thing will be ready for General Burgoyne's paffing the lakes by the time you and he fhall have adjufted the plan of the expedition.

It is the King's further pleafure that you put under the command of Lieutenant Colonel St. Leger,

Detachment from the 8th regiment	—	—	100
Detachment from the 34th regiment	—	—	100
Sir John Johnfon's regiment of New York	—	—	133
Hanau chaffeurs —	—	—	342

675

Together with a fufficient number of Canadians and Indians; and after having furnifhed him with proper artillery, ftores, provifions, and every other neceffary article for his expedition, and fecured to him every affiftance in your power to afford and procure, you are to give him orders to proceed forthwith to and down the Mohawk River to Albany, and put himfelf under the command of Sir William Howe.

I fhall write to Sir William Howe from hence by the firft packet; but you will neverthelefs endeavour to give him the earlieft intelligence of this meafure, and alfo direct Lieutenant General Burgoyne, and Lieutenant Colonel St. Leger, to neglect no opportunity of doing the fame, that they may receive inftructions from Sir William Howe. You will at the fame time inform them, that, until they fhall have received orders from Sir William Howe, it is his Majefty's pleafure that they act as exigencies may require, and in fuch manner as they fhall judge moft proper for making an impreffion on the rebels, and bringing them to obedience; but that in fo doing, they muft never lofe view of their intended junctions with Sir William Howe as their principal objects.

In cafe Lieutenant General Burgoyne or Lieutenant Colonel St. Leger fhould happen to die, or be rendered, through illnefs, incapable of executing thofe great trufts, you are to nominate to their refpective commands, fuch officer or officers as you fhall think beft qualified to fupply the place of thofe whom his Majefty has in his wifdom at prefent appointed to conduct thefe expeditions.

U

Copy

APPENDIX.

Copy of a Letter from Lieutenant General Burgoyne *to Lord* George Germain, *dated* Quebec, May 14, 1777.

[Private.]

MY LORD,

I TAKE the opportunity of a veſſel diſpatched by Sir Guy Carleton to England, to inform your Lordſhip of my arrival here the 6th inſtant. And though my preſent ſituation, as acting under a ſuperior upon the ſpot, may make an official correſpondence unneceſſary, I cannot perſuade myſelf I ſhall not appear guilty of impropriety in aſſuming the honour of a private and confidential one, relatively to the objects of my deſtination.

From my preſent information, I have reaſon to expect the preparations for opening the campaign to be very forward on our part. Due exertions were uſed in the courſe of the winter, and the uncommon mildneſs of the weather greatly favoured them, to convey proviſions to Chamblé and St. John's. One large victualler arrived after I left the St. Lawrence laſt November; all reſidues of other victuallers have been collected; I am in hopes of finding a ſufficiency of proviſion to enable me to croſs the Lake Champlain at leaſt, without the arrival of the Corke fleet. I hope alſo to find artillery ſtores enough to feel the pulſe of the enemy at Ticonderoga. Should their ſituation and reſolution be ſuch as to make great artillery preparations requiſite, I ſhall certainly be under the neceſſity of waiting at Crown Point the arrival of the ordnance ſhips from England. A good body of the Indians I am aſſured are ready to move upon the firſt call, and meaſures are taking for bringing them forthwith to proper redezvous.

I cannot ſpeak with ſo much confidence of the military aſſiſtance I am to look for from the Canadians. The only corps yet inſtituted, or that I am informed can at preſent be inſtituted, are three independent companies of 100 men each, officered by Seigneurs of the country, who are well choſen; but they have not been able to engage many volunteers. The men are chiefly drafted from the militia, according to a late regulation of the legiſlative council. Thoſe I have yet ſeen afford no promiſe of uſe of arms—aukward, ignorant, diſinclined to the ſervice, and ſpiritleſs. Various reaſons are aſſigned for this change in the natives ſince the time of the French government. It may partly be owing to a diſuſe of arms, but I believe principally to the unpopularity of their Seigneurs, and to the poiſon which the emiſſaries of the rebels have thrown into their minds. Should I find the new companies up the country better compoſed, or that the well affected parties can be prevailed upon to turn out volunteers, though but for a ſhort occaſion, as they did laſt year, I ſhall move Sir Guy to exert further meaſures to augment my numbers.

The army will fall ſhort of the ſtrength computed in England; the want of the camp equipage, cloathing, and many other neceſſary articles, will cauſe inconvenience; I am neverthelefs determined to put the troops deſtined for my command immediately in motion; and, aſſiſted by the ſpirit and health in which they abound, I am confident in the proſpect of overcoming difficulties and diſappointments.

Having ſettled all meaſures with Sir Guy Carleton, both for this purpoſe and for the expeditious tranſport of the ſtores as they may arrive, and having already diſpatched inſtructions to Captain Lutwidge, who commands the fleet upon Lake Cham-

Champlain, to fecure the navigation, in which I clearly fee he will find no trouble, I fhall proceed in perfon this afternoon for Montreal, and from thence make my final arrangements for purfuing the King's orders.

I fhould think myfelf deficient in juftice and in honour, were I clofe my letter without mentioning the fenfe I entertain of General Carleton's conduct; that he was anxioufly defirous of leading the military operations out of the province, is eafi-ly to be difcerned; but his deference to his Majefty's decifion, and his zeal to give effect to his meafures in my hands, are equally manifeft, exemplary, and fatisfactory. I fhall take every poffible means to tranfmit to your Lordfhip an account of my pro-ceedings from time to time, and have the honour to be, with perfect refpect,

Your Lordfhip's moft obedient and moft humble fervant,

J. BURGOYNE.

P. S. I have mentioned nothing of intelligence concerning the enemy, con-cluding that Sir Guy Carleton will tranfmit the material part of it, and in a manner more full than in my power to do. I underftand they have laboured hard to ftrengthen Ticonderoga, and threaten a vigorous refiftance there, and that they have built fome veffels on Lake George, as your Lordfhip may remember I had forefeen.

Copy of a Letter from Lieutenant General Burgoyne *to Lord* George Germain, *dated*
Montreal, May 19, 1777.

Second
No. V.

MY LORD,

I HAD the honour to write to your Lordfhip the day I left Quebec, having rea-fon to imagine this letter may reach that place in time to be difpatched with my former one, I cannot omit the occafion to inform your Lordfhip, that the hopes I expreffed of being able to put the troops in motion without waiting the arrival of the fleets from England and Ireland, are confirmed.

The only delay is occafioned by the impracticability of the roads, owing to late extraordinary heavy rains, and this difficulty will be fpeedily removed, by exerting the fervices of the parifhes as foon as the weather clears. In the mean time, I am employing every means that water carriage will admit for drawing the troops and ftores towards their point. I truft, I fhall have veffels fufficient to move the army and ftores together, and in that cafe, will take poft at once, within fight of Ticon-deroga, and only make ufe of Crown Point for my hofpital and magazine.

A continuation of intelligence from different fpies and deferrers, confirms the de-fign of the enemy to difpute Ticonderoga vigoroufly. They are alfo building bow-gallies at Fort George, for the defence of that Lake, &c. fortifying on the road to Skenefborough.

It is configned to the New England colonies, to furnifh fupplies of men and pro-vifion to oppofe the progrefs of my army, and they have undertaken the tafk, upon condition of being exempt from fupplying Mr. Wafhington's main army.

It is my defign, while advancing to Ticonderago, and during the fiege of that poft, for a fiege I apprehend it muft be, to give all poffible jealoufy on the fide of Connecticut. If I can by manœuvre lead the enemy to fufpect, that after the reduc-tion of Ticonderago, my views are pointed that way, the Connecticut forces will be

U 2

very

very cautious of leaving their own frontier, and I may gain a ftart that may much expedite and facilitate my progrefs to Albany.

Your Lordfhip may reft affured, that, whatever demonftration I may endeavour to impofe on the enemy, I fhall *really* make no movement that can procraftinate the great objeft of my orders.

I have the honour to be, &c.

J. BURGOYNE.

No. VI.   *Subftance of the Speech of Lieutenant-General* Burgoyne *to the* Indians *in Congrefs, at the Camp upon the River* Bouquet, *June* 21, 1777, *and their Anfwer, tranflated.*

[*In Lieutenant-General* Burgoyne's, June 22, 1777.]

CHIEFS and WARRIORS,

THE great King, our common father, and the patron of all who feek and deferve his proteftion, has confidered with fatisfaction the general conduct of the Indian tribes from the beginning of the troubles in America. Too fagacious and too faithful to be deluded or corrupted, they have obferved the violated rights of the parental power they love, and burned to vindicate them. A few individuals alone, the refufe of a fmall tribe, at the firft were led aftray, and the mifreprefentations, the fpecious al. lurements, the infidious promifes and diverfified plots, in which the rebels are exer-cifed, and all of which they employed for that effect, have ferved only in the end to enhance the honour of the tribes in general, by demonftrating to the world, how few and how contemptible are the apoftates. It is a truth known to you all, that thefe pitiful examples excepted, and they probably have before this day hid their faces in fhame, the collective voices and hands of the Indian tribes over this vaft con-tinent, are on the fide of juftice, of law, and of the King.

The reftraint you have put upon your refentment in waiting the King your father's call to arms, the hardeft proof, I am perfuaded, to which your affection could have been put, is another manifeft and affected mark of your adherence to that principle of connection to which you were always fond to allude, and which it is mutually the joy and the duty of the parent to cherifh.

The clemency of your father has been abufed, the offers of his mercy have been defpifed, and his farther patience would, in his eyes, become culpable, in as much as it would withold redrefs from the moft grievous oppreffions in the provinces that ever dif-graced the hiftory of mankind. It therefore remains for me, the General of one of his Majefty's armies, and in this council his reprefentative, to releafe you from thofe bonds which your obedience impofed.—Warriors, you are free—Go forth in might of your valour and your caufe ; ftrike at the common enemies of Great-Britain and America—difturbers of public order, peace, and happinefs—deftroyers of commerce, parricides of the ftate.

The circle round you, the chiefs of his Majefty's European forces, and of the Princes his allies, efteem you as brothers in the war ; emulous in glory and in friend-fhip, we will endeavour reciprocally to give and to receive examples ; we know how to value, and we will ftrive to imitate your perfeverance in enterprize, and your conftancy to refift hunger, wearinefs, and pain. Be it our tafk, from the dictates of

our

our religion, the laws of our warefare, and the principles and interest of our policy, to regulate your passions when they overbear, to point out were it is nobler to spare than to revenge, to discriminate degrees of guilt, to suspend the up-lifted stroke, to chastise, and not to destroy.

This war to you, my friends, is new ; upon all former occasions in taking the field you held yourselves authorized to destroy wherever you came, because every where you found an enemy. The case is now very different.

The King has many faithful subjects dispersed in the provinces, consequently you have many brothers there ; and these people are the more to be pitied, that they are persecuted, or imprisoned, wherever they are discovered, or suspected, and to dissemble, is, to a generous mind, a yet more grievous punishment.

Persuaded that your magnanimity of character, joined to your principles of affection to the King, will give me fuller controul over your minds, than the military rank with which I am invested, I enjoin your most serious attention to the rules which I hereby proclaim for your invariable observation during the campaign.

I positively forbid bloodshed, when you are not opposed in arms.

Aged men, women, children, and prisoners, must be held sacred from the knife or hatchet, even in the time of actual conflict.

You shall receive compensation for the prisoners you take, but you shall be called to account for scalps.

In conformity and indulgence to your customs, which have affixed an idea of honour to such badges of victory, you shall be allowed to take the scalps of the dead, when killed by your fire, and in fair opposition ; but on no account, or pretence, or subtlety, or prevarication, are they to be taken from the wounded, or even dying; and still less pardonable, if possible, will it be held, to kill men in that condition, on purpose, and upon a supposition, that this protection to the wounded, would be thereby evaded.

Base lurking assassins, incendiaries, ravagers, and plunderers of the country, to whatever army they may belong, shall be treated with less reserve ; but the latitude must be given you by order, and I must be the judge of the occasion.

Should the enemy, on their part, dare to countenance acts of barbarity towards those who may fall into their hands, it shall be yours also to retaliate ; but till severity shall be thus compelled, bear immoveable in your hearts this solid maxim, it cannot be too deeply impressed, that the great essential reward, worthy service of your alliance, the sincerity of your zeal to the King your father, and never-failing protector, will be examined, and judged upon the test only of your steady and uniform adherence to the orders and counsels of those to whom his Majesty has intrusted the direction and the honour of his arms.

Answer from an old Chief of the Iroquois.

I stand up in the name of all the nations present, to assure our father, that we have attentively listened to his discourse, We receive you as our father, because when you speak, we hear the voice of our great father beyond the great lake.

We rejoice in the approbation you have expressed of our behaviour.

We have been tried and tempted by the Bostonians ; but we have loved our father, and our hatchets have been sharpened upon our affections.

In

In proof of the fincerity of our profeffions, our whole villages able to go to war, are come forth. The old and infirm, our infants and wives, alone remain at home.

With one common affent we promife a conftant obedience to all you have ordered, and all you fhall order ; and may the Father of Days give you many and fuccefs.

No. VII.   *Copy of a Letter from General* Burgoyne *to Lord* George Germain, *dated* Skenefborough, July 11th, 1777.

I HAVE the honour to inform your Lordfhip, that the enemy, difloged from Ti-conderoga and Mount Independant, on the 6th inftant, and were driven, on the fame day, beyond Skenefborough on the right, and to Humerton on the left, with the lofs of 128 pieces of cannon, all their armed veffels and bateaux, the greateft part of their baggage and ammunition, provifion, and military ftores, to a very large amount.

This fuccefs has been followed by events equally fortunate and rapid. I fubjoin fuch a detail of circumftances as the time will permit ; and for his Majefty's further information, I beg leave to refer your Lordfhip to Captain Gardner, my aid de camp, whom I thought it neceffary to difpatch with news fo important to the King's fervice and fo honourable to the troops under my command.

Journal of the late principal Proceedings of the Army.

Having remained at Crown-Point three days to bring up the rear of the army, to eftablifh the magazines and the hofpital, and to obtain intelligence of the enemy, on the

30th June.   I ordered the advanced corps, confifting of the Britifh light infantry and grenadiers, the 24th regiment, fome Canadians and Savages, and ten pieces of light artillery, under the command of Brigadier General Frafer, to move from Putnam Creek, where they had been encamped fome days, up the weft fhote of the lake to Four-Mile-Point, fo called from that diftance off the fort of Ticoderoga. The German referve, confifting of the Brunfwick chaffeurs, light infantry and gre-nadiers under Lieutenant Colonel Breyman were moved at the fame time to Richard-fon's farm, oppofite to Putnam Creek.

1ft July.   The whole army made a movement forward. Brigadier Frafer's corps occupied the ftrong poft called Three-Mile-Point, on the weft fhore ; the German referve the eaft-fhore oppofite : the army encamped in two lines, the right wing at the Four-Mile-Point, the left wing nearly oppofite, on the eaft fhore.

The Royal George, and Inflexible frigates, with the gun-boats, were anchored at this time juft without the reach of the enemy's batteries, and covered the lake from the weft to the eaft fhores. The reft of the fleet had been fome time without guns, in order to affift in carrying provifions over Lake Champlain.

The enemy appeared to be pofted as follows. A brigade occupied the old French lines on the height to the north of the fort of Ticonderoga. Thefe lines were in good repair, and had feveral intrenchments behind them, chiefly calculated to guard the north-weft flank, and were further fuftained by a block-houfe. They had, farther to,
                              their

their left, a poft at the faw-mills, which are at the foot of the carrying-place to Lake George, and a block-houfe upon an eminence above the mills, and a block-houfe and hofpital at the entrance of the lake.

Upon the right of the lines, and between them 'and the old fort, there were two new block-houfes and a confiderable battery clofe to the water edge.

It feemed that the enemy had employed their chief induftry, and were in the greateft force upon Mount Independence, which is high and circular, and upon the fummit, which is Table Land, was a ftar fort, made of pickets, and well fupplied with artillery, and a large fquare of barracks within it. The foot of the hill, on the fide which projects into the lake, was intrenched and had a ftrong abbattis clofe to the water. This intrenchment was lined with heavy artillery, pointed down the lake flanking the water battery, above defcribed, and fuftained by another battery about half way up the hill. On the weft fide the hill runs the main river, and in its paffage is joined by the water which comes down from Lake George. The enemy had here a bridge of communication, which could not at this time be reconnoitred. On the eaft fide of the hill the water forms a fmall bay, into which falls a rivulet after having encirculed in its courfe part of the hill to the fouth caft. The fide to the fouth could not be feen, but was defcribed as inacceffible.

About nine in the morning a fmoke was obferved towards Lake George, and the July 2. Savages brought in a report that the enemy had fet fire to the further block-houfe and had abandoned the faw-mills, and that a confiderable body were advancing from the lines towards a bridge upon the road which led from the faw-mills towards the right of the Britifh camp. A detachment of the advanced corps was immediately put in march, under the command of Brigadier Frafer, fupported by the fecond brigade and fome light artillery, under the command of Major General Phillips, with orders to proceed to Mount Hope, which is to the north of the lines, to reconnoitre the enemy's pofition, and to take advantage of any poft they might abandon or be driven from. The Indians under Captain Frafer, fupported by his company of markfmen, were directed to make a circuit to the left of Brigadier Frafer's line of march, and endeavour to cut off the retreat of the enemy to their lines ; but this defign mifcarried through the impetuofity of the Indians, who attacked too foon, and in front; and the enemy were thereby able to retire with the lofs of one officer and a few men killed, and one officer wounded. Major General Phillips took poffeffion of the very advantageous poft of Mount Hope this night, and the enemy were thereby entirely cut off from all communication with Lake George.

Mount Hope was occupied in force by General Frafer's whole corps. The firft July 3. Britifh brigade, and two entire brigades of artillery. The fecond brigade, Britifh, encamped upon the left of the firft, and the brigade of Gall, having been drawn from the eaft fhore to occupy the ground where Frafer's corps had originally been ; the line became compleat, extending from Three-Mile-Point to the weftermoft part of Mount Hope ; on the fame day, Major General Reidefel encamped on the eaft fhore in a parallel line with Three-Mile-Point, having pufhed the referve forward near the rivulet which encircles Mount Independence. The enemy cannonaded the camps of Mount Hope and of the German referve during moft part of this day, but without effect.

The army worked hard at their communications and got up the artillery, tents, July 4. baggage and provifions ; the enemy at intervals continued the cannonade upon the camps, which was not in any inftance returned.

The

The Thunderer Radeau, carrying the battering train and stores, having been warped up from Crown Point, arrived this day, and immediately began to land the artillery.

5th July. Lieutenant Twiss, the commanding engineer, was ordered to reconnoitre Sugar Hill, on the south side of the communion from Lake George into Lake Champlain; which had been possessed in the night by a party of light infantry. It appeared at first to be a very advantageous post, and it is now known that the enemy had a council some time ago upon the expediency of possessing it; but the idea was rejected, upon the supposition that it was impossible for a corps to be established there in force. Lieutenant Twiss reported this hill to have the entire command of the works and buildings both of Ticonderoga and Mount Independence, at the distance of about 1400 yards from the former, and 1500 from the latter; that the ground might be levelled so as to receive cannon, and that the road to convey them, though difficult, might be made practicable in twenty-four hours. This hill also commanded, in reverse, the bridge of communication; saw the exact situation of their vessels; nor could the enemy, during the day, make any material movement or preparation, without being discovered, and even having their numbers counted,

It was determined that a battery should be raised on Sugar Hill for light twenty-four pounders, medium twelves, and eight-inch howitzers. This very arduous work was carried on so rapidly that the battery would have been ready the next day.

It is a duty in this place to do some justice to the zeal and activity of Major General Phillips, who had the direction of the operation, and having mentioned that most valuable officer, I trust it cannot be thought a digression to add, that it is to his judicious arrangements and indefatigable pains, during the general superintendency of preparation which Sir Guy Carleton entrusted to him in the winter and spring, that the service is indebted for its present forwardness. The prevalence of contrary winds and other accidents having rendered it impossible for any necessaries prepared in England for the opening of the campaign, yet to reach the camp.

6th July. Soon after day-light an officer arrived express, on board the Royal George, where in the night I took up my quarters, as the most centrical situation, with information from Brigadier Fraser that the enemy were retiring, and that he was advancing with his picquets, leaving orders for the brigade to follow as soon as they could accoutre, with intention to pursue by land. This movement was very discernible, as were the British colours, which the Brigadier had fixed upon the fort of Ticonderoga. Knowing how safely I could trust to that officer's conduct, I turned my chief attention to the pursuit by water, by which route I understood one column were retiring in two hundred and twenty bateaux, covered by five armed gallies.

The great bridge of communication, through which a way was to be opened, was supported by twenty-two sunken piers of large timber, at nearly equal distances; the space between were made of separate floats, each about fifty feet long, and twelve feet wide, strongly fastened together by chains and rivets, and also fastened to the sunken piers. Before this bridge was a boom, made of very

3   B.   large

large pieces of timber, faftened together by rivetted bolts and double chains, made of iron an inch and an half fquare.   •

The gun-boats were inftantly moved forward, and the boom and one of the intermediate floats were cut with great dexterity and difpatch, and Commodore Lutwidge, with the officers and feamen in his department, partaking the general animation, a paffage was formed in half an hour for the frigates alfo, through impediments which the enemy had been labouring to conftruct fince laft autumn.

During this operation Major General Reidefel had paffed to Mount Independence, with the corps, Breyman, and part of the left wing. He was directed to proceed by land, to fuftain Brigadier Frafer, or to act more to the left, if he faw it expedient fo to do.

The 62d regiment Britifh, and the Brunfwick regiment of Prince Frederick, were ftationed at Ticonderoga and Mount Independence, in the place of the parties of Frafer's brigade, which had been left in poffeffion of the artillery and ftores, and the reft of the army was ordered to follow up the river as they could be collected, without regard to the place in the line.

About three in the afternoon I arrived with the Royal George and Inflexible, and the beft failing gun-boats at South Bay, within three miles of Skenefborough, at which latter place the enemy were pofted in a ftockaded fort, and their armed gallies in the falls below.

The foremoft regiments, viz. the 9th, 20th, and 21ft, were immediately difembarked, and afcended the mountains with the intention of getting behind the fort, and cutting off the retreat of the enemy; but their precipitate flight rendered this manœuvre ineffectual. The gun-boats and frigates continued their courfe to Skenefborough Falls, where the armed veffels were pofted. Captain Carter, with part of his brigade of gun-boats, immediately attacked, and with fo much fpirit, that two of the veffels very foon ftruck; the other three were blown up, and the enemy having previoufly prepared combuftible materials, fet fire to the fort, mills, ftorehoufes, bateaux, &c. and retired with the detachment left for that purpofe, when the main body having gone off when the troops were afcending the mountain. A great quantity of provifions and fome arms were here confumed, and moft of their officers' baggage was burnt, funk, or taken. Their lofs is not known; about 30 prifoners were made, among which were two wounded officers

During thefe operations upon the right, Brigadier General Frafer continued his purfuit to Caftletown till one o'clock, having marched in a very hot day from four o'clock in the morning till that time. Some ftragglers of the enemy were picked up, from whom the Brigadier learned that their rear guard was compofed of chofen men, and commanded by Colonel Francis, one of their beft officers. During the time that the men were refrefhing, Major General Reidefel came up, and arrangements for continuing the purfuit having been concerted, Brigadier Frafer moved forward again, and during the night lay upon his arms, in an advantageous fituation, three miles nearer the enemy.

At three in the morning he renewed his march, and about five his advanced 7th July. fcouts difcovered the enemy's centries, who fired their pieces and joined the main body. The Brigadier obferving a commanding ground to the left of his light infantry, immediately ordered it to be poffeffed by that corps; and a confiderable body of the enemy attempting the fame, they met. The enemy were driven back to their original poft; the advanced guard under Major Grant was by this time engaged, and the grenadiers were advanced to fuftain them, and to prevent the right flank from being turned. The Brigadier remained on the left, where the enemy long defended themfelves by the aid of logs and trees, and after being repulfed, and prevented getting to the Caftletown road by the grenadiers, they rallied, and renewed the action; and upon a fecond repulfe, attempted their retreat by Pitsford Mountain. The grenadiers fcrambled up a part of that afcent, appearing almoft inacceffible, and gained the fummit before them, which threw them into confufion; they were ftill greatly fuperior in numbers, and confequently in extent, and the brigadier, in momentary expectation of the Brunfwickers, had latterally drawn from his left to fupport his right. At this critical moment General Reidefel, who had preffed on, upon hearing the firing, arrived with the foremoft of his columns, viz. the chaffeurs company and eighty grenadiers and light infantry. His judgment immediately pointed to him the courfe to take; he extended upon Brigadier Frafer's left flank. The chaffeurs got into action with great gallantry, under Major Barner. They fled on all fides, leaving dead upon the field Colonel Francis and many other officers, with upwards of 200 men; above 600 were wounded, moft of whom perifhed in the woods, attempting to get off, and one colonel, feven captains, ten fubalterns, and 210 men were made prifoners; above 200 ftand of arms were alfo taken.

The number of the enemy before the engagement amounted to 2000 men. The Britifh detachment under Brigadier General Frafer (the parties left the day before at Ticonderoga not having been able to join) confifted only of 850 fighting men.

The bare relation of fo fignal an action is fufficient for its praife. Should the attack againft fuch inequality of numbers, before the German brigade came up, feem to require explanation, it is to be confidered that the enemy might have efcaped by delay; that the advanced guard on a fudden found themfelves too near the enemy to avoid action without retreating; and that Brigadier Frafer had fuppofed the German troops to be very near. The difference of time in their arrival was merely accidental. The Germans pufhed for a fhare in the glory, and they arrived in time to obtain it. I have only to add, that the exertions of Brigadier Frafer on this day were but a continuance of that uniform intelligence, activity and bravery, which diftinguifh his character upon all occafions, and entitle him to be recommended, in the moft particular manner, to his Majefty's favour.

The officers and foldiers of this brigade have prevented any diftinctions of individuals by a general and equal difplay of fpirit.

The country people about Skenefborough having reported that part of the enemy were ftill retreating, the 9th regiment was detached, with orders to take poft near Fort Anne, and obferve the enemy's motions. This was effected, but with great difficulty, as the roads were almoft impracticable, and the bridges broken. The other troops were employed all that day and night in dragging fifty bateaux over the carrying place at Wood Creek, to facilitate the movement of the reft of the firft brigade to Fort Anne, to diflodge the enemy.

8th July.   A report was received from Lieutenant Colonel Hill (9th regiment) that the enemy had been reinforced in the night by a confiderable body of frefh men; that he could not retire with his regiment before them, but he would maintain his ground. The two remaining regiments of the firft brigade were ordered to quicken
their

their march, and upon fecond intelligence of the enemy, and firing being heard, the 20th regiment was ordered forward with two pieces of artillery, and Major General Phillips was fent to take the command. A violent ftorm of rain, which lafted the whole day, prevented the troops from getting to Fort Anne fo foon as was intended ; but the delay gave the 9th regiment an opportunity of diftinguifhing themfelves, by ftanding and repulfing an attack of fix times their number. The enemy finding the pofition not to be forced in front, endeavoured to turn it ; and from the fuperiority of their numbers that inconvenience was to be apprehended ; and Lieutenant Colonel Hill found it neceffary to change his pofition in the height of action : fo critical an order was executed by the regiment with the utmoft fteadinefs and bravery. The enemy, after an attack of three hours, were totally repulfed, and fled towards Fort Edward, fetting fire to Fort Anne, but leaving a faw-mill and a block-houfe in good repair, which were afterwards poffeffed by the king's troops.

The 9th regiment acquired, during their expedition, about thirty prifoners, fome ftores and baggage, and colours of the 2d Hampfhire regiment.

One unlucky accident happened, to counterbalance, in fome degree, this fuccefs. Captain Montgomery, an officer of great merit, was wounded early in the action, and was in the act of being dreffed by the furgeon when the regiment changed ground ; being unable to help himfelf, he and the furgeon were taken prifoners. I fince hear he has been well treated, and is in a fair way of recovery at Albany.

The army very much fatigued (many parts of it having wanted their provifions for two days, almoft the whole their tents and baggage) affembled in their prefent pofition. The right wing occupies the heights of Skenefborough in two lines ; the right flank to the mountains, covered by the regiment of Reidefel's dragoons, *en potence*; the left to the Wood Creek.

                                                                   9th and 10th July.

The Brunfwick troops under Major General Reidefel upon Caftletown River, with Breyman's corps upon the communication of roads leading to Putney and Rutland ; the regiment of Heffe Hanau are pofted at the head of Eaft Creek, to preferve the communication with the camp at Caftletown River, and fecure the bateaux.

Brigadier Frafer's corps is in the centre, ready to move on either wing of the army.

The fcattered remains of the enemy are at Fort Edward, on the Hudfon's River, where they have been joined, as I am informed, by General Putnam, with a confiderable corps of frefh troops.

Roads are opening for the army to march to them by Fort Anne, and the Wood Creek is clearing of fallen trees, funken ftones, and other obftacles, to give paffage to bateaux for carrying artillery, ftores, provifions and camp equipage. Thefe are laborious works ; but the fpirit and zeal of the troops are fufficient to furmount them. Some little time muft alfo be allowed for the fupplies of provifions to overtake us. In the mean time all poffible diligence is ufing at Ticonderoga to get the gun-boats, provifion veffels, and a proper quantity of bateaux into Lake George. A corps of the army will be ordered to penetrate by that route, which will afterwards be the route for the magazines ; and a junction of the whole is intended at Fort Edward.

I tranf-

I tranfmit to your Lordfhip herewith returns of the killed and wounded, and lifts of fuch parts of provifions and ftores, taken from the enemy, as could be collected in fo fbort a time.

I have the honour to be, with the greateft refpect,
Your Lordfhips, &c.

No. VIII. *Copy of a Letter from Lieutenant General* Burgoyne *to Lord* George Germain, *dated* Skenefborough, July 11, 1777.

[Private.]

MY LORD,

HAVING given your Lordfhip a detail, in my public letter of this date, of the late tranfactions, I now do myfelf the honour to ftate to your Lordfhip, fuch circum_ ftances as appear to me more proper for a private communication.

Mr. Peters and Mr. Jeffup, who came over to Canada laft autumn, and propofed to raife battalions, one from the neighbourhood of Albany, the other from Charlotte county, are confident of fuccefs as the army advances. Their battalions are now in embryo, but very promifing ; they have fought, and with fpirit. Sir Guy Carleton has given me blank commiffions for the officers, to fill up occafionally, and the agree_ ment with them is, that the commiffions are not to be fo effective, till two thirds of the battalions are raifed. Some hundreds of men, a third part of them with arms, have joined me fince I have penetrated this place, profeffing themfelves loyalifts, and wifhing to ferve, fome to the end of the war, fome for the campaign. Though I am without inftructions upon this fubject, I have not hefitated to receive them, and as faft as companies can be formed, I fhall poft the officers till a decifion can be made upon the meafure by my fuperiors. I mean to employ them particularly upon detach_ ments, for keeping the country in awe, and procuring cattle ; their real ufe I expect will be great in the prefervation of the national troops : but the impreffion which will be caufed upon public opinion, fhould provincials be feen acting vigoroufly in the caufe of the King, will be yet more advantageous, and, I truft, fully juftify the ex_ pence.

The manifefto, of which I enclofed your Lordfhip a copy in my laft difpatches, and herewith fend a duplicate, has great effect where the country is not in the power of the rebels ; where it is, the committees turn all their efforts to counteract it. They watch or imprifon all fufpected perfons, compel the people in general to take arms, and to drive the cattle, and to burn the corn, under penalty of immediate death. Great numbers have been hanged. Should thefe wretches fucceed to make a defert of the country, by fire and maffacre, it will at leaft be a pleafing reflection, that while advantages are reaped from the clement part of the manifefto, they, and not the King's troops, are the executioners of its threats.

Your Lordfhip will have obferved, I have made no mention of the Indians, in the purfuit from Ticonderoga. It is not poffible to draw them in many refpects from the plunder of that place, and I confidentially acknowledge this is not the only inftance in which I have found little more than a name. If, under the management of their conductors, they are indulged, for interefted reafons, in all the caprices and humours of fpoiled children, like them they grow more unreafonable and importunate upon

2   every

every new favour; were they left to themfelves, enormities too horrid to think of would enfue, guilty and innocent, women and infants, would be a common prey.

This is the character of the lower Canadian Indians, who alone have been with the army hitheito. I am informed the Outawas, and other remote nations, who are within two days march of joining me, are more brave and more tractable; that they profels war, not pillage. They are under the directions of a M. St. Luc, a Canadian gentleman of honour and parts, and one of the beft partizans the French had laft war, and of one Langlade, the very man who projected and executed with thefe very nations the defeat of General Braddock. My firft intention was to turn this whole corps to the Connecticut immediately, to force a fupply of provifions, to intercept reinforcements, and to confirm the jealoufy I have in many ways endeavoured to excite in the New England provincés; but finding that the enemy are labouring to remove their magazines from Forts George and Edward, and every where deftroying the roads, and preparing to drive and burn the country towards Albany, I have determined to employ them, to prevent, if poffible, by their terror, the continuance of thofe operations. And after arriving at Albany, they may be employed to renew the alarm towards Connecticut and Bofton.

Your Lordfhip will pardon me if I a little lament that my orders do not give me the latitude I ventured to propofe in my original project for the campaign, to make a real effort inftead of a feint upon New England. As things have turned out, were I at liberty to march in force immediately by my left, inftead of my right, I fhould have little doubt of fubduing before winter the provinces where the rebellion originated.

If my late letters reach Mr. Howe, I ftill hope this plan may be adopted from Albany; in the mean while my utmoft exertions fhall continue, according to my inftructions, to force a junction.

I have fent fome Indians through the woods, in the hope of their reaching St. Leger, with the account of my progrefs; now is the critical time for his pufh upon the Mohawk. I have certain intelligence that all the country round Fort Stanwix is in alarm: but I imagine it proceeds from the appearance of fome Savages detached by Colonel Butler, not apprehending St. Leger can be got quite fo forward.

Camp near Saratoga, Auguft 20, 1777.   Second No. VIII.

To Lord George Germaine.

My Lord,

IN my laft difpatch (a duplicate of which will be inclofed herewith) I had the honour to inform your Lordfhip of the proceedings of the army under my command to the 30th of July.

From that period to the 15th of Auguft every poffible meafure was employed to bring forward bateaux, provifions, and ammunition from Fort George to the firft navigable part of Hudfon's River, a diftance of eighteen miles, the roads in fome parts fteep, and in others wanting great repair. Of the horfes furnifhed by contract in Canada not more than a third part was yet arrived. The delay was not imputable to negleɛ, but to the natural accidents attending ſo long and intricate a combination of land and water carriage. Fifty team of oxen, which had been collected in the country through which I had marched, were added to aſſiſt the tranſpoit; but theſe reſources together were found far inadequate to the purpoſes of feeding the army, and forming a magazine at the ſame time. Exceeding heavy rains augmented the impediments. It was often neceſſary to employ ten or twelve oxen upon a ſingle bateau; and after the utmoſt exertions for the fifteen days above ſtated, there were not above four days proviſion before hand, nor above ten bateaux in the river.

Intelligence had reached me that Lieutenant Colonel St. Leger was before Fort Stanwix, which was defended. The main army of the enemy oppoſed to me was at Stillwater, a place between Saratoga and the mouth of the Mohawk.

A rapid movement forward appeared to be of the utmoſt conſequence at this period. The enemy could not have proceeded up the Mohawk without putting themſelves between two fires, in caſe Colonel St. Leger ſhould have ſucceeded; and at beſt being cut off by my army from Albany. They muſt either therefore have ſtood an action, have fallen back towards Albany, or have paſſed the Hudſon's River, in order to ſecure a retreat to New England, higher up. Which ever of theſe meaſures they had taken, ſo that the King's army had been enabled to advance, Colonel St. Leger's operations would have been aſſiſted, a junction with him probably ſecured, and the whole country of the Mohawk opened. To maintain the communication with Fort George during ſuch a movement, ſo as to be ſupplied by daily degrees at a diſtance, continually increaſing, was an obvious impoſſibility. The army was much too weak to have afforded a chain of poſts. Eſcorts for every ſeparate tranſport would have been a ſtill greater drain; nor could any have been made ſo ſtrong as to force their way through ſuch poſitions as the enemy might take in one night's march from the White Creek, where they had a numerous militia. Had the enemy remained ſupine, through fear or want of comprehending ſo palpable an advantage, the phyſical impoſſibility of being ſupplied by degrees from Fort George was ſtill in force, becauſe a new neceſſity of land carriage for nine miles ariſes at Stillwater; and in the proportion that carriages had been brought forward to that place, the tranſport muſt have ceaſed behind.

The alternative therefore was ſhort; either to relinquiſh the favourable opportunity of advancing upon the enemy, or to attempt other reſources of ſupply.

It was well known that the enemy's ſupplies in live cattle, from a large tract of country, paſſed by the route of Mancheſter, Arlington, and other parts of the Hampſhire Grants, to Bennington, in order to be occaſionally conveyed from thence to the main army. A large depoſit of corn and of wheel carriages was alſo formed at the ſame place, and the uſual guard was militia, though it varied in numbers from day to day. A ſcheme was formed to ſurpriſe Bennington. The poſſeſſion of the cattle and carriages would certainly have enabled the army to leave their diſtant magazines, and to have acted with energy and diſpatch: ſucceſs would alſo have anſwered many ſecondary purpoſes.

Lieut. Col. Baume, an officer well qualified for the undertaking, was fixed upon to command. He had under him 200 diſmounted dragoons of the regiment of Riedeſel, Captain Fraſer's markſmen, which were the only Britiſh, all the Canadian volunteers, a party of the Provincials who perfectly knew the country, 100 Indians, and two light pieces of cannon; the whole detachment amounted to about 500 men. The inſtructions were poſitive to keep the regular corps poſted while the light troops felt

4   their

their way, and not to incur the danger of being furrounded, or having a retreat cut off.

In order to facilitate this operation, and to be ready to take advantage of its fuccefs, the army moved up the eaft fhore of Hudfon's River. On the 14th, a bridge was formed of rafts, over which the advanced corps paffed and encamped at Saratoga. Lieutenant Colonel Breyman's corps were pofted near Batten Kill, and upon intelligence from Colonel Baume, that the enemy were ftronger at Bennington than expected, and were aware of his attack, that corps, confifting of the Brunfwick grenadiers, light infantry and chaffeurs, were fent forward to fuftain him.

It fince appears that Lieutenant Colonel Baume, not having been able to complete his march undifcovered, was joined at a place called Sancoix Mills, about four miles fhort of Bennington, by many people profeffing themfelves to be Loyalifts. A provincial gentleman of confidence who had been fent with the detachment, as knowing the country and the character of the inhabitants, was fo incautious as to leave at liberty fuch as took the oath of allegiance.

His credulity and their profligacy caufed the firft misfortune. Colonel Baume was induced to proceed without fufficient knowledge of the ground. His defign was betrayed ; the men who had taken the oaths were the firft to fire upon him ;. he was attacked on all fides. He fhewed great perfonal courage, but was overpowered by numbers.

During this time Lieutenant Colonel Breyman was upon the march through a heavy rain ; and fuch were the other impediments ftated in that officer's report, of bad roads, tired horfes, difficulties in paffing artillery, carriages, &c.. that he was from eight in the morning of the 15th to four in the afternoon of the following day making about twenty-four miles.

He engaged, fought gallantly, and drove the enemy from three feveral heights ; but was too late to fuccour Colonel Baume, who was made prifoner, and a confiderable part of his dragoons were killed or taken. The failure of ammunition, from the accidental breaking to pieces of a tumbril, unfortunately obliged Lieutenant Colonel Breyman to retire conquering troops, and to leave behind two pieces of cannon, befides two which had been loft by Lieutenant Colonel Baume. The Indians made good their retreat from the firft affair, as did Captain Frafer, with part of his company, and many of the Provincials and Canadians.

The lofs, as at prefent appears, amounts to about 400 men, killed and taken in both actions, and twenty-fix officers, moftly prifoners ;. but men who were difperfed in the woods drop in daily. A correct return fhall be tranfmitted to your Lordfhip the firft opportunity.

This, my Lord, is a true ftate of the event. I have not dwelt upon errors, becaufe in many inftances they were counterbalanced by fpirit. The enemy will of courfe find matter of parade in the acquifition of four pieces of cannon : but that apart, they have fmall caufe of exultation ; their lofs in killed and wounded being more than double to ours, by the confeffion of their prifoners and deferters, and of many inhabitants who were witneffes to the burial of their dead.

The chief fubject of regret on our fide, after that which any lofs of gallant men naturally occafions, is the difappointment of not obtaining live cattle, and the lofs of time in bringing forward the magazines.

This

This heavy work is now nearly completed, and a new bridge of boats is thrown over the Hudfon's River, oppofite to Saratoga, the former one of rafts having been carried away by the fwell of water after the late continual rains. When enabled to move, nothing within my feale of talent fhall be left unattempted to fulfil his Majefty's orders, and I hope circumftances will be fuch, that my endeavours may be in fome degree affifted by a co-operation of the army under Sir William Howe.

I have the honour to be, with great refpect,

Your Lordfhip's
moft obedient and moft humble fervant,

(Signed.)   J. BURGOYNE.*

No. IX.   *Copy of a Letter fiom Lieutenant General Burgoyne to Lord George Germain, dated Camp, near Saratoga, Auguft 20, 1777.*

[Private.]

MY LORD,

I NEED not enlarge upon the concern I have in communicating any finifter events. I am perfuaded your Lordfhip will give me credit for partaking every fentiment that your Lordfhip, or any other man warmed with principle and zeal in this conteft, can feel.

In regard to the affair of Saintcoick, I have only to add to the public account, that if ever there was a fituation to juftify enterprize and exertion, out of the beaten track of military fervice, it was that in which I found myfelf. Had I fucceeded, I fhould have effected a junction with St. Leger, and been now before Albany. And I flatter myfelf, I need only mention thofe views, to fhew that in hazarding this expedition I had the foundeft principles of military reafoning on my fide, viz. that the advantages to be expected from fuccefs were in a great degree fuperior to the evils that could attend mifcarriage. The fecondary purpofes, to which I alluded in the public letter, were to try the affections of the country ; to complete the Provincial corps, many recruits for which were unable to efcape from their villages without a force to encourage and protect them ; and to diftract the councils of the enemy, by continuing their jealoufy towards New England.

Major General Reidefel has preffed upon me repeatedly the mounting his dragoons, the men were animated with the fame defire, and I conceived it a moft favourable occafion to give into their ideas and folicitations, becaufe in exerting their zeal to fulfil their favourite purpofe, they neceffarily would effect the greater purpofe of my own. The reft of the troops were felected from fuch as would leaft weaken the folid ftrength of the army, in cafe of ill fuccefs ; and I thought it expedient to take a little trial of the Provincials and Canadians before I might have occafion for them in more important actions.

The original detachment could not have been made larger without opening roads, and other preparations of time, nor fhould I have thought it juftifiable to expofe the beft troops to lofs upon a collateral action. Had my inftructions been followed, or could Mr. Breyman have marked at the rate of two miles an hour any given twelve hours out of the two and thirty, fuccefs would probably have enfued, misfortune would certainly have been avoided. I did not think it prudent, in the prefent crifis, to mark thefe circumftances to the public fo ftrongly as I do in confidence to your

Lord-

---

* The letter that follows, No. 9, is alfo materially referrable to No. 8.

Lordſhip ; but I rely, and I will venture to ſay I expeƈt, becauſe I think juſtice will warrant the expeƈtation, that while, for the ſake of public harmony, that neceſſary principle for conduƈting nice and laborious ſervice, I colour the faults of the execution,. your Lordſhip will, in your goodneſs, be my advocate to the King, and to the world,. in vindication of the plan.

The conſequences of this affair, my Lord, have little effeƈt upon the ſtrength or ſpirits of the army ; but the proſpeƈt of the campaign in other reſpeƈts, is far leſs proſperous than when I wrote laſt. In ſpite of St. Leger's viƈtory, Fort Stanwix holds out obſtinately. I am afraid the expeƈtations of Sir J. Johnſon greatly fail in the tiſing of the country. On this ſide I find daily reaſon to doubt the ſincerity of the reſolution of the profeſſing loyaliſts. I have about 400, but not half of them armed, who may be depended upon ; the reſt are trimmers, merely aƈtuated by intereſt. The great bulk of the country is undoubtedly with the Congreſs, in principle and in zeal ; and their meaſures are executed with a ſecrecy and diſpatch that are not to be equalled. Wherever the King's forces point, militia, to the amount of three or four thouſand aſſemble in twenty-four hours ; they bring with them their ſubſiſtence, &c. and, the alarm over, they return to their farms. The Hampſhire Grants in particular, a country unpeopled and almoſt unknown in the laſt war, now abounds in the moſt aƈtive and moſt rebellious race of the continent, and hangs like a gathering ſtorm upon my left. In all parts the induſtry and managment in driving cattle, and removing corn, are indefatigable and certain ; and it becomes impraƈticable to move without portable magazines. Another moſt embarraſſing circumſtance, is the want of communication with Sir William Howe ; of the meſſengers I have ſent, I know of two being hanged, and am ignorant whether any of the reſt arrived. The ſame fate has probably attended thoſe diſpatched by Sir William Howe ; for only one letter is come to hand, informing me that his intention is for Penſylvania ;. that Waſhington has detached Sullivan, with 2500 men to Albany ; that Putnam is in the Highlands, with 4000 men. That after my arrival at Albany, the movements of the enemy muſt guide mine ; but that he wiſhed the enemy might be driven out of the province before any operation took place againſt the Conneƈticut ; that Sir Henry Clinton remained in the command in the neighbourhood of New-York, and would aƈt as occurrences might direƈt.

No operation, my Lord, has yet been undertaken in my favour : the highlands have not even been threatened. The conſequence is, that Putnam has detached two brigades to Mr. Gates, who is now ſtrongly poſted near the mouth of the Mohawk-. River, with an army ſuperior to mine in troops of the Congreſs, and as many militia as he pleaſes. He is likewiſe far from being deficient in artillery, having received all the pieces that were landed from the French ſhips which got into Boſton.

Had I a latitude in my orders, I ſhould think it my duty to wait in this poſition, or perhaps as far back as Fort Edward, where my communication with Lake George would be perfeƈtly ſecure, till ſome event happened to aſſiſt my movement forward ; but my orders being poſitive to " force a junƈtion with Sir William Howe," I apprehend I am not at liberty to remain inaƈtive longer than ſhall be neceſſary to colleƈt twenty-five days proviſion, and to receive the reinforcement of the additional companies, the German drafts and recruits now (and unfortunately only now) on Lake Champlain. The waiting the arrival of this reinforcement is of indiſpenſible neceſſity, becauſe from the hour I paſs the Hudſon's River and proceed towards Albany, all

Y   ſafety

safety of communication ceafes. I muft expect a large body of the enemy from my left will take poft behind me. I have put out of the queftion the waiting longer than the time neceffary for the foregoing purpofes, becaufe the attempt, then critical, depending on adventure and the fortune that often accompanies it, and hardly juftifiable but by orders from the ftate, would afterwards be confummately defperate. I mean my Lord, that by moving foon, though I fhould meet with infurmountable difficulties to my progrefs, I fhall at leaft have the chance of fighting my way back to Ticonderoga, but the feafon a little further advanced, the diftance encreafed, and the march unavoidably tardy, becaufe furrounded by enemies, a retreat might be fhut by impenetrable bars or the elements, and at the fame time no poffible means of exiftence remain in the country.

When I wrote more confidently, I little forefaw that I was to be left to purfue my way through fuch a tract of country, and hofts of foes, without any co-operation from New-York ; nor did I then think the garrifon of Ticonderoga would fall to my fhare alone, a dangerous experiment would it be to leave that poft in weaknefs, and too heavy a drain it is upon the life-blood of my force to give it due ftrength.

I yet do not defpond.—Should I fucceed in forcing my way to Albany, and find that country in a ftate to fubfift my army, I fhall think no more of a retreat, but at the worft fortify there and await Sir W. Howe's operations.

Whatever may be my fate, my Lord, I fubmit my actions to the breaft of the King, and to the candid judgment of my profeffion, when all the motives become public ; and I reft in the confidence, that whatever decifion may be paffed upon my conduct, my good intent will not be queftioned.

I cannot clofe fo ferious a letter without expreffing my fulleft fatisfaction in the behaviour and countenance of the troops, and my compleat confidence that in all trials they will do whatever can be expected from men devoted to their King and country.

I have the honour to be, &c.

J. BURGOYNE.

P. S. Upon re-perufing this letter, I am apprehenfive that the manner in which I have expreffed myfelf, refpecting the reinforcement being only upon Lake Champlain, may feem ambiguous.—I do not mean to impute the delay to any thing but accidents, nor do I mean to conteft Sir Guy Carleton's reafoning upon not complying with my requifitions to garrifon Ticonderoga, I only lament it.

No. X.

Copy of a Letter from Sir William Howe *to Lieutenant General* Burgoyne, *dated* New-York, July *the* 17th, 1777.

DEAR SIR,

I have received yours of the fecond inftant on the 15th, have fince heard from the rebel army of your being in poffeffion of Ticonderoga, *which is a great event, carried without lofs.* I have received your two letters, *viz.* from Plymouth and Quebec, your laft of the 14th May, and fhall obferve the contents. There is a report of a meffenger of yours to me having been taken, and the letter difcovered in a double wooden canteen, you will know if it was of any confequence; nothing of it has tranfpired to us. I will obferve the *fame rules* in writing to you, as you propofe, in your

letters

letters to me. Wafhington is waiting our motions here, and has detached Sullivan with about 2500 men, as I learn, to Albany. My intention is for Penfylvania, where I expect to meet Wafhington, but if he goes to the northward contrary to my expectations, and you can keep him at bay, be affured - I fhall foon be after him to relieve you.

After your arrival at Albany, the movements of the enemy will guide yours ; but my wifhes are; that the enemy be drove out of this province before any operation takes place in Connecticut. Sir Henry Clinton remains in the command here, and will act as occurrences my direct. Putnam is in the highlands with about 4000 men. Succefs be ever with you.

Yours, &c.

WILLIAM HOWE.

Sir Guy Carleton's Letter.*

Second No. X.

S I R,   *Quebeck, November 12, 1777.*

I received your letter of the 20th of October, with your public difpatches by Captain Craig, the 5th inftant, and heartily condole with you upon the very difagreeable accounts they contain, all which I fincerely lamented, both on the public account and your own.

This unfortunate event, it is to be hoped, will in future prevent minifters from pretending to direct operations of war, in a country at three thoufand miles diftance, of which they have fo little knowledge as not to be able to diftinguifh between good, bad, or interefted advices, or to give pofitive orders in matters, which from their nature, are ever upon the change ; fo that the expedience or propriety of a meafure at one moment, may be totally inexpedient or improper in the next.

Having given over all hopes of being relieved this fall. I determined upon fending home Captain Foy, to furnifh his Majefty's confidential fervants, and my fucceffor, with the beft information in my power, of the ftate of affairs in this province, that they may form the better judgment of what they have to do.

I am, &c.

Army from Canada *under Lieutenant General* Burgoyne.

Total Rank and File, 1ft of July, 1777. [*Sick included.*]

No. XI.

Britifh.			Britifh.	Brought over	2660
9th regiment	—	542	53d	—	537
20th	---	528	62d	—	541
21ft	—	528	Grenadiers and light infantry companies from 29th, 31ft, and 34th		
24th	—	528			
47th	—	524	regiments	—	329
	Carried over	2660		Carried over	4067

* This letter, which was never printed before, only regards the view of the evidence, page 96.

A P P E N D I X.

Brought over	4067
Left in Canada out of the above	343

British. Total —	3,724
Germans, 1st July 3727	
Left in Canada 711	

For the campaign, Germans	30,16

Regular troops, total —	6,740

Garrison left out of the above at Ticonderoga.

British rank and file	462
German rank and file	448
	910

To force a passage to Albany	5,830
1st July, British artillery —	257
German artillery —	100

Bat men, servants, &c. in the above.

Recruits under Lieut. Nutt —	154
Canadians — —	148
Indians never more than	500

Before Septemb. fell off to	90
Provincials at most —	682
1st October, no more than	456

In September the additional companies joined near Fort Miller, in all — — 300

Regulars killed, wounded, and prisoners in the campaign, 1777.

British.		Killed.	Wounded.	Prisoners.	Total
	Officers	26	47	19	
	Serjeants	15	33	14	
	Drummers	3	5	6	
	R. & File	207	549	449	1285
Germans.					
	Officers	10	16	29	
	Serjeants	12	28	59	
	Drummers	1	8	18	
	R. & File	141	225	575	941

No. XII. *First Application from Major General* Phillips *relative to Horses.* Dated Montreal, June 4, 1777.

SIR,

I TAKE the liberty of informing your Excellency, that there has yet been no arrangement made for marching the field artillery by land, should the corps of troops upon an expedition under your command in the course of the campaign quit the lakes Champlain and George, and the rivers.

I have, upon the strictest information which could be procured, reason to believe, that neither carriages nor horses will be to be had nearer than Albany, should the route of your army be that way, and even in that country, it will necessarily require a considerable time before any can be got; all which must necessarily delay the operations of the campaign, after the reduction of Ticonderoga. I therefore submit to your Excellency's consideration whether horses and such ammunition-carriages as may be wanted should not be procured for the service of the campaign, for the field artillery attached to the corps of troops your Excellency is to command this campaign?

I have the honour to be Sir,

With the greatest respect,

Your Excellency's most obedient and most humble servant,

M. PHILLIPS, Major General,

commanding the royal artillery in Canada.

His Excellency
Lieutenant General Burgoyne.

4

Copy

Copy of a Letter to Major General Phillips, *refpecting Horfes.* Dated Montreal,
June 4, 1777.

SIR,

I have the honour of your letter of this day's date, informing me that no arrangement
has yet been made for moving the field artillery by land ; and that upon the beft information you can obtain, neither carriages nor horfes can be procured on the other fide
Lake Champlain nearer than Albany.

In confequence of this reprefentation, I have to requeft you, to give in your opinion
upon the mode of procuring horfes and carriages from this country, com,,ining the
confiderations of difpatch, fufficiency, œconomy towards government, and I wifh to
know the opinion as foon as poffible.

I am with trueft regard, Sir,

Your obedient humble fervant,

J. BURGOYNE, Lieutenant-General.

Major-General Phillips.

Extracts of Letters from Major General Phillips, *&c.*

Extract of a Letter from Major General Phillips *to Lieutenant General* Burgoyne.

Montreal, *June* 5, 1777.

I HAVE the honour of your Excellency's letter to me of yefterday, in anfwer to
one I wrote on the fubject of the field-artillery being fupplied with horfes, &c. &c.

You are pleafed, Sir, to order me to give an opinion upon the mode of procuring
horfes and carriages from this country, combining the confideration of difpatch,
fufficiency, and œconomy towards government.

There are but two modes of procuring horfes for the fervice, fuppofing the country
is not to furnifh them upon Corvées, the one is by purchafing of horfes upon the
account of government, the other by contract.

The firft of thefe modes has always appeared to me difficult, uncertain, and full
of openings for every fpecies of impofition, and the exprnce uncertain.—Government
muft truft various people to buy horfes, and in this country it will not be poffible to
procure any perfons who will not immediately purfue the views of gaining money to
themfelves with a confideration for the King's fervice. Add to this, that it will become fuch a charge, that many commiffaries muft be appointed, and various other
officers of that fort, &c, which being a mixture of infpectors into the purchafes of
horfes, and neceffarily alfo at times the being purchafers, it will be difficult ever to
afcertain the price, and feldom that the goodnefs of horfes can be depended on.

I have feen in my fervice this mode attempted, but it has to my knowledge failed.
I muft allow, that could it be carried into execution complete, it would be the cheapeft
for government: but taking into confideration the various impofitions which will arife,
and that the fetting out on a plan of this nature will require a very large fum of money,

ney, perhaps from 20,000l. to 30,000l. to be intrusted into various hands, I freely give it as my opinion that it is not a perfect plan. The contracting for a certain number of horses at a fixed price for the hire, by day reduces the whole to a very simple, and therefore generally a certain plan. It depends in the setting out, by making as cheap, as fair, and just a bargain on the part of government as can be. And being so made, that the military and civil officers do their duty, by attending to the receiving of horses only as they are fitting for service. The contractor has his interest so directly connected with fulfilling his contract, as upon failure it ceases, that he will exert all means to do it, and the care of government will be that it be done honestly and compleatly.

I have thus obeyed your Excellency's orders, and given an opinion which I submit entirely to your consideration.

Extract of a Letter to Nathaniel Day, *Esq. Commissary General, &c. dated* Montreal, *June 4th,* 1777.

I BEG the favour of you to calculate what number of horses and carriages (supposing them such as are in common use in Canada) will be sufficient for conveying by land thirty days provision for 10,000 men, together with about 1000 gallons of rum, and you will please to make me your report as soon as possible.

Extract of a Letter to Sir Guy Carleton.

Montreal, June 7, 1777.

HAVING had the honor to represent to your Excellency the necessity of being provided with a certain number of horses and carriages for the artillery, victual, and other indispensible purposes of the army, when it shall be obliged to quit the borders of the lakes and rivers; and having understood from your Excellency that such provision could not be made by the ordinary methods of corvée, and that if proposed without compulsion upon the country the effect would be precarious, dilatory, and expensive; I have the honour now to lay before your Excellency proposals for contracts for an expeditious supply of horses for the artillery, and 500 carts, with two horses each, for the other purposes.

I am too ignorant of the prices of the country to offer any judgment upon the reasonableness of these proposals; nor have I any long acquaintance with Mr. Jordan, or other motive for wishing him the preference, if other persons can be found equally capable, responsible, and expeditious. I have only thus far interfered, upon a conviction, after considering the route the King's orders direct, and taking all possible methods of information upon the supply to be expected as we proceed, that to depend upon the country altogether would be to hazard the expedition.

Your Excellency will observe, that in order to save the public expence as much as possible, I have reduced this requisition much below what would be adequate to the service, and I mean to trust to the resources of the expedition for the rest; 500 carts will barely carry fourteen days provisions at a time, and Major General Phillips means

2   to

to demand as few horfes as poffible, fubject to whatever future augmentations future fervices may require; the prefent number wanted will be about 400; there will then remain unprovided for (for expeditious movement) the tranfport of bateaux from Lake George to Hudfon's River, and the carriage of the tents of the army, and many other contingencies that I need not trouble your Excellency to point out to you.

Extract of a Letter to General Harvey.

Montreal, May 19, 1777.

YOU have permitted me, as formerly, to write to you confidentially. I take the firft conveyance to renew a correfpondence fo pleafing and honourable to myfelf, and that may, in fome cafes, become beneficial to the public fervice. It fhall never be employed but to convey truths, to do juftice to facts and perfons, and to fecure myfelf in the continuance of an efteem fo valuable to me as yours againft appearances and mifreprefentations.

I have reafon to be exceedingly fatisfied with all that has been done, and with moft things that are doing: exertions have been made during the winter, which was remark- ably favourable, in all the departments, and preparations are very forward; thofe that have been committed to the directions of General Phillips have been executed with a diligence, precifion, and forefight, that entitle him to the fulleft praife. The troops are in a ftate of health almoft unprecedented, and their fpirits and general improvement are equally objects of great pleafure and promife. To this agreeable reprefentation I have the happinefs to add, that Sir Guy Carleton has received me and the orders I brought in a manner that, in my opinion, does infinite honour to his public and private character.

That he fhould have wifhed for the lead in active and important military operations, is very natural. That he thinks he has fome caufe of refentment for the general tenor of treatment he has received from fome of the minifters is difcernible; but neither his difappointment nor his perfonal feelings operate againft his duty; and I am convinced he means to forward the King's meafures, entrufted to my hands, with all the zeal he could have employed had they refted in his own.

My intention is, during my advance to Ticonderoga, and fiege of that poft, for a fiege I apprehend it muft be, to give all poffible jealoufy on the fide of Connecticut. If I can by manœuvre make them fufpect that after the reduction of Ticonderoga my views are pointed that way, it may make the Connecticut forces very cautious of leaving their own frontiers, and much facilitate my progrefs to Albany. I mention this intention only to Lord George and yourfelf, and I do it left from any intelligence of my motions that may reach England indirectly, it fhould be fuppofed I have fuffer- ed myfelf to be diverted from the main object of my orders. The King and his Majefty's minifters may reft affured that whatever demonftrations I may endeavour to impofe upon the enemy, I fhall really make no movement that can procraftinate my progrefs to Albany.

One thing more occurs. I had the furprife and mortification to find a paper handed about at Montreal, publifhing the whole defign of the campaign, almoft as accurately as if it had been copied from the Secretary of State's letter. My own cau-

tion

tion has been fuch that not a man in my own family has been let into the fecret. Sir
Guy Carleton's, I am confident, has been equal ; I am therefore led to doubt whether
imprudence has not been committed from private letters from England, and wifh you
would afk my friend D'Oyley, to whom my very affectionate compliments, whether
there is any perfon within the line of minifterial communication that he can fufpect to
be fo unguarded ? It is not of great confequence here, except as far as regards St.
Leger's expedition ; but fuch a trick may be of moft prejudicial confequence in other
cales, and fhould be guarded againft.

Extract of a Letter to General Harvey.

Camp on the River Bouquet, near Lake Champlain, June 22, 1777.

I HAVE had to contend againft wet weather that rendered the roads almoft impracticable at the carrying places, and confequently the paffage of the bateaux and
exceedingly dilatory, befides a great deal of contrary wind. Indeed the combination
of land and water movement, bad roads, inactivity and fometimes difobedience in the
country, and a thoufand other difficulties and accidents, unknown in other fervices,
difconcert all arrangements. I do not mention this upon my own account, as I do
not hold myfelf refponfible for delays within the province of Canada; but I mention
it to do juftice to others, who, I really think, have infinite merit in overcoming the
obftructions we have met with, and who ought to be juftified againft fome acquain-
tances of yours and mine, who travel acrofs a map very faft, and are very free in their
comments, when others, who have ten times their knowledge and refources, do not
anfwer their predictions and expectations.

I have been exceedingly diftreffed in regard to the brigadiers of this army. Sir
Guy Carleton, the day I took leave of him, put into my hands an extract of a letter
from the Secretary at War, approving the appointment of thofe gentlemen, but
obferving, that whenever any of them fhould *lead their brigades out of the province of
Canada, in order to join the troops under General Howe,* there would be a neceffity for
their command ceafing as brigadiers, &c.

Were this to be put in execution, according to the letter of the order, and the geo-
graphical limits of Canada, and fuppofing Major General Phillips at the fame time
to be employed folely in the artillery, I fhould find myfelf at the head of an army to
undertake a fiege, and afterwards purfue objects of importance, and poffibly of time,
without a fingle intermediate Britifh officer between the Lieutenant General, commanding *pro tempore* in chief, and a Lieutenant Colonel. It would be prepofterous
and impertinent in me to fay one word more to you as an officer, upon the impoffibility of methodizing or conducting fuch an army with fuch a total deficiency of ftaff.
Had Lord Barrington condefcended to have communicated his intentions to me in
London, I think I could have convinced him of the impropriety. As it is, I muft
conclude that the fpirit of the order goes only to prevent thofe gentlemen bearing a
higher rank and pay than fenior lieutenant colonels ferving in the fame army ; and
that therefore there can be no fault in keeping it dormant till the junction takes place.
In other words, I look upon mine to be the Canada army till fuch time as I am in
communication with General Howe, fo as to make part of his force, and confequently
                                                                        without

without meafuring degrees north and fouth, that the arrangements made in Canada, and approved of by the King, remain in force till that time.

I am perfuaded, my dear General, you will fupport me in this liberty, if fuch it is to be called, not only as the abfolute order and method of the fervice depends upon it, but alfo to avoid to thefe gentlemen, who have really great merit, the vexation and the ridicule of being deprived of their rank and pay in the houɽ of that very fervice, with a view to which their appointment was originally made. I think I can anfwer, that the junction made, and the reafons for reverting to their former ranks, become obvious, they will fubmit to his Majefty's pleafure without a murmur.

Extract of a Letter from Lieutenant General Burgoyne *to General* Harvey.

Head Quarters, Skenesborough, July 11, 1777.

THE mere compliment of fervice I have given to the troops in orders, and in the relation defigned for the Gazette, is not doing them fufficient juftice. It is a duty in me further, through you, and I know I fhall impofe a pleafing tafk on you, to affure the King that their behaviour is as uniformly good in the camp as in action.

After what I have publicly mentioned of Frafer I am fure I need not prefs you in his favour. I cannot but feel confident in the hope that his Majefty's grace will find its way through all obftacles to prevent fo difcouraging a circumftance as the return of this gallant officer to the mere duty of lieutenant colonel, at the head of one battalion, after having given afcendancy to the King's troops, and done honour to his profeffion, by the moft fpirited actions in critical periods of two fucceffive campaigns.

You will obferve, Sir, both in the public letter and in the order of battle, which Captain Gardner will put into your hands, that Major General Phillips is occafionally employed feparately from the ftrict line of his department. This does not proceed from inattention to the explanation of his Majefty's pleafure two years ago; but from abfolute neceffity. The ftaff being compofed without any Britifh major general, Brigadier Frafer being pofted where he is of infinite ufe, at the head of the advanced corps, the fervice would fuffer in the moft material degree if the talents of General Phillips were not fuffered to extend beyond the limits of the artillery, and I hold myfelf fully juftified in continuing the great ufe of his affiftance under this extenfion, by what I underftand to be the fignification of the King's pleafure to Sir Guy Carleton, viz. *That this meafure muft not be made a precedent*, but not forbidding it during the prefent exigency.

I flatter myfelf the King will be fatisfied with the diligence ufed in taking the field, as well as with the fubfequent operations; if not, my difappointment can only proceed from my own deficiency in ftating the embarraffments I found, notwithftanding previous preparations and cordial affiftances. Remote fituations of the troops, currents, winds, roads, want of materials for caulking the veffels, inactivity and defertion of the Canadian corvées, were all againft me. A great difficulty lay in providing horfes and carriages for the bare tranfport of provifions and tents, when we fhould arrive at Fort George, or any other place where the army fhould have no refource of water carriage. I found an active, and I think a reafonable contractor, who fupplied this neceffity at a much cheaper rate than it could have been done any other way.

I in-

I inclofe a copy of the contract to the treafury, to which I refer you. You will ob. ferve that I have limited the number to the mere indifpenfible purpofes of provifions and tents, trufting to the country for the further affiftance of officers baggage and the other attirail of an army. Experience already fhews me that I judged right in not trufting to the country for more; for had this precaution been omitted, I fhould be bound faft to the fpot where I am, or obliged to return by water to Ticonderoga.

I avow alfo to you my advice to General Carleton to grant commiffions to two pro. vincial battalions, to be raifed from Albany and Charlotte County, by a Mr. Jeffup and a Mr. Peters, upon condition that the commiffions fhould not take place till two thirds of the corps fhould be effective, provincial corps, acting zealoufly in the King's caufe, muft have great impreffion upon public opinion, and will, befides, in fact be of fingular ufe to the cafe and prefervation of the regular troops.

Upon this principle, therefore, I have not hefitated further to receive and to pay fuch loyalifts as have come in with their arms fince the fuccefs of Ticonderoga, and wifh to be employed. Though I have not power to grant commiffions, I poft the officers, and form them into companies till the meafure can be decided by thofe who have more authority.

I hope all thefe articles of expence will meet with the fupport of your opinion; and have only to add, that as no job fhall be done myfelf, fo will I ufe all efforts to pre. vent fuch being done by others.

I am indifpenfibly obliged to wait fome time on this pofition, to clear roads and make bridges, which is great labour in this country, and to bring up a ftock of provifion, and alfo to give time to the gun-boats, bateaux, and provifion veffels to be put into Lake George to fcour that lake, and fecure the future route of the maga- zines. I propofe to poffefs Fort Edward at the fame time that the force is ready to move down the lake, by which means, if the enemy do not evacuate Fort George, the garrifon muft inevitably be caught. In the mean while I have ordered Reidefel to make roads, reconnoitre the country, and make all other poffible feints of a march to the Connecticut, and by fome other meafures I hope to give alarms that way.

INSTRUCTIONS for Lieutenant Colonel Baume, *on a fecret expedition to the Con- necticut River.*

Amendments made by Gen. Burgoyne.

[*The erafures were made by Gen. Burgoyne.**]

THE object of your expedition is to try the affections of the country, to difconcert the councils of the enemy, to mount the Reidefel's dragoons, to com- pleat Peters's corps, and to obtain large fupplies of cattle, horfes, and carriages.

The feveral corps, of which the in- clofed is a lift, are to be under your command.

The

---

* The erafures are printed in Italics, and the amendments in the oppofite column.

Amendments by¹ General Burgoyne.

The troops muft take no tents, and what little baggage is carried by officers muft be on their own bat horfes.

You are to proceed *by the route* from Batten Kill to Arlington, and take poft there, *fo as to fecure the pafs from Man_chefter. You are to remain at Arlington* till the detachment of the Provincials, under the command of Captain Sherwood, fhall join you from the fouthward.

You are then to proceed to Manchefter, where you will take poft fo as to fecure the pafs of the mountains on the road from Manchefter to Rockingham ; from hence you will detach the Indians and light troops to the northward, toward Otter Creek. On their return, and alfo receiving intelligence that no enemy is in force *in the neighbourhood of Rockingham* (1) you will proceed by the road over the mountains to Rockingham,where you will take poft. This will be the moft diftant part on the expedition. (2)

(1) *upon the Connecticut River,*

You are to remain there *as long as neceffary to fulfil the intention of the expedition fi om thence* (3) and you are afterwards to defcend *by the Connecticut* River to Brattlebury, and from that place, by the quickeft march, you are to return by the great road to Albany.

During your whole progrefs your detachments are to have orders to bring in to you all horfes fit to mount the dragoons under your command, or to ferve as bat horfes to the troops, *they are likewife to bring in* (4) faddles and bridles as can be found. (5)

Your parties are likewife to bring in waggons and other convenient carriages, with as many draft oxen as will be neceffary to draw them and all cattle fit for flaughter (milch cows excepted) which are to be left for the ufe of the inhabitants.

(2) *And muft be proceeded upon with caution, as you will have the defile of the mountains behind you, which might make a retreat difficult ; you muft therefore endeavour to be well informed of the force of the enemy's militia in the neighbouring country.*

Should you find it may with prudence be effected.

(3) *while the Indians and light troops are detached up the river.*

(4) *together with as many.*

(5) *The number of horfes requifite, befides thofe necefary for mounting the regiment of dragoons, ought to be* 1300. *If you can bring more for the ufe of the army it will be fo much the better.*

Z. 2

tants. Regular receipts, in the form hereto fubjoined, are to be given in all places where any of the abovementioned articles are taken, to fuch perfons as have remained in their habitations, and otherwife complied with the terms of General Burgoyne's manifefto; but no receipts to be given to fuch as are known to be acting in the fervice of the rebels. (6).

Amendments by General Burgoyne.

(6) *As you will have with you perfons perfectly acquainted with the abilities of the country, it may perhaps be advifeable to tax the feveral diftricts with the portions of the feveral articles, and limit the hours for their delivery; and fhould you find it necef-fary to move before fuch delivery can be made, hoftages of the moft refpectable people fhould be taken, to fecure their following you the enfuing day. All poffible means are to be ufed to prevent plundering.*

As it is probable that Captain Sherwood, who is already detached to the fouthward, and will join you at Arlington, will drive in a confiderable quantity of cattle and horfes to you, you will therefore fend in this cattle to the army, with a proper detachment from Peters's corps, to cover them, in order to difencumber yourfelf; but you muft always keep the regiments of dragoons compact.

The dragoons themfelves muft ride, and take care of the horfes of the regiment. Thofe horfes which are deftined for the ufe of the army muft be tied together by ftrings of ten each, in order that one man may lead ten horfes. You will give the unarmed men of Peters's corps to conduct them, and inhabitants whom you can truft. You muft always take your camps in good pofition, but at the fame time where there is pafture, and you muft have a chain of centinels round your cattle and horfes when grazing.

Colonel Skeene will be with you as much as poffible, in order to affift you with his advice, to help you to diftinguifh the good fubjects from the bad, to procure you the beft intelligence of the enemy, and to chufe thofe people who are to bring me the accounts of your progrefs and fuccefs.

When you find it neceffary to halt for a day or two, you muft always entrench the camp of the regiment of dragoons, in order never to rifk an attack or affront from the enemy.

As

Amendments by General Burgoyne.

You will use all poffible means to make the country believe that the troops under your command are the advanced corps of the army, and that it is intended to pafs the Connecticut on the road to Bofton. You will likewife *have it infinuated* (7) that the main army from Albany is to be joined at Springfield by a corps of troops from Rhode Ifland.

You will fend off occafionally cattle or carriages, to prevent being too much incumbered ; and will give me as frequent intelligence of your fituation as poffible.

It is highly probable that the corps under Mr. Warner, now fuppofed to be at Manchefter, will retreat before you ; but fhould they, contrary to expectation, be able to collect in great force, and poft themfelves advantageoufly, it is left to your difcretion to attack them or not, always bearing in mind that your corps is too valuable to let any confiderable lofs be hazarded on this occafion.

Should any corps be moved from Mr. Arnold's main army, in order to intercept your retreat, you are to take as ftrong a poft as the country will afford, and fend the quickeft intelligence to me, and you may depend on my making fuch a movement as fhall put the enemy between two fires, or otherwife effectually fuftain you.

It is imagined the progrefs of the whole of this expedition may be effected in about a fortnight, but every movement of it muft depend upon your fuccefs in obtaining fuch fupply of provifions as will enable you to fubfift for your return to the army, in cafe you can get no more. (8)

All perfons acting in committees, or any officers acting under the directions of Congrefs, either civil or military, are to be made prifoners.

As you will return with the regiment of dragoons mounted, you muft always have a detachment of Captain Frafer's or Peters's corps in front of the column, and the fame in the rear, in order to prevent your falling into an ambufcade when you march through the woods.

(7) *infinuate*

(8) *And fhould not the army be able to reach Albany before your expedition fhould be compleated, I will find means to fend you notice of it, and give your route another direction.*

Batten

SIR, *Batten Kill, 12th August,* 1777.

I HAD the honour of acquainting your Excellency, by a man sent yesterday evening by Colonel Skeene to head-quarters, of the several corps under my command being encamped at Saratoga, as well as of my intention to proceed the next morning at five o'clock; the corps moved at that time, and marched a mile, when I received a letter from Brigadier General Fraser, signifying your Excellency's order to post the corps advantageously on Batten Kill, till I should receive fresh instructions from your Excellency; the corps is now encamped at that place, and wait your Excellency's orders. I will not trouble you, Sir, with the various reports which spread, as they seem rather to be founded on the different interests and feelings of the people who occasion them.

I have the honour to be, most respectfully,
Your Excellency's most obedient and humble servant,
F. BAUME.

The reinforcement of fifty chasseurs, which
your Excellency was pleased to order,
joined me last night at eleven o'clock.

General Burgoyne.

SIR, *Cambridge, 13th August,* 1777.

IN consequence of your Excellency's orders I moved this morning at four o'clock, with the corps under my command; and after a march of sixteen miles arrived at Cambridge at four in the evening. On the road I received intelligence of forty or fifty of the rebels being left to guard some cattle. I immediately ordered thirty of the provincials and fifty savages to quicken their march, in hopes to surprize them. They took five prisoners in arms, who declared themselves to be in the service of the Congress; yet the enemy received advice of our approach, and abandoned the house they were posted in. The provincials and savages continued their march about a mile, when they fell in with a party of fifteen men, who fired upon our people, and immediately took to the woods with the greatest precipitation. The fire was quick on our side, but I cannot learn if the enemy sustained any loss. A private of Captain Sherwood's company was the only one who was slightly wounded in the thigh. From the many people who came from Bennington they agree that the number of the enemy amounted to 1800. I will be particularly careful, on my approach at that place, to be fully informed of their strength and situation, and take the precautions necessary to fulfil both the orders and instructions of your Excellency.

I cannot ascertain the number of cattle, carts, and waggons taken here, as they have not been as yet collected. A few horses have been also brought in, but am sorry to acquaint your Excellency that the savages either destroy or drive away what is not paid for with ready money. If your Excellency would allow me to purchase the horses from the savages, stipulating the price, I think they might be procured cheap, otherwise they ruin all they meet with, their officers and interpreters not having it in their power to controul them. Your Excellency may depend

3   on

on hearing how I proceed at Bennington, and' of my fuccefs there : praying my re_
fpectful compliments to General Reidefel,

I am, moft refpectfully, Sir,

Your moft obedient and humble fervant,

F. BAUME.

P. S. The names of the men taken in arms are as follows.

George Duncan,	John Bell,
David Slarrow,	Matt. Bell.
Samuel Bell,	

Hugh More, a noted rebel furrendered himfelf yefterday evening.
The exprefs left Cambridge at 4 o'clock on the morning of the 14th of Auguft.

SIR,   *Sancoick, 14th Auguft,* 1777, *9 o'clock.*
I have the honour to inform your excellency, that I arrived here at eight in the
morning, having had intelligence of a party of the enemy being in poffeffion of a
mill, which they abandoned at our approach, but in their ufual way fired from the
bufhes, and took their road to Bennington ; a favage was flightly wounded ; they
broke down the bridge which has retarded our march above an hour, they left in
the mill about feventy-eight barrels of very fine flour, 1000 bufhels of wheat, 20
barrels of falt, and about 1000l. worth pearl and pot afh. I have ordered thirty provincials and an officer to guard the provifion and the pafs of the bridge. By five prifoners taken here, they agree that 1500 to 1800 men are in Bennington, but are fuppofed to leave it on our approach ; I will proceed fo far to-day as to fall on the
the enemy to-morrow early, and make fuch difpofition as I think neceffary from the
intelligence I may receive. People are flocking in hourly, but want to be armed ;
the favages cannot be controuled, they ruin and take every thing they pleafe.

I am,

Your excellency's moft obedient,

humble fervant,

F. BAUME.

Beg your excellency to pardon the hurry of this letter,
it is wrote on the head of a barrel.

General Burgoyne.

Inftructions to Colonel Skeene, *upon the expedition to Bennington.*

SIR,
I requeft the favour of you to proceed with Lieutenant Colonel Baume, upon an
expedition of which he has the command, and which will march this evening, or
to-morrow morning.

The objects of his orders are to try the affections of the country ; to difconcert the
councils of the enemy; to mount the regiment of Reidefel dragoons ; to compleat
Lieutenant Colonel Peters's corps, and to procure a large fupply of horfes for the ufe
of the troops, together with cattle and carriages,

The

The route marked for this expedition is to Arlington and Manchefter, and in cafe it fho uld be found that the enemy is not in too great force upon the Connecticut river, it is intended to pafs the mountains to Rockingham, and defcend the river from thence to Brattlebury. Some hours before the corps marches for Arlington, Colonel Peters with all his men are to fet forward for Bennington, and afterwards are to join at Arlington.

Receipts are ordered to be given for all horfes and cattle taken from the country.

Lieutenant Colonel Baume is directed to communicate to you the reft of his inftructions, and to confult with you upon all matters of intelligence, negotiation with the inhabitants, roads, and other means depending upon a knowledge of the country for carrying his inftructions into execution.

I rely upon your zeal and activity for the fulleft affiftance, particularly in having it underftood in all the country through which you pafs, that the corps of Lieutenant Colonel Baume is the firft detachment of the advanced guard, and that the whole army is proceeding to Bofton, expecting to be joined upon the route by the army from Rhode Ifland.

I need not recommend to you to continue the requifites of the fervice with every principle of humanity in the mode of obtaining them ; and it may be proper to inform the country that the means to prevent their cattle and horfes being taken for the future, will be to refift the enemy when they fhall prefume to force them, and drive them voluntarily to my camp.

I have the honour to be, &c. &c. &e.

J. BURGOYNE.

CALCULATION

CALCULATIONS of the Number of Carts that will carry Provisions for the following Number of Men.

	1 Day.	2 Days.	3 Days.	4 Days.	5 Days.	6 Days.	7 Days.	8 Days.	9 Days.	10 Days.	11 Days.	12 Days.	13 Days.	14 Days.	15 Days.	16 Days.	17 Days.	18 Days.	19 Days.	20 Days.	30 Days.	60 Days.	90 Days.
s	38	75	113	150	188	226	263	300	338	375	413	452	490	526	564	600	638	678	716	750	1125	2250	3375
s	19	38	57	75	94	113	132	150	169	188	207	226	245	263	282	300	319	339	358	375	563	1125	1688
ts	15	30	45	60	75	90	105	120	135	150	165	180	195	210	225	240	255	270	285	300	450	900	1350
ts	12	23	34	45	57	68	79	90	102	113	124	135	147	158	169	180	192	203	214	225	338	676	1014
rts	8	15	23	30	38	45	53	61	68	75	83	90	98	105	113	120	128	135	143	150	225	450	675
rts	4	8	12	15	19	23	27	31	35	39	42	45	49	53	57	60	64	68	72	75	113	226	339
rts	2	4	6	8	10	12	14	16	18	20	21	23	25	27	29	30	32	34	36	38	57	113	171

The above Table made, allowing 3 pounds weight to the Ration and 800 pounds to the Cart Load.

NATHANIEL DAY, Commissary General.

Extract of a Letter from Lieutenant General Burgoyne, *to Sir* Guy Carleton, *dated Head-Quarters, at Skenesborough House,* 11th *July,* 1777.

I REQUEST your Excellency to take into confideration the expediency of fupplying from Canada, a garrifon for Ticonderoga.

My communication will widen fo much as I proceed, the drain upon the army for pofts will be fo confiderable, not to fpeak of detachments and fafe-guards to protect and to awe the country, that if that firft diminution is not replaced, my effective ftrength may become inadequate to the fervices intended. My prefent intelligence is that Putnam is collecting an army to oppofe me at Saratoga. Fort Edward is alfo talked of to fuftain a fiege.

Your excellency will, I am fure, agree with me that Ticonderoga, or fome other fortified poft on the South part of Lake Champlain, ought to be confidered on the frontiers of the province of Canada. I am aware of the difficulties that arife from the manner in which the Secretary of State's orders are penned; but I fubmit to your Excellency, whether, under the principle laid down in the beginning of the order, and afterwards repeated, *that* 3000 *men were held fufficient for the defence of that province,* you would not be juftified in fparing for the purpofe of this garrifon, the overplus of the 3000 that may remain after compleating my army.

And notwithftanding the corps for the Canada fervice are precifely named by the Secretary of State, I would further fubmit whether, upon my preffing requifition, the garrifon might not juftifiably be furnifhed by detachment, even though there was no overplus, under the following words of the order; *after having fecured to him,* (Lieutenant General Burgoyne) *every affiftance which it is in your power to afford and procure.* Your Excellency's zeal for the fervice and favour towards me, will be better interpreters for the latitude I propofe, than any thing I can further fuggeft; my prefent purpofe, Sir, is to get a fufficient number of gun-boats upon the Lake George to fcour that lake as expeditioufly as poffible, to fupport them with a proper force to attack Fort George on that fide, while with the main of the army as foon as refrefhed and fupplied, I attack Fort Edward from hence, and therebycut off the communication from Albany to Fort George, and confequently prevent the fuccour or retreat of that garrifon.

Extract of a Letter from Lieutenant General Burgoyne, *to Sir* Guy Carleton, *Head-Quarters, near Fort Anne,* July 29th 1777.

THE conftruction your excellency puts upon the orders of the Secretary of State, is too full and decifive for me to prefume to trouble you further upon the fubject of a garrifon for Ticonderoga from Canada, I muft do as well as I can, but I am fure your Excellency, as a foldier, will think my fituation a little difficult. A breach into my communication muft either ruin my army entirely, or oblige me to return in force to reftore, which might be the lofs of the campaign. To prevent a breach, Ticonderoga and Fort George muft be in very refpectable ftrength, and I muft befides have pofts at Fort Edward and other carrying-places. Thefe drains added to common accidents and loffes of fervice, will neceffarily render me very inferior in
point

point of numbers to the enemy, whom I muſt expect always to find ſtrongly poſted. I aſk pardon for dwelling ſo much upon this ſubject, and have only to add my re-queſt to your Excellency to forward the additional companies as expeditiouſly as may be.

Copy of Lieutenant-General Burgoyne's *Letter to Colonel* Baume.

Near Saratoga, Auguſt 14, 1777. *Seven at Night.*

S I R,

THE accounts you have ſent me are very ſatisfactory, and I have no doubt of every part of your proceeding continuing to be the ſame.

I beg the favour of you to report whether the road you have paſſed is practicable, and if ſo, if it is convenient for a conſiderable corps with cannon.

Should you find the enemy too ſtrongly poſted at Bennington, and maintaining ſuch a countenance as may make an attack imprudent, I wiſh you to take a poſt where you can maintain yourſelf till you receive an anſwer from me, and I will either ſupport you in force, or withdraw you.

You will pleaſe to ſend off to my camp, as ſoon as you can, waggons, and draft cattle, and likewiſe ſuch other cattle as are not neceſſary for your ſubſiſtence.

Let the waggons and carts bring off all the flour and wheat they can that you do not retain for the ſame purpoſe. This tranſport muſt be under the charge of a com-miſſion officer.

I will write you at full to-morrow in regard to getting horſes out of the hands of the ſavages.

In the mean time any you can collect from them, fit to mount the regiments, at a low price, ſhall be allowed.

I am with great eſteem, Sir,
Your moſt obedient humble ſervant.

J. BURGOYNE.

Colonel St. Leger's *Account of Occurrences at* Fort Stanwix.

A MINUTE detail of every operation ſince my leaving La Chine, with the de-tachment entruſted to my care, your Excellency will permit me to reſerve to a time of leſs hurry and mortification than the preſent, while I enter into the intereſting ſcene before Fort Stanwix, which I inveſted the 3d of Auguſt, having previouſly puſhed forward Lieutenant Bird of the King's reigment, with thirty of the King's troops and two hundred Indians, under the direction of Captains Hare and Wilſon, and the chiefs Joſeph and Bull, to ſeize faſt hold of the lower landing-place, and there-by cut off the enemy's communication with the lower country.—This was done with great addreſs by the lieutenant, though not attended with the effect I had promiſed myſelf, occaſioned by the ſlackneſs of the Meſſaſagoes. The brigade of proviſion and ammunition boats I had intelligence of, being arrived and diſembarked before this party had taken poſt.

The fourth and fifth were employed in making arrangements for opening Wood Creek (which the enemy, with the indefatigable labour of one hundred and fifty men, for fourteen days, had most effectually choaked up) and the making a temporary road from Pine Ridges upon Fish Creek, sixteen miles from the fort, for a present supply of provision and the transport of our artillery: the first was effected by the diligence and zeal of Captain Bouville, assisted by Captain Harkimer of the Indian department, with one hundred and ten men, in nine days; while Lieutenant Lundy, acting as assistant quarter-master general, had rendered the road in the worst of weather, sufficiently practicable to pass the whole artillery and stores, with seven days provision, in two days.

On the 5th, in the evening, intelligence arrived by my discovering parties on the Mohawk River, that a reinforcement of eight hundred militia, conducted by General Herkimer, were on their march to relieve the garrison, and were actually at that instant at Orifka, an Indian settlement, twelve miles from the fort. The garrison being apprised of their march by four men, who were seen enter the fort in the morning, through what was thought an impenetrable swamp, I did not think it prudent to wait for them, and thereby subject myself to be attacked by a sally from the garrison in the rear, while the reinforcement employed me in front. I therefore determined to attack them on the march, either openly or covertly, as circumstances should offer. At this time, I had not two hundred and fifty of the King's troops in camp; the various and extensive operations I was under an absolute necessity of entering into, having employed the rest; and therefore, could not send above eighty white men, rangers and troops included, with the whole corps of Indians. Sir John Johnson put himself at the head of this party, and began his march that evening at five o'clock, and met the rebel corps at the same hour the next morning. The impetuosity of the Indians is not to be described on the sight of the enemy (forgetting the judicious disposition formed by Sir John, and agreed to by themselves, which was, to suffer the attack to begin with the troops in front, while they should be on both flanks and rear) they rushed in, hatchet in hand, and thereby gave the enemy's rear an opportunity to escape. In relation to the victory, it was equally complete, as if the whole had fallen; nay more so, as the two hundred who escaped only served to spread the panic wider; but it was not so with the Indians; their loss was great (I must be understood Indian computation, being only about thirty killed, and the like number wounded, and in that number some of their favourite chiefs and confidential warriors were slain.) On the enemy's side, almost all their principal leaders were slain. General Herkimer has since died of his wounds. It is proper to mention, that the four men detached with intelligence of the march of the reinforcement, set out the evening before the action, and consequently the enemy could have no account of the defeat, and were in possession only, of the time appointed for their arrival; at which, as I suspected, they made a sally with two hundred and fifty men towards Lieutenant Bird's post, to facilitate the entrance of the relieving corps, or bring on a general engagement, with every advantage they could wish.

Captain Hoyes was immediately detached to cut in upon their rear, while they engaged the lieutenant. Immediately upon the departure of Captain Hoyes, having learned that Lieutenant Bird, misled by the information of a cowardly Indian, that Sir John was pressed, had quitted his post to march to his assistance, I marched
the

the detachment of the King's regiment, in fupport of Captain Hoyes, by a road in fight of the garrifon, which, with executive fire from his party, immediately drove the enemy into the fort, without any further advantage than frightening fome fquaws and pilfering the packs of the warriors which they left behind them. After this affair was over, orders were immediately given to compleat a two-gun battery, and mortar beds, with three ftrong redoubts in their rear, to enable me, in cafe of another attempt, to relieve the garrifon by their regimented troops, to march out a larger body of the King's troops.

Captain Lernoult was fent with 110 men to the lower landing place, where he eftablifhed himfelf with great judgment and ftrength, having an enclofed battery of a three-pounder oppofed to any fally from the fort, and another to the fide of the country, where a relief muft approach; and the body of his camp deeply entrenched and abbatifed.

When by the unabating labour of officers and men (the fmallnefs of our numbers never admitting of a relief, or above three hours ceffation for fleep or cooking) the batteries and redoubts were finifhed, and new cheeks and axle-trees made for the fix-pounders, thofe that were fent being reported rotten and unferviceable.

It was found that our cannon had not the leaft effect upon the fod-work of the fort, and that our royals had only the power of teizing, as a fix-inch plank was a fufficient fecurity for their powder magazine, as we learnt from the deferters. At this time Lieutenant Glenic of the artillery, whom I had appointed to act as affiftant engineer, propofed a converfion of the royals (if I may ufe the expreffion) into howitzers. The ingenuity and feafability of this meafure ftriking me very ftrongly, the bufinefs was fet about immediately, and foon executed, when it was found that nothing prevented their operating with the defired effect but the diftance, their chambers being too fmall to hold a fufficiency of powder. There was nothing now to be done but to approach the town, by fap to fuch a diftance that the rampart might be brought within their portice, at the fame time all materials were preparing to run a mine under their moft formidable haftion.

In the midft of thefe operations intelligence was brought in by our fcouts, of a fecond corps of 1000 men being on their march. The fame zeal no longer animated the Indians; they complained of our thinnefs of troops and their former loffes. I immediately called a council of the chiefs; encouraged them as much as I could; promifed to lead them on myfelf, and bring into the field 300 of the beft troops. They liftened to this, and promifed to follow me, and agreed that I fhould reconnoitre the ground propereft for the field of battle the next morning, accompanied by fome of their chief warriors, to fettle the plan of operations. When upon the ground appointed for the field of battle, fcouts came in with the account of the firft number fwelled to 2000; immediately after a third, that General Burgoyne's army, was cut to pieces, and that Arnold was advancing, by rapid and forced marches, with 3000 men. It was at this moment I began to fufpect cowardice in fome, and treafon in others; however I returned to camp, not without hopes, with the affiftance of my gallant coadjutor, Sir John Johnfon, and the influence of the fuperintending colonels, Claus and Butler, of inducing them to meet the enemy. A council, according to their cuftom, was called, to know their refolutions, before the breaking up of which I learned that 200 were already decamped. In about an hour

they

they infifted that I fhould retreat, or they would be obliged to abandon me. I had
no other party to take, and a hard party it was to troops who could do nothing
without them, to yield to their refolves ; and therefore propofed to retire at night,
fending on before my fick, wounded, artillery, &c. down the Wood Creek, covering them by our line of march.

This did not fall in with their views, which were no lefs than treacheroufly committing ravage upon their friends, as they had loft the opportunity of doing it
upon their enemies. To effect this they artfully caufed meffengers to come in,
one after the other, with accounts of the nearer approaches of the rebels ; one and
the laft affirmed that they were within two miles of Captain Lernoult's poft. Not
giving entire credit to this, and keeping to my refolution of retiring by night, they
grew furious and abandoned ; feized upon the officers' liquor and cloaths, in fpite
of the efforts of their fervants ; and became more formidable than the enemy we
had to expect. I now thought it time to call in Captain Lernoult's poft, retiring
with the troops in camp to the ruined fort called William, in the front of the
garrifon, not only to wait the enemy, if they thought proper to fally, but to protect the boats from the fury of the favages, having fent forward Captain Hoyes,
with his detachment, with one piece of cannon, to the place where Bull Fort
ftood, to receive the troops who waited the arrival of Captain Lernoult. Moft of
the boats were efcorted that night beyond Canada Creek, where no danger was to
be apprehended from the enemy. The creek at this place bending from the road,
has a deep cedar fwamp between. Every attention was now turned to the mouth
of the creek, which the enemy might have poffeffed themfelves of by a rapid
march by the Oneyda Caftle. At this place the whole of the little army arrived by
twelve o'clock at night, and took poft in fuch a manner as to have no fears of any
thing the enemy could do. Here we remained till three o'clock next morning,
when the boats which could come up the Creek arrived, or rather that the rafcally
part of all nations of the Indians would fuffer to come up ; and proceeded acrofs
Lake Oneyda to the ruined fort of Brereton, where I learnt that fome boats were
ftill labouring down the creek, after being lightened of the beft part of their freight
by the Meffafagoes. Captain Lernoult propofed, with a boat full of armed men,
to repafs the lake that night, to relieve them from their labour, and fupply them
with provifion. This tranfaction does as much honour to the humanity as to the
gallantry of this valuable officer.

On my arrival at the Onondago Falls I received an anfwer to my letter from
your Excellency, which fhewed, in the cleareft light, the fcenes of treachery that
had been practifed upon me. The meffenger had heard indeed on his way that they
were collecting the fame kind of rabble as before, but that there was not an enemy
within forty miles of Fort Stanwix.

Soon after my arrival here I was joined by Captain Lernoult, with the men and
boats he had been in fearch of. I mean immediately to fend off, for the ufe of the
upper garrifon, all the overplus provifion I fhall have, after keeping a fufficiency to
carry my detachment down, which I mean to do with every expedition in my power
the moment this bufinefs is effected, for which purpofe I have ordered here the
fnow. The floop is already gone from this with her full lading.

Officers

Officers from each corps are fent to Montreal to procure neceffaries for the men, who are in a moft deplorable fituation from the plunder of the favages, that no time may be loft to join your army.

I have the honour to be, with the greateft refpect,

Sir, your Excellency's moft obedient,

Ofwego, Aug. 27, 1777.   and moft faithful fervant,

BARRY ST. LEGER.

His Excellency General Burgoyne.

Copy of a Letter from Lieutenant-General Burgoyne *to Lord* George Germain, *dated*   No. XIV.
at Albany, 20*th* October, 1777.

MY LORD,

NO poffibility of communication with your Lordfhip having exifted fince the beginning of September, at which time my laft difpatch was fent away, I have to report to your Lordfhip the proceedings of the army under my command from that period : a feries of hard toil, inceffant effort, ftubborn action ; till difabled in the collateral branches of the army by the total defection of the Indians ; the defertion or timidity of the Canadians and Provincials, fome individuals excepted ; difappointed in the laft hope of any timely co-operation from other armies ; the regular troops reduced by loffes from the beft part to 3500 fighting men, not 2000 of which were Britifh ; only three days provifions upon fhort allowance in ftore ; invefted by an army of 16,000 men, and no apparent means of retreat remaining, I called into council all the generals, field officers, and captains commanding corps, and by their unanimous concurrence and advice, I was induced to open a treaty with Major General Gates.

Your Lordfhip will fee, by the papers tranfmitted herewith, the difagreeable profpect which attended the firft overtures ; and when the terms concluded are compared, I truft that the fpirit of the councils I have mentioned, which under fuch circumftances dictated inftead of fubmitting, will not be refufed a fhare of credit.

Before I enter upon the detail of thefe events, I think it a duty of juftice, my Lord, to take upon myfelf the meafure of having paffed the Hudfon's River, in order to force a paffage to Albany. I did not think myfelf authorifed to call any men into council, when the peremptory tenor of my orders and the feafon of the year admitted no alternative.

Provifions for about thirty days having been brought forward, the other neceffary ftores prepared, and the bridge of boats completed, the army paffed the Hudfon's River on the 13th and 14th of September, and incamped on the heights, and in the plain of Saratoga, the enemy being then in the neighbourhood of Stillwater.

The whole army made a movement forward, and incamped in a good pofition in a   15th. place called Dovacote.

It being found that there were feveral bridges to repair, that work was begun under   16th. cover of ftrong detachments, and the fame opportunity was taken to reconnoitre the country.

The army renewed their march, repaired other bridges, and encamped upon ad-   17th. vantageous ground about four miles from the enemy.

The enemy appeared in confiderable force to obftruct the further repair of bridges,   18th. and with a view, as it was conceived, to draw on an action where artillery could not be

4

· be employed. A small loss was sustained in skirmishing, but the work of the bridges was effected.

Sept. 19. The passages of a great ravine, and other roads towards the enemy, having been reconnoitred, the army advanced in the following order.

Brigadier General Fraser's corps, sustained by Lieutenant Colonel Breyman's corps, made a circuit, in order to pass the ravine commodiously, without quitting the heights, and afterwards to cover the march of the line to the right. These corps moved in three columns, and had the Indians, Canadians, and Provincials upon their fronts and flanks. The British line led by me in person passed the ravine in a direct line south, and formed in order of battle as fast as they gained the summit, where they waited to give time to Fraser's corps to make the circuit, and to enable the left wing and artillery, which, under the commands of Major General Phillips, and Major General Reidesel, kept the great road and meadows near the river in two columns, and had bridges to repair, to be equally ready to proceed. The 47th regiment guarded the bateaux.

The signal guns, which had been previously settled to give notice of all the columns being ready to advance, having been fired between one and two o'clock, the march continued. The scouts and flankers of the column of the British line were soon fired upon from small parties but with no effect. After about an hour's march, the picquets, which made the advanced guard of that column, were attacked in force, and obliged to give ground, but they soon rallied and were sustained.

On the first opening of the wood I formed the troops. A few cannon-shot dislodged the enemy at a house from whence the picquets had been attacked, and Brigadier General Fraser's corps had arrived with such precision in point of time, as to be found upon a very advantageous height on the right of the British.

In the mean time the enemy, not acquainted with the combination of the march, had moved in great force out of their intrenchments, with a view of turning the line upon the right, and being checked by the disposition of Brigadier General Fraser, countermarched, in order to direct their great effort to the left of the British.

From the nature of the country, movements of this sort, however near, may be effected without a possibility of their being discovered.

About three o'clock the action began by a very vigorous attack on the British line, and continued with great obstinacy till after sunset. The enemy being continually supplied with fresh troops, the stress lay upon the 20th, 21st, and 62d regiments, most parts of which were engaged near four hours without intermission; the 9th had been ordered early in the day to form in reserve.

The grenadiers and 24th regiment were some part of the time brought into action, as were part of the light infantry, and all these corps charged with their usual spirit.

The riflemen, and other parts of Breyman's corps, were also of service; but it was not thought advisable to evacuate the heights where Brigadier General Fraser was posted otherwise than partially and occasionally.

Major General Phillips upon first hearing the firing found his way through a difficult part of the wood to the scene of action, and brought up with him Major Williams and four pieces of artillery, and from that moment I stood indebted to that gallant and judicious second, for incessant and most material services, particularly for restoring the action in a point which was critically pressed by a great superiority of fire, and to which he led up the 20th regiment at the utmost personal hazard.

3   Major

Major-General Riedefel exerted himfelf to bring up a part of the left wing, and arrived in time to charge the enemy with regularity and bravery.

Juft as the light clofed, the enemy gave ground on all fides, and left us completely mafters of the field of battle, with the lofs of about five hundred men on their fide, and, as fuppofed, thrice that number wounded.

The darknefs preventing a purfuit, the prifoners were few.

The behaviour of the officers and men in general was exemplary. Brigadier-General Frafer took his pofition in the beginning of the day with great judgment, and fuftained the action with conftant prefence of mind and vigour. Brigadier-General Hamilton was the whole time engaged and acquitted himfelf with great honour, activity and good conduct.

The artillery in general was diftinguifhed, and the brigade under Captain Jones, who was killed in the action, was confpicuoufly fo.

The army lay upon their arms the night of the 19th, and the next day took a, pofition nearly within cannon fhot of the enemy, fortifying their right, and extending their left to the brow of the heights, fo as to cover the meadows through which the great river runs, and where their bateaux and hofpitals were placed. The 47th regiment, the regiment of Heffe Hanau, and a corps of Provincials incamped in the meadows as a further fecurity.

It was foon found that no fruits, honour excepted, were attained by the preceding victory, the enemy working with redoubled ardor to ftrengthen their left : their right was already unattackable.

On our fide it became expedient to erect ftrong redoubts for the protection of the magazines and hofpital, not only againft a fudden attack, but alfo for their fecurity. in cafe of a march to turn the enemy's flank.

A meffenger arrived from Sir Harry Clinton with a letter in cypher, informing September me of his intention to attack Fort Montgomery in about ten days from the date 21. of his letter, which was the 12th inftant. This was the only meffenger of many that I apprehend were difpatched by Sir William Howe, and him that had reached my camp fince the beginning of Auguft. He was fent back the fame night to inform Sir Harry of my fituation, and of the neceffity of a diverfion to oblige General Gates to detach from his army, and my intention to wait favourable events in that pofition, if poffible, to the 12th of October.

In the courfe of the two following days, two officers in difguife, and other confidential perfons, were difpatched by different routes with verbal meffages to the fame effect, and I continued fortifying my camp and watching the enemy, whofe numbers increafed every day.

I thought it advifable on the 3d of October to diminifh the foldiers' ration in order to lengthen out the provifions, to which meafure the army fubmitted with the utmoft chearfulnefs. The difficulties of a retreat to Canada were clearly forefeen, as was the dilemma, fhould the retreat be effected, of leaving at liberty fuch an army as General Gates's to operate againft Sir William Howe.

This confideration operated forcibly to determine me to abide events as long as poffible, and I reafoned thus. The expedition I commanded was evidently meant at firft to be *hazarded*. Circumftances might require it fhould be *devoted*. A critical junction of Mr. Gates's force with Mr. Wafhington might poffibly decide the fate of the war; the failure of my junction with Sir Harry Clinton, or the loss of my retreat to Canada could only be a partial misfortune.

In this situation things continued till the seventh, when no intelligence having been received of the expected co-operation, and four or five days for our limited stay in the camp only remained, it was judged advisable to make a movement to the enemy's left, not only to discover whether there were any possible means of forcing a passage should it be necessary to advance, or of dislodging him for the convenience of a retreat, but also to cover a forage of the army which was in the greatest distress on account of the scarcity.

A detachment of fifteen hundred regular troops with two twelve pounders, two howitzers, and six six-pounders, were ordered to move, and were commanded by myself, having with me Major-General Phillips, Major-General Reidesel, and Brigadier-General Fraser.

The guard of the camp upon the heights was left to Brigadier-General Hamilton and Specht, the redoubts and the plain to Brigadier General Gall; and as the force of the enemy immediately in their front consisted of more than double their numbers, it was not possible to augment the corps that marched, beyond the numbers above stated.

I formed the troops within three-quarters of a mile of the enemy's left, and Captain Fraser's rangers, with Indians and Provincials, had orders to go by secret paths in the woods to gain the enemy's rear, and by shewing themselves there to keep them in a check.

The further operations intended, were prevented by a very sudden and rapid attack of the enemy on our left, where the British grenadiers were posted to support the left wing of the line. Major Acland at the head of them sustained the attack with great resolution; but the enemy's great numbers enabling them in a few minutes to extend the attack along the front of the Germans, which were immediately on the right of the grenadiers, no part of that body could be removed to make a second line to the flank, where the stress of the fire lay. The right was at this time engaged, but it was soon observed that the enemy were marching a large corps round their flank to endeavour cutting off their retreat. The light infantry and part of the 24th regiment which were at that post were therefore ordered to form a second line, and to secure the return of the troops into camp. While this movement was proceeding the enemy pushed a fresh and strong reinforcement to renew the action upon the left, which, overpowered by a great superiority, gave way, and the light infantry and 24th regiment were obliged to make a quick movement to save that point from being entirely carried, in doing which, Brigadier-General Fraser was mortally wounded.

The danger to which the lines were exposed becoming at this moment of the most serious nature, orders were given to Major-General Phillips and Reidesel to cover the retreat, while such troops as were most ready for the purpose, returned for the defence of them. The troops retreated hard pressed, but in good order; they were obliged to leave six pieces of cannon, all the horses having been killed, and most of the artillery-men, who had behaved as usual with the utmost bravery under the command of Major Williams, being either killed or wounded.

The troops had scarcely entered the camp when it was stormed with great fury, the enemy rushing to the lines under a severe fire of grape-shot and small arms.

4   The

APPENDIX.

The poſt of the light infantry under Lord Balcarras aſſiſted by ſome of the line, which threw themſelves by order into the intrenchments, was defended with great ſpirit, and the enemy led on by General Arnold was finally repulſed, and the General wounded ; but unhappily the intrenchments of the German reſerve, commanded by Lieutenant-Colonel Breymann, who was killed, were carried, and although ordered to be recovered, they never were ſo, and the enemy by that misfortune gained an opening on our right and rear. The night put an end to the action.

Under the diſadvantages thus apparent in our ſituation, the army was ordered to quit the preſent poſition during the night and take poſt upon the heights above the hoſpital.

Thus by an entire change of front, to reduce the enemy to form a new diſpoſition. This movement was effected in great order and without loſs, though all the artillery and camp were removed at the ſame time. The army continued offering battle to the enemy in their new poſition the whole day of the 8th.

Intelligence was now received that the enemy were marching to turn the right, and no means could prevent that meaſure but retiring towards Saratoga. . The army began to move at nine o'clock at night, Major-General Reideſel commanding the van-guard, and Major-General Phillips the rear.

This retreat, though within muſquet-ſhot of the enemy, and encumbered with all the baggage of the army, was made without loſs, but a very heavy rain and the difficulties of guarding the bateaux which contained all the proviſions, occaſioned delays which prevented the army reaching Saratoga till the night of the 9th, and the artillery could not paſs the fords of the Fiſh-kill till the morning of the 10th.

At our arrival near Saratoga, a corps of the enemy, between five and ſix hundred, were diſcovered throwing up intrenchments on the heights, but retired over a ford of the Hudſon's River at our approach, and joined a body poſted to oppoſe our paſſage there.

It was judged proper to ſend a detachment of artificers under a ſtrong eſcort to repair the bridges and open a road to Fort-Edward on the weſt ſide of the river. The 47th regiment, Captain Fraſer's markſmen, and Mackoy's Provincials, were ordered for that ſervice, but the enemy appearing on the heights of the Fiſh-kill in great force, and making a diſpoſition to paſs and give us battle : the 47th regiment and Fraſer's markſmen were recalled ; the Provincials left to cover the workmen at the firſt bridge run away upon a very flight attack of a ſmall party of the enemy, and left the artificers to eſcape as they could, without a poſſibility of their performing any work.

During theſe different movements the bateaux with proviſions were frequently fired upon from the oppoſite ſide of the river, and ſome of them were loſt, and ſeveral men were killed and wounded in thoſe which remained.

The attacks upon the bateaux were continued, ſeveral were taken and retaken, October but their ſituation being much nearer to the main force of the enemy than to ours, it 11. was found impoſſible to ſecure the proviſions any otherwiſe than by landing them and carrying them upon the hill : this was effected under fire, and with great difficulty.

The poſſible means of further retreat were now conſidered in councils of war, compoſed of the general officers, minutes of which will be tranſmitted to your Lordſhip.

The

The only one that feemed at all practicable was, by a night march to gain Fort-Edward with the troops carrying their provifion upon their backs; the impoffibility of repairing bridges, putting a conveyance of artillery and carriages out of the queftion, it was propofed to force the ford at Fort-Edward, or the ford above it. Before this attempt could be made, fcouts returned with intelligence that the enemy were intrenched oppofite thefe fords, and poffeffed a camp in force on the high ground between Fort-Edward and Fort-George with cannon. They had alfo parties down the whole fhore to watch our motions, and pofts fo near to us, upon our own fide of the water as muft prevent the army moving a fingle mile undifcovered.

The bulk of the enemy's army was hourly joined by new corps of militia and volunteers, and their numbers together amounted to upwards of 16,000 men. Their pofition, which extended three parts in four of a circle round us, was from the nature of the ground unattackable in all parts.

In this fituation the army took the beft pofition poffible and fortified, waiting till the 13th at night, in the anxious hope of fuccours from our friends, or the next defirable expectation, an attack from our enemy.

During this time the men lay continually upon their arms, and were cannonaded in every part, even rifle-fhot and grape-fhot came into all parts of the line, though without any confiderable effect.

At this period an exact account of the provifions was taken, and the circumftances ftated in the opening of this letter became compleat.

The council of war was extended to all the field officers and captains commanding corps of the army, and the event enfued which I am fure was inevitable, and which, I truft, in that fituation was honourable, but which it would be fuperfluous and melancholy to repeat.

After the execution of the treaty, General Gates drew together the force that had furrounded my pofition, and I had the confolation to have as many witneffes as I have men under my command, of its amounting to the numbers mentioned above.

During the events ftated above, an attempt was made againft Ticonderoga by an army affembled under Major General Lincoln, who found means to march with a confiderable corps from Huberton undifcovered, while another column of his force paffed the mountains between Skenefborough and Lake George, and on the morning of the 18th of September a fudden and general attack was made upon the carrying place at Lake George, Sugar Hill, Ticonderoga, and Mount Independence. The fea officers commanding the armed floop ftationed to defend the carrying place, as alfo fome of the officers commanding at the pofts of Sugar Hill and at the Portage were furprifed, and a confiderable part of four companies of the 53d regiment were made prifoners; a block-houfe, commanded by Lieutenant Lord of the 53d, was the only poft on that fide that had time to make ufe of their arms, and they made a brave defence till cannon taken from the furprifed veffel was brought againft them.

After ftating and lamenting fo fatal a want of vigilance, I have to inform your Lordfhip of the fatisfactory events which followed.

The enemy having twice fummoned Brigadier General Powell, and received fuch anfwer as became a gallant officer entrufted with fo important a poft, and having tried during the courfe of four days feveral attacks, and being repulfed in all, retreated without having done any confiderable damage.

Brigadier General Powell, from whofe report to me I extract this relation, gives great commendations to the regiment of Prince Frederick, and the other troops ftationed

tioned at Mount Independence. The Brigadier also mentions with great applause the behaviour of Captain Taylor of the 21ft regiment, who was accidentally there on his route to the army from the hofpital, and Lieutenant Beecroft of the 24th regiment, who with the artificers in arms defended an important battery.

On the 24th inftant, the enemy, enabled by the capture of the gun-boats and bateaux which they had made after the furprife of the floop, to embark upon Lake George, attacked Diamond Ifland in two divifions.

Captain Aubrey and two companies of the 47th regiment, had been pofted at that ifland from the time the army paffed the Hudfon's River, as a better fituation for the fecurity of the ftores at the fouth end of Lake George than Fort George, which is on the continent, and not tenable againft artillery and numbers, The enemy were repulfed by Captain Aubrey with great lofs, and purfued by the gun-boats under his command to the caft fhore, where two of their principal veffels were retaken, together with all the cannon. They had juft time to fet fire to the other bateaux, and retreated over the mountains.

I beg leave to refer your Lordfhip for further particulars to my aid-de-camp, Lord Peterfham, and I humbly take occafion to recommend to his Majefty's notice that nobleman, as one endued with qualities to do important fervices to his country in every ftation to which his birth may lead. In this late campaign in particular, his behaviour has been fuch as to entitle him to the fulleft applaufe, and I am confident his merit will be thought a fufficient ground for preferment, though deprived of the *eclat* and fort of claim which generally attends the delivery of fortunate difpatches.

I have only to add, my Lord, a general report of the killed and wounded; I do not give it correct, the hurry of the time and the feparation of the corps having rendered it impoffible to make it fo. The Britifh officers have bled profufely and moft honourably; thofe who remain unwounded have been equally forward, and the general officers from the mode of fighting have been more expofed than in other fervices. Among the reft of this ftation, I have had my efcapes. It depends upon the fentence his Majefty fhall pafs upon my conduct; upon the judgment of my profeffion, and of the impartial and refpectable parts of my country, whether I am to efteem them bleffings or misfortunes.

I have the honour to be,

(Signed.)   J. BURGOYNE.

Copy of a Letter from Lieutenant-General Burgoyne *to Lord* George Germain, *dated* Albany, 20th October, 1777.

Second No. XIV.

[*Private, by Lord* Peterfham.]

MY LORD,

I HAVE little to add to my public letter refpecting the courfe of unfuccefsful events, therein detailed. I reft my confidence in the juftice of the King and his councils, to fupport the General they thought proper to appoint to as arduous an undertaking, and under as pofitive a direction, as perhaps a cabinet ever framed. It will, I am fure, be remembered, my Lord, that a preference of exertions was the only latitude given me, and that to force a junction with Sir William Howe, or at leaft a paffage to Albany, was the principle, the letter, and the fpirit of my orders.

Indeed

3

Indeed the appearances at the time I paffed the Hudfon's-River, though fubject to doubt in fome inftances, as I then wrote your Lordfhip, were upon a general view, fuch as I am perfuaded would have rendered inaction cenfurable, had my orders, inftead of being peremptory, been difcretionary. Promifes of the profeffing loyalifts were not then brought to the teft; the fpirit of the enemy, in combat againft regular Britifh troops, had only been tried at Ticonderago, at Huberton, at Skenefborough, and Fort Anne; in all which places it had failed; the total difappointment of effectual co-operation, could not be forefeen or fuppofed; and fure I am, had I then made fuppo-fition that any thing like what has happened, might have happened, and remained cautioufly pofted, no exertion attempted, my conduct would have been held indefen-fible by every clafs and diftinction of men in government, in the army, and in the public.

The expediency of advancing being admitted, the confequences have been honou-rable misfortunes. The Britifh have perfevered in a ftrenuous and bloody pro-grefs. Had the force been all Britifh, perhaps the perfeverance had been longer; but as it was, will it be faid, my Lord, that in the exhaufted fituation defcribed, and in the jaws of famine, and invefted by quadruple numbers, a treaty which faves the army to the ftate, for the next campaign, was not more than could have been expected? I call it faving the army, becaufe if fent home, the ftate is thereby enabled to fend forth the troops now deftined for her internal defence; if exchanged, they become a force to Sir William Howe, as effectually, as if any other junction had been made.

I fhould now hold myfelf unjuftifiable if I did not confide to your Lordfhip, my opinion, upon a near infpection, of the rebel troops. The ftanding corps which I have feen, are difciplined. I do not hazard the term, but apply it to the great funda-mental points of military inftitution, fobriety, fubordination, regularity and courage. The militia are inferior in method and movement, but not a jot lefs ferviceable in woods. My conjectures were very different after the affair of Ticonderago, but I am convinced they were delufive; and it is a duty to the ftate to confefs it.

The panic of the rebel troops is confined, and of fhort duration; the enthufiafim is extenfive and permanent.

It is a juftice to Major General Phillips, to inform your Lordfhip, that when the crifis of our fituation at Saratoga arrived, he very handfomely offered to hazard his perfon by making a circuit through the woods, and attempt to throw himfelf into Ticondera-go, to defend that place, fhould it be the object of the enemy to endeavour the re-taking it.

In regard to myfelf, I am funk in mind and body; but while I have a faculty of either, it fhall be exerted for the King's fervice. I fhall wait in the neighbourhood of Bofton, the orders of Sir William Howe.

I have the honour to be, &c.

J. BURGOYNE.

Minutes of a Council of War, held on the Heights of Saratoga, Oct. 12.

PRESENT.

Lieutenant General BURGOYNE, Major General PHILIPS,
Major General REIDESEL, Brigadier General HAMILTON.

THE Lieutenant General states to the council the present situation of affairs.

The enemy in force, according to the best intelligence he can obtain, to the amount of upwards of 14,000 men, and a considerable quantity of artillery, are on this side the Fish-kill, and threaten an attack. On the other side the Hudson's River, between this army and Fort Edward, is another army of the enemy, the numbers unknown; but one corps, which there has been an opportunity of observing, is reported to be about 1500 men. They have likewise cannon on the other side the Hudson's River, and they have a bridge below Saratoga church, by which the two armies can communicate.

The bateaux of the army have been destroyed, and no means appear of making a bridge over the Hudson's River, were it even practicable from the position of the enemy.

The only means of retreat, therefore, are by the ford at Fort Edward, or taking the mountains in order to pass the river higher up by rafts, or by any other ford which is reported to be practicable with difficulty, or by keeping the mountains, to pass the head of Hudson's River, and continue to the westward of Lake George all the way to Ticonderoga; it is true, this last passage was never made but by Indians, or very small bodies of men.

In order to pass cannon or any wheel carriages from hence to Fort Edward, some bridges must be repaired under fire of the enemy from the opposite side of the river, and the principal bridge will be a work of fourteen or fifteen hours; there is no good position for the army to take to sustain that work, and if there were, the time stated as necessary, would give the enemy on the other side the Hudson's River an opportunity to take post on the strong ground above Fort Edward, or to dispute the ford while General Gates's army followed in the rear.

The intelligence from the lower part of Hudson's River is founded upon the concurrent reports of prisoners and deserters, who say it was the news in the enemy's camp, that Fort Montgomery was taken; and one man, a friend to government, who arrived yesterday, mentions some particulars of the manner in which it was taken.

The provisions of the army may hold out to the 20th; there is neither rum nor spruce beer.

Having committed this state of facts to the consideration of the council, the General requests their sentiments on the following propositions.

1st. To wait in the present position an attack from the enemy, or the chance of favourable events.

2d. To attack the enemy.

3d. To retreat repairing the bridges as the army moves for the artillery, in order to force the passage of the ford.

4th. To retreat by night, leaving the artillery and the baggage; and should it be found impracticable to force the passage with musquetry, to attempt the upper ford, or the passage round Lake George.

5th. In

In cafe the enemy, by extending to their left, leave their rear open, to march rapidly for Albany.

Upon the firſt propoſition reſolved, that the ſituation would grow worſe by delay, that the proviſion now in ſtore not more than ſufficient for the retreat, ſhould impediments intervene, or a circuit of country become neceſſary; and as the enemy did not attack when the ground was unfortified, it is not probable they will do it now, as they have a better game to play.

The ſecond unadviſable and deſperate, there being no poſſibility of reconnoitering the enemy's poſition, and his great ſuperiority of numbers known.

The third impracticable.

The fifth thought worthy of conſideration by the Lieutenant-General, Major-General Phillips, and Brigadier-General Hamilton; but the poſition of the enemy yet gives no opening for it.

Reſolved, that the fourth propoſition is the only reſource, and that to effect it, the utmoſt ſecrecy and ſilence is to be obſerved; and the troops are to be put in motion from the right in the ſtill part of the night, without any change in the diſpoſition.

N. B. It depended upon the delivery of ſix days proviſion in due time, and upon the return of ſcouts, who had been ſent forward to examine by what route the army could probably move the firſt four miles undiſcovered, whether the plan ſhould take place on that day, or on the morrow.

The ſcouts on their return reported, that the enemy's poſition on the right was ſuch, and they had ſo many ſmall parties out, that it would be impoſſible to move without our march being immediately diſcovered.

Minutes and Proceedings of a Council of War, conſiſting of all the general Officers and Field Officers, and Captains commanding Corps, on the Heights of Saratoga, Oct-ober 13.

THE Lieutenant-General having explained the ſituation of affairs, as in the preceding council, with the additional intelligence, that the enemy was intrenched at the fords of Fort Edward, and likewiſe occupied the ſtrong poſition on the Pine-plains between Fort George and Fort Edward, expreſſed his readineſs to undertake at their head any enterpriſe of difficulty or hazard that ſhould appear to them within the compaſs of their ſtrength or ſpirit. He added, that he had reaſon to believe a capitulation had been in the contemplation of ſome, perhaps of all, who knew the real ſituation of things; that upon a circumſtance of ſuch conſequence to national and perſonal honour, he thought it a duty to his country, and to himſelf, to extend his council beyond the uſual limits; that the aſſembly preſent might juſtly be eſteemed a full repreſentation of the army; and that he ſhould think himſelf unjuſtifiable in taking any ſtep in ſo ſerious a matter, without ſuch a concurrence of ſentiments as ſhould make a treaty the act of the army, as well as that of the general.

The firſt queſtion therefore he deſired them to decide was, Whether an army of 3500 fighting men, and well provided with artillery, were juſtifiable, upon the principles of national dignity and military honour, in capitulating in any poſſible ſituation?

Reſolved,

Refolved, nem. con. in the affirmative.

Queftion 2. Is the prefent fituation of that nature?

Refolved, nem. con. That the prefent fituation juftifies a capitulation upon honourable terms.

The Lieutenant-General then drew up the meffage, marked No. 2, and laid it before the council. It was unanimoufly approved, and upon that foundation the treaty opened.

October 14. Major Kingfton having delivered the meffage marked No. 2, returned with the propofals marked No. 3, and the council of war being affembled again, the Lieutenant-General laid the propofals before them, when it was refolved unanimoufly to reject the 6th article, and not to admit of it in any extremity whatever.

The Lieutenant-General then laid before the council the anfwers to Major-General Gates's propofals, as marked in the fame paper, together with his own preliminary propofals, which were unanimoufly approved of.

October 15. The council being affembled again, Major-General Gates's anfwers to Lieutenant-General Burgoyne's propofals were laid before them, whereupon it was refolved, that they were fatisfactory, and a fufficient ground for proceeding to a definitive treaty.

No. 2. *Major* Kingfton *delivered the following Meffage to Major-General* Gates, October 14.

AFTER having fought you twice, Lieutenant-General Burgoyne has waited fome days, in his prefent pofition, determined to try a third conflict againft any force you could bring to attack him.

He is apprifed of the fuperiority of your numbers, and the difpofition of your troops to impede his fupplies, and render his retreat a fcene of carnage on both fides. In this fituation he is impelled by humanity, and thinks himfelf juftifiable by eftablifhed principles and precedents of ftate, and of war, to fpare the lives of brave men upon honourable terms. Should Major-General Gates be inclined to treat upon that idea, General Burgoyne would propofe a ceffation of arms during the time neceffary to communicate the preliminary terms by which, in any extremity, he and his army mean to abide.

No. 3. *Major-General* Gates's *Propofals; together with Lieutenant-General* Burgoyne's *Anfwers.*

I. General Burgoyne's army being exceedingly reduced by repeated defeats, by defertion, ficknefs, &c. their provifions exhaufted, their military horfes, tents, and baggage, taken or deftroyed, their retreat cut off, and their camp invefted, they can only be allowed to furrender prifoners of war.

Anfwer. Lieutenant-General Burgoyne's army, however reduced, will never admit that their retreat is cut off, while they have arms in their hands.

II. The officers and foldiers may keep the baggage belonging to them. The generals of the United States never permit individuals to be pillaged.

C c

III.

III. The troops under his Excellency General Burgoyne will be conducted by the moſt convenient route to New England, marching by eaſy marches, and ſufficiently provided for by the way.

Anſwer. This article is anſwered by General Burgoyne's firſt propoſal, which is here annexed.

IV. The officers will be admitted on parole ; may wear their ſide-arms, and will be treated with the liberality cuſtomary in Europe, ſo long as they, by proper behaviour, continue to deſerve it ; but thoſe who are apprehended having broke their parole, as ſome Britiſh officers have done, muſt expect to be cloſe confined.

Anſwer. There being no officer in this army under, or capable of being under the deſcription of breaking parole, this article needs no anſwer.

V. All public ſtores, artillery, arms, ammunition, carriages, horſes, &c. &c. muſt be delivered to commiſſaries appointed to receive them. .

Anſwer. All public ſtores may be delivered, arms excepted.

VI. Theſe terms being agreed to and ſigned, the troops under his Excellency General Burgoyne's command may be drawn up in their encampments, where they will be ordered to ground their arms, and may thereupon be marched to the river ſide, to be paſſed over in their way towards Bennington.

Anſwer. This article inadmiſſible in any extremity. Sooner than this army will conſent to ground their arms in their encampment, they will ruſh on the enemy, determined to take no quarter.

VII. A ceſſation of arms to continue till ſun-ſet, to receive General Burgoyne's anſwer.

(Signed)

HORATIO GATES.

Camp at Saratoga, Oct. 14.

Major Kingſton met the Adjutant-General of Major-General Gates's army, October 14th, at ſun-ſet, and delivered the following meſſage :

If General Gates does not mean to recede from the 6th article, the treaty ends at once.

The army will to a man proceed to any act of deſperation, rather than ſubmit to that article.

The ceſſation of arms ends this evening.

No. XVI.

Brigades	Brigadiers	Colonels	Lieutenant Colonels	Majors	Captains	First Lieutenants	Second Lieutenants	Ensigns	Chaplains	Adjutants	Quarter Masters	Pay Masters	Surgeons	Mate	Serjeants	Drums and Fifes	Present fit for Duty	Sick present	Sick absent	On Command	On Furlough	Total
General Nixon's	1	3	4	3	27	25	28	24	1	4	4	2	4	3	104	52	1257	55	87	73	9	1481
Poor's	1	2	5	4	24	23	26	28	1	3	3	4	3	5	110	50	1132	48	64	61	11	1316
Learned's	1	4	3	4	26	21	23	30	1	3	3	3	2	4	121	54	1498	57	51	44	8	1658
Glover's	1	3	5	4	30	26	23	27	1	4	4	4	4	3	120	58	1776	69	94	86	23	2048
Paterson's	1	4	3	4	28	22	24	26	1	3	4	4	3	4	108	49	1255	61	77	53	12	1458
Warner's	1	5	4	3	24	27	22	26	0	3	3	3	2	3	96	40	1572	95	83	68	32	1850
Stark's	1	3	3	4	27	30	24	22	0	3	4	3	4	2	101	48	220	25	32	1019	7	1303
Bailey's	1	4	4	2	28	26	22	24	0	2	2	2	2	3	93	37	897	30	23	48	13	1011
Whipple's	1	3	4	4	24	27	23	25	1	3	4	2	3	2	104	49	112	18	21	897	27	1075
Brickett's	1	2	4	3	26	23	27	30	0	2	2	1	1	2	83	37	776	21	37	31	4	869
Fellows's	1	4	4	4	22	26	24	28	0	3	3	4	2	4	113	51	132	40	31	884	10	1097
Woolcut's	1	1	3	3	20	23	21	25	0	2	2	1	1	1	96	47	843	27	34	38	7	949
Ten Brock's	1	4	2	3	24	22	27	30	0	4	4	1	3	3	105	44	987	54	65	553	14	1673
Artillerists	0	0	1	1	6	5	5	0	0	1	1	0	0	2	22	12	438	17	25	8	2	490
Cavalry	0	0	1	3	8	6	7	0	0	0	1	0	0	2	16	8	321	5	7	12	1	346
Total	12	44	45	49	344	332	326	345	5	42	43	30	37	43	1392	636	13216	622	731	3875	180	18624

B. Exclusive of the numbers in the above Return, there are, the upper staff of the army, the bateau-men, the artificers, and followers of the camp.

Colonel Morgan's corps of rifle-men, and the light-infantry, are included in the brigades.

(Signed.)

HORATIO GATES, Major General.

No. XVII.   *Extracts from the Minutes of the last Council of War, excepting the names of the officers, and the notes they gave.*

QUESTION.

General Gates having, in anfwer to General Burgoyne's meffage, given a folemn affirmation on his honour, that no detachment has been made from his army during the negociation of the treaty, is the treaty, in its prefent fituation, binding on this army, or is the general's honour engaged for the figning it ?

[Here follow the names of the officers as they voted.]

The lieutenant general's opinion being clear, that he is not bound by what has paffed, he would not execute the treaty upon the fole confideration of the point of honour, notwithftanding the refpectable majority againft him.

He is likewife far from being convinced that this army, by great exertions and by great enduring in point of provifions, might not yet be relieved ; but he is compelled to yield on the following confiderations.

The treaty was generally thought a moft advantageous one before the intelligence arrived. That intelligence is refuted, and ocular demonftration of its falfity pledged as far as relates to General Gates's force ; the other parts are only founded on hearfay, and not to be depended upon.

Should General Clinton be where reported, yet the diftance is fuch as to render any relief from him improbable during the time our provifions could be made to laft.

- - - - - - - declares his poft untenable, and fays, if this convention is not figned, he apprehends there will be confiderable defertion.

- - - - - - - fays he thinks the 47th regiment not to be depended on.

- - - - - - - is of the fame opinion.

- - - - - - - thinks the 62d regiment is difheartened by the fituation of their poft, and not equal to their former exertions.

Several officers think the men in general feem to have got the convention in their heads as defirable.

Many of the beft officers are abfent by ficknefs and wounds from all the corps.

Though the other officers at the head of the Britifh corps think they can anfwer for the fpirit of their men, if attacked on their prefent ground, it is evident the moft fanguine do not think any part of the army in that elevation and alacrity of fpirit neceffary for undertaking defperate enterprizes.

To break off the treaty now renders a future renewal of it hopelefs, as our condition muft every hour grow worfe.

A defeat is fatal to the army. A victory does not fave it, as they have neither provifions to advance nor retreat againft an enemy who by experience we know are capable of rallying at every advantageous poft.

And that the life and property of every provincial and dependant of this army depends upon the execution of this treaty.

POSTSCRIPT to the APPENDIX.

[Though the following Letters are not referred to in any Part of the Defence,
it is hoped they will not be deemed superfluous.]

Extract of a Letter from Major General Phillips, *to Lieutenant General* Burgoyne,
dated Cambridge, September 29, 1778.

My Dear Sir,

THE Boston news papers, have given extracts from English and New York papers, wherein you are mentioned; your arrival, your speeches in parliament; and a variety of other matters concerning you. I do not always give credit to news papers, and therefore, the publishers at Boston will excuse me, if in the instance of news I do not give them, in my opinion, more veracity than I allow the news compilers at London.

I will not plague you about our situation, as you will know it, by my assuring you it is almost exactly as you left us; so no more about it. The troops here depend upon you their chief, in whatever may relate to them; their interest; their honour. It is not doubted but you will exert yourself, that the officers may gain preferment in common, with other parts of the army. That you will have the goodness to exert yourself in behalf of their situation, respecting the very great expence of living; and endeavour to procure the allowance of forage money. And in short, that you will use all your powers of perfuasion and interest for these troops, which have served under you with zeal, and with honour; and endeavour, by serving their situation and promoting their honour, to alleviate misfortunes which nor fortitude nor valour could prevent, and which they suffer, however, with resignation and patience. I am most perfectly convinced of your affectionate, I will say your grateful regard for us all; and I leave myself and the troops to your friendly care; to your humanity; to your honour.

You cannot expect a letter of entertainment; I have not even a power of making it one of intelligence. It shall be however, a letter of perfect sincerity, and in the fullest sense of it I profess to be,
My dear Sir,
Your very sincere Friend, and faithful Servant,
(Signed)　　　　　　　　　　　W. PHILLIPS.

P. S. I enclose you the Copy of a Memorial to the Secretary at War, I am sure you will assist it.

Copy

A P P E N D I X.

Copy of a Letter from Lieutenant General Burgoyne *to Lord* Amherst, *inclofing the Memorial referred to in the above, dated* November 6, 1778.

My Lord,

THE heavy misfortune I fuftain in being precluded the King's prefence, touches me in no point more nearly, than in the prevention of doing juftice to the various and extenfive merits of the army I had the honour to command. That the confequences of my fuppofed, or real errors, fhould involve pretenfions and interefts of fo many gallant officers is a painful reflection; and it can only be alleviated by the trueft fenfe of the truft to be repofed in your Lordfhip, for the general protection of the fervice. The inclofed memorial was accompanied with expreffions of reliance, in the name of the whole army, upon my efforts to fupport it. The officers in New England little conceive my prefent fituation : I take the firft opportunity to tranfmit their caufe to your Lordfhip's happier aufpices, with this folemn declaration, which I have mentioned upon different public occafions, and which I can omit no occafion to repeat, that there is not a Britifh officer who ferved under me during the campaign of 1777, to whom I can impute blame; that the inftances are very numerous wherein particular diftinction is due; and as a body, they have a claim to my fincereft refpect for their zeal in the King's fervice, and to my utmoft gratitude for their attention to me perfonally.

I have the honour to be, &c. &c. &c.

J. BURGOYNE.

F I N I S.

ADVERTISEMENT.

In Plan IV. the third and fourth positions of the army in the engagement of 19th of September may appear upon a cursory view to want precision. The inequalities of the ground could not be distinctly marked upon so small a scale ; and the continual shift of the positions of separate corps, as they were attacked by corps of the enemy, which frequently, from the thickness of the wood, they did not see, made it equally difficult to mark regularly the position of the whole at any one time.

The position of the armies on the 8th of September in Plate V. requires also some explanation. From the smallness of the scale, the position of the enemy could only be shewn upon the plain near the river ; but it is to be observed, it extended over the ground of General Burgoyne's former encampment, and in front of the redoubts upon the hill.

N. B. The papers respecting the expedition to Bennington, referred to by mistake, under No. IV. page 103, will be found in the Appendix under No. XII. after Lieutenant Colonel Baume's instructions.

The account of the expedition of Lieutenant Colonel St. Leger, referred to also, by mistake, under No. V. will be found in the Appendix under No. XIII.

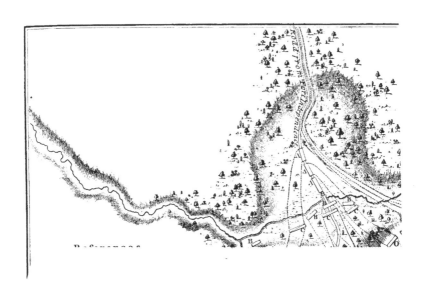

References

Road to Crown Point

S

Gen! Frazer which was

while it was forming.

hed to cover the Right Wing?

rick Comp! of Chasseurs.

n! Reidesel

after Gen! Reidesel arrived.

n.

d were carried.

previous to the Action

P

of the

HUB

under BRIG.

supported by M.

on

Drawn by P. Gerlac

Engrav

SCALE *of* 200 Paces to

100   200   300   400   500

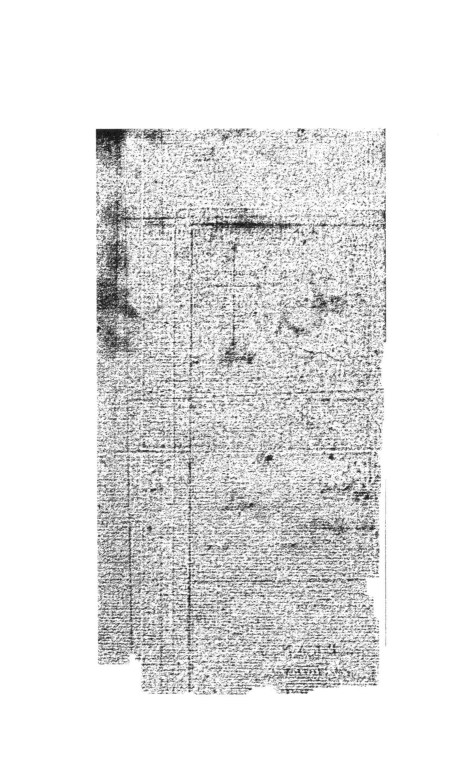

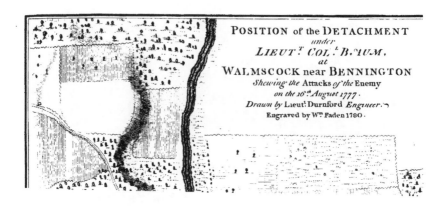

POSITION of the DETACHMENT
under
LIEUT.ᵀ COL.ᴸ B.ᵃIUM.
at
WALMSCOCK near BENNINGTON
Shewing the Attacks *of the* Enemy
on the 16.ᵗʰ August 1777.
Drawn by Lieut.ᵗ Durnford *Engineer.*
Engraved by Wᵐ. Faden 1780.

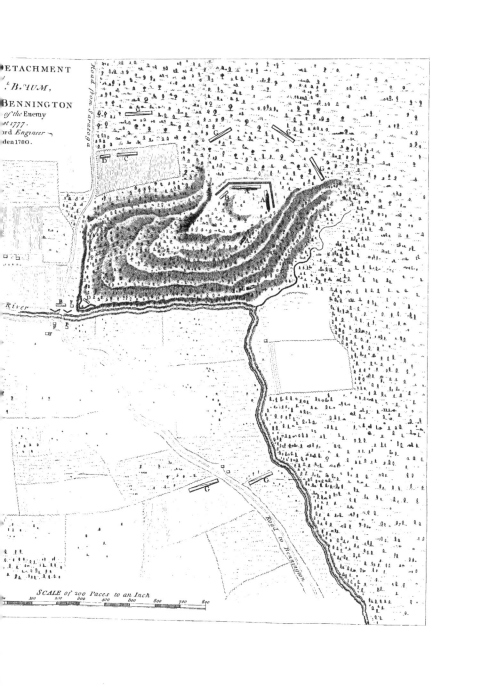

ETACHMENT
B.cIUM,

BENNINGTON
of the Enemy
at 1777.
ord Engineer
den 1780.

Road from Saratoga

G

G

B

A

G

G

A

A

River

B

F

G

G

Road to Bennington

SCALE of 200 Paces to an Inch

100   200   300   400   500   600   700   800

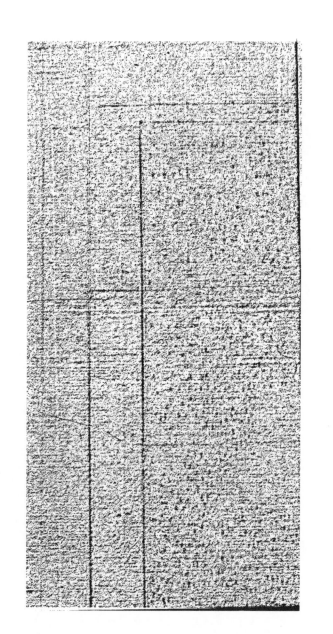

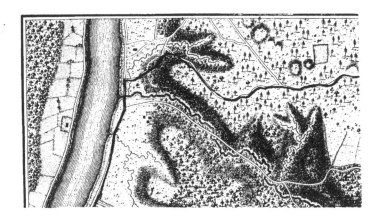

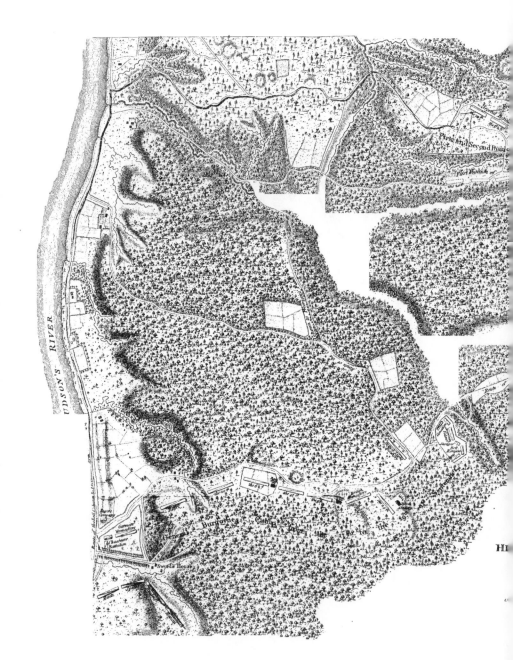

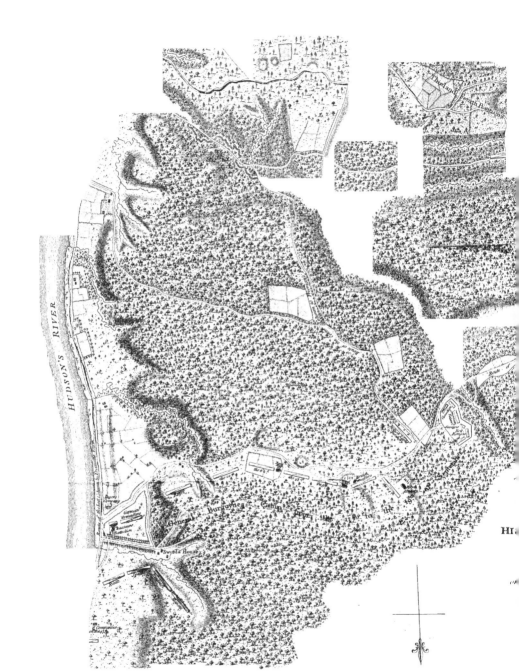

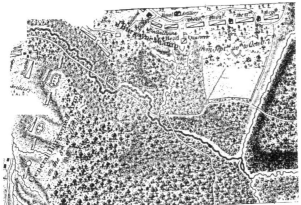

London, published as the Act

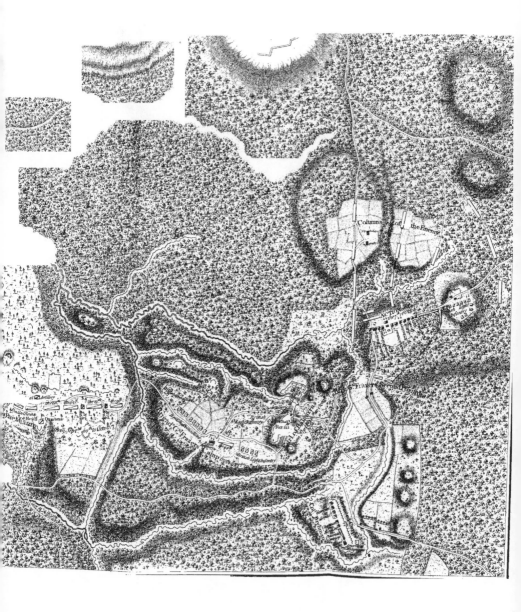

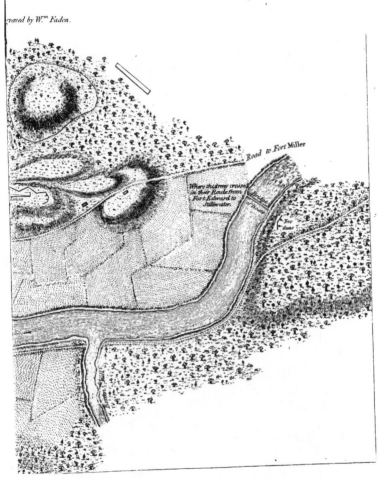

Road to Fort Miller

Where this Army croſsed
in their Route from
Fort Edward to
Stillwater.

five
Guns

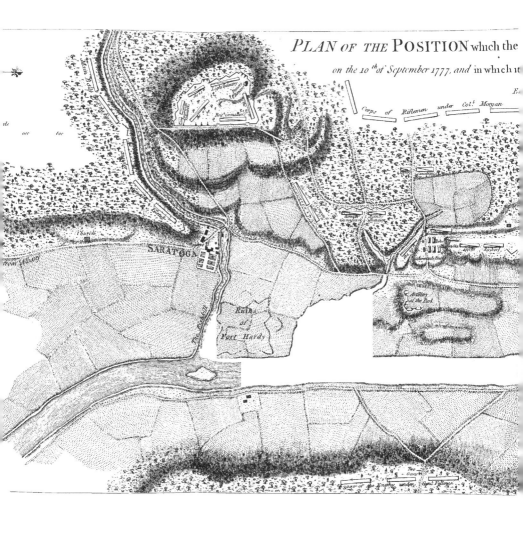

PLAN OF THE POSITION which the

on the 10ᵗʰ of September 1777, and in which it

Corps of Riflemen under Colᵗ Morgan

SARATOGA

Ruins of Fort Hardy

SD - #0037 - 230822 - C0 - 229/152/13 - PB - 9781330990100 - Gloss Lamination